Lifelong Action Learning and Resea

A Tribute to the Life and Pioneering Work of Ortrun Zuber-Skerritt

COVER ARTWORK

A single spark can start a prairie fire.

This Chinese proverb captures the essence of Ortrun Zuber-Skerritt's understanding of life and learning, reflection and action, research and publication. The cover painting by Wolfram Achenbach, Ortrun's beloved brother, captures this understanding beautifully. A highly respected medical specialist in Germany, Wolfram came into painting later in life. He enjoyed Australian summers at Ortun's Bribie Island getaway near Brisbane, where thoughts of Australian nature – in this painting, the typical bushfire – would flow through his brush. Today, sparks of constructive thought and action shape the lives of many people touched by Ortrun's contagious enthusiasm for building a better world.

Lifelong Action Learning and Research

A Tribute to the Life and Pioneering Work of Ortrun Zuber-Skerritt

Edited by

Judith Kearney
Griffith University, Brisbane, Australia

and

Maureen Todhunter
Griffith University, Brisbane, Australia

SENSE PUBLISHERS
ROTTERDAM/BOSTON/TAIPEI

A C.I.P. record for this book is available from the Library of Congress.

ISBN: 978-94-6300-137-3 (paperback)
ISBN: 978-94-6300-138-0 (hardback)
ISBN: 978-94-6300-139-7 (e-book)

Published by: Sense Publishers,
P.O. Box 21858,
3001 AW Rotterdam,
The Netherlands
https://www.sensepublishers.com/

Printed on acid-free paper

TABLE OF CONTENTS

Part III: Communities of Practice

Part IV: Futures

Part V: Concluding Reflection

CARSTEN ZUBER

FOREWORD

Ortrun Zuber-Skerritt is my mother. When her long time colleagues, collaborators and friends, Judith Kearney and Maureen Todhunter, told me about their then covert plans for this Festschrift project, I felt grateful and thrilled at such a recognition of her life's work and deeply touched to be asked to write the foreword.

As a loving son, I view Mum's work through a lens that is in no way objective or dispassionate. It is, however, a unique perspective, which I hope will add a very personal layer to the fabric of this publication.

My mother is the product of a traditional, protestant German family. Her father was in many ways the stereotypical headmaster of the day – a strict yet loving family patriarch whom she revered. Her mother was a professional homemaker (in every sense of the term) whose life revolved around her husband and children, and whose energy, resourcefulness and perseverance enabled her to singlehandedly provide for Mum and her two siblings for almost a decade, during and immediately after WW2 while my grandfather was a PoW. Mum inherited these qualities in large doses, serving her well professionally and personally.

Two other family members also left a defining influence on Mum's character and psyche. They are her 'onkel Frieda', a benevolent uncle with whom she spent much time as a young girl and whose encouragement, sense of fun and generous nature left a deep impression. And her brother Wolfram, a mischievous child who developed into a highly successful oncologist and haematologist, an extraordinary, larger than life character with whom she shared a deep, loving and extraordinary bond. His life was cut short by motor neurone disease, a tragedy lessened only for the fact he left a beautiful son Ulf, who is also adored by Mum. It is entirely fitting that Wolfram's painting (a hobby he developed as an adult) adorns the cover of this book.

Mum's work is often described as pioneering and this descriptor extends to her life more broadly. It is difficult today to imagine what it meant, in 1971, for a single working mother to emigrate from Germany to the other side of the world. The courage to leave the security of a tenured teaching job in Germany and the support structure associated with a large and loving (though not always harmonious) family cannot be overstated. Consistent with perceptions prevailing at the time, when my grandparents farewelled their daughter at Frankfurt airport in 1971 they imagined Australia to be a land of creepy crawlies and bush, of towns where kangaroos roamed the streets. Air travel was the domain of the wealthy and moving overseas was a one way journey. They thought they would never see their daughter or grandson again.

Of course, Mum saw the opportunity, the freedom and the lifestyle that this young and vibrant society could provide and threw herself into building our new life with a passion that only migrants can truly appreciate. She worked so hard to make sure I retained German language skills and every year she managed to send me back to Germany at Christmas time to ensure that familial and cultural bonds remained intact. This loving and generous act, for which I am forever grateful, was expensive (air travel in the 1970s was significantly more expensive than today, in relative terms) and required significant sacrifice over the course of the year.

Aside from the gift of a fierce intellect, a number of character traits enabled her to succeed in those early days and endure to this day. The first is her work ethic. Mum has always worked hard. Really hard. In those early days in Australia this was a differentiator that helped her to advance her career – even in the face of discriminatory conduct that today would be regarded as unacceptable. A good insight into the work ethic, principle and single minded persistence that enabled a divorced migrant woman with a strong German accent to overcome adversity in the mid-1970s lies in the way she dealt with the first (and by no means last) major obstacle in her career. Even with a solid teaching, research and publication record and a recently completed PhD under her belt, she was denied a promotion that merit-based criteria dictated was not simply deserved but well overdue. Moreover, it was made clear to her that she would not be considered for promotion in the future. Mum's response – after picking herself up from the canvas – was to complete a second PhD and to continue publishing extensively, until it became impossible to deny her the promotion. I cite this as one of the many examples of her indefatigable and optimistic spirit.

Despite the time, energy and commitment Mum devoted to her own and others' career development, as a young son I always felt loved, included and cared for deeply. I knew Mum was always there for me when I needed her. I'm still not sure how she managed that.

The work ethic, persistence, determination, optimism and energy I have identified here are shared by almost all successful leaders in every walk of life. But other values that shape Mum's life profoundly as an academic, a citizen, a community member and friend are a little more rare and elude many successful people. These are fairness, kindness and generosity.

The philosophy with which Mum has approached interaction with others is encapsulated neatly in the adage of keeping a hard head and a soft heart. Of course, no-one achieves this ideal all the time. But I believe it best describes the way she has lived her life and the example she has set.

In the mid-1980s my mother first discovered the work of Reg Revans and other early pioneers of Action Learning. She felt an intrinsic alignment with this approach to learning – and its broader underpinning philosophy – and this inspired both a pivotal time in her career and a transformational moment for her personally. Action Learning lit a fire within her that continues to burn to this day. That's another reason why the cover of this book is so meaningful and apt. As an intimate observer of my mother's life, I saw work become a true vocation for her, one that expanded both her professional and personal horizons. The 'true believers' of Action Learning and Action Research (ALAR) will appreciate the holistic application that its principles carry.

In my (somewhat biased) view, one of my mother's great skills is the ability to translate theory into tangible action. The enormous potential of ALAR was clear to her by the late 1980s, yet at that time the work was conducted in isolated pockets throughout the world. Those were days before the internet, video-conferencing and other technologies that enable us to connect far and wide in seconds, so opportunities to collaborate and share this progressive thinking in a truly global sense were limited. Her vision to provide a structured forum to bring together disparate proponents of the new discipline became the first world congress held in Brisbane in 1990. The congress became a catalyst for establishing the Action Learning Action Research and Process Management Association in 1991. It also provided a foundation stone upon which future congresses and a wealth of future developments have been built.

At a professional level, one of the early outworkings of this expanded thinking lay in the practical application of ALAR principles to develop leadership development programs for private and public sector executives. Although relatively commonplace today, back in the 1980s there was a deep divide – and mutual distrust – between industry and academia. Together with a small number of like-minded individuals, such as Bob Dick, my mother recognised that an ALAR framework could provide a very effective and practical way to bridge this divide and for industry leaders to develop their own skill sets and qualifications and to then establish similar frameworks throughout their businesses (ripple effect), for the betterment of staff and businesses as a whole. The outcome here was building learning organisations!

This work has continued and evolved over the years and as ALAR has increasingly been accepted and adopted in first world countries, Mum has shifted her focus to applying these principles in underprivileged communities. The possibilities to make a quantum difference to improving life in these communities and to help to break the shackles of poverty by providing a framework to help individuals within these communities to recognise, harness and develop their own abilities appealed to my mother. She first became aware of these possibilities through the work of inspirational pioneers such as the late Orlando Fals Borda, whom she first met in 1992. For the past two decades her energy has been increasingly devoted in this direction, primarily in South Africa but also in other disadvantaged communities such as within the Samoan community on the outskirts of Brisbane not so far from where she lives. It is work of which I am very proud.

A great many colleagues and friends (so often intertwined) have made a real difference to her professional and personal life. These relationships have been nourishing and fulfilling for the highly social person who my mother is. I would like to pay particular tribute to Judith Kearney and Maureen Todhunter, who share her values and her passion for ALAR and who have played an enormous role, including in South Africa in the last decade in particular, and Judith also with the Samoan community. Through their shared journey both Judith and Maureen have become trusted friends and confidantes.

And finally to you, *meine liebe* Mum, I'd like to express how proud I am of the positive difference your work has made – and continues to make – in so many lives. I'm grateful for the example you have set for me through the values you have lived out – especially in tough times. I hope to pass these on to your grandson. But most of all I want you to know that I love you very much.

Carsten Zuber
Melbourne

ACKNOWLEDGEMENTS

This book comprises the efforts, creative minds and energies of numerous people in tribute to the work and life of Ortrun Zuber-Skerritt. As well as the contributing authors of chapters and short tributes are, in particular, Robyn White through her formatting flair and Jo Anne Pomfrett through proofreading. The production team at Sense Publishers has provided excellent technical and editorial support.

LIST OF FIGURES

LIST OF TABLES

ABOUT THE AUTHORS

Richard Bawden

Throughout his four decade long experience in leadership positions within academia, Richard Bawden has placed a great deal of emphasis on the management of processes as the basis for effective education, action research, community engagement and organisational development. Of particular importance in this context has been his concern for the impact of worldview beliefs, values and attitudes and for the challenges that these represent to truly transformative learning and the critically creative management of change. He remains deeply committed to the application of systems principles and practices as conceptual frameworks and pragmatic guides respectively for dealing with complex, often chaotic circumstances that systems-of-interest typically confront from the environments in which they are embedded.

Pip Bruce Ferguson

Pip Bruce Ferguson is an educational consultant and researcher. She has spent most of her professional life in New Zealand, including as Director at Pip Bruce Ferguson Consultancies, as Teaching Developer at University of Waikato, Research Manager at Te Wananga o Aotearoa, and Senior Lecturer at Auckland University of Technology. From 2014 she is Teaching and Learning Developer at Dublin City University. Pip has always been an advocate for equity and social justice.

Mary Brydon-Miller

Mary Brydon-Miller, PhD directs the University of Cincinnati's Action Research Center and is Professor of Educational and Community-based Action Research in the College of Education, Criminal Justice, and Human Services. She is a participatory action researcher who conducts work in both school and community settings. She recently completed work on the *Sage Encyclopedia of Action Research* with co-editor David Coghlan. Other publications focus on the development of new frameworks for understanding research ethics in community. She recently completed a Fulbright Research Fellowship at Keele University in the United Kingdom where her work focussed on developing new strategies to inform the ethical conduct of community-based research.

David Coghlan

David Coghlan is an action research scholar and an Adjunct Professor at the School of Business, Trinity College Dublin, Ireland, and a Fellow Emeritus of the college. Recent co-authored books include *Collaborative Strategic Improvement through Network Action Learning* (2011), *Doing Action Research in Your Own Organization* (4th ed. 2014). He is co-editor (with Mary Brydon-Miller) of *The Sage Encyclopedia of Action Research*. He is currently on the editorial boards of *Action Research, Action Learning: Research and Practice*, among others.

Bob Dick

In the past Bob Dick has been shop assistant, electrician, draftsperson, recruitment officer and psychologist. For the past 30 years he has been academic, publisher, consultant, facilitator, and of course person. His consultancy and facilitation primarily help people learn action research, qualitative evaluation, change management, and the communication and facilitation skills which are a foundation for these. In this work he uses highly participative methods to help others to improve their practice while also trying to improve his own. When he isn't doing these things he thinks about them. He maintains one of the world's premier action research websites at Southern Cross University. He lives in the leafy western suburbs of Brisbane, in sub-tropical Australia, with his partner of 30 years, Camilla. He may be contacted at bdick@scu.edu.au.

Chris Kapp

Chris Kapp is an Emeritus Professor in Higher Education at the University of Stellenbosch in South Africa. He was the first Director of the Academic Staff Development Unit at the university from 1984 to 1996. From 1997 to 2007 he was the first Director of the Centre for Higher and Adult Education at the University of Stellenbosch. In his career he successfully supervised 44 Masters and 33 PhD candidates and has been an examiner for more than 50 theses. He has published more than 20 articles and has facilitated more than 130 weeklong workshops on 'Writing for Publication' and more than 80 weeklong workshops on 'The Science and Art of Postgraduate Supervision and Assessment.'

Judith Kearney

Judith Kearney PhD is Director of Community Partnerships in the School of Education and Professional Studies at Griffith University. In this role she works with academics, industry groups and community organisations to progress partnerships that promote engaged scholarship. Judith's preferred methodology is Participatory Action Learning and Action Research (PALAR). She has used this methodology in partnerships with refugee and migrant communities, especially Pacific Island migrant communities. Judith is a member of the Griffith Institute for Educational Research. Much of her research aims to develop capacity within communities to promote educational and employment opportunities across the lifespan. A range of publications has resulted from this work.

Ron Passfield

Ron Passfield is co-owner and Director of Merit Solutions Australia, established in 1996 to provide human resource consultancy services to all levels of the public sector in Australia. He is also an Adjunct Professor with the Australian Institute of Business (AIB), an accredited higher education provider offering action research and action learning-based degrees up to and including PhD. Ron's involvement in action learning and action research began in 1976. He was a founding member of ALARPM and President from 2002 to 2007 and was co-founder and Editor of the *ALAR Journal*. He worked as a manager in the Australian Public Service for 15 years and lectured at Griffith University for 10 years in organisation change and development. He has been actively engaged as an action learning and action research consultant since 1999 when he left Griffith University to work from home as a freelance academic and organisation consultant.

Eileen Piggot-Irvine

Eileen Piggot-Irvine is a Professor of Leadership at Royal Roads University (Victoria, Canada) and an Adjunct Professor at both Griffith University (Brisbane) and Unitec (Auckland). She was formerly Director of the New Zealand Action Research and Review Centre (NZARRC), Director of the New Zealand Principal and Leadership Centre (NZPLC) and Senior Lecturer at Massey University, and Head of the Education Management Centre, at Unitec. She has published four books, multiple book chapters, approximately 50 journal articles and presented too many keynotes etc. to count. In the last six years she has directed 11 evaluation contracts (several at a national level) and recently won a national Canadian grant to lead a team of researchers investigating the impact of action research. She may be contacted at Eileen.piggotirvine@royalroads.ca.nz

Shankar Sankaran

Shankar Sankaran is the Professor of Organisational Project Management at the Faculty of Design Architecture and Building at the University of Technology Sydney (UTS) and an Associate Editor of the *Sage International Encyclopaedia of Action Research* (2014). Shankar has been an advocate of Action Research (AR) since he completed his PhD in 1999 using this methodology. He is a distinguished fellow of the AR Centre, University of Cincinnati and Chair of the AR Special

Integration Group at the International Society for the Systems Sciences (ISSS). He is a chief investigator in an Australian Research Council project that used AR as a meta-methodology. Shankar has supervised eight doctoral students using AR as their methodology. He has also been a special issue editor for *Action Research.*

Doris Santos

Doris Santos has an MA in Linguistics and an MPhil at the Universidad Nacional de Colombia. She has a PhD from Charles Sturt University, Australia. She conducts participatory action research, critical ethnography and critical discourse analysis research projects on higher education issues. She is the leader of the inter-university research group Estudios del Discurso (Discourse Studies) and a member of the Collaborative Action Research Network (CARN); the Pedagogy, Education and Praxis Network (PEP); Association of Latin American Discourse Studies (AED); and the Australian Association for Research in Education (AARE).

Richard Teare

Richard Teare is President of the Global University for Lifelong Learning (GULL) which he co-founded in 2007. In this capacity he has helped to create learning and development applications for many organisations and in different parts of the world. He is the co-author (with Ortrun Zuber-Skerritt) of *Lifelong Action Learning for Community Development* (Sense Publishers, 2013), the first in a series of books about GULL's work with communities. Prior to his current role, he held professorships at four UK universities and he has been a journal editor for more than 25 years. His academic publications include 20 co-authored and edited books on aspects of service management and organisational learning. GULL's mission is a source of self-help and encouragement to low income communities and for an overview of GULL's work see: www.gullonline.org

Maureen Todhunter

Maureen Todhunter is an academic copy editor through Griffith University, Brisbane. She also facilitates workshops on academic writing and publishing in Australia and South Africa. She works in community radio, refugee community support and wildlife appreciation.

Yoland Wadsworth

Yoland Wadsworth has been a pioneer practitioner, facilitator and theorist in the development of transformative research and evaluation methodologies in Australia, including participatory, dialogic and 'whole systems' action research in health, community and human services for over 38 years. She has authored Australia's best-selling research methodology texts *Do It Yourself Social Research* and *Everyday Evaluation on the Run* and the final work in this methodology trilogy: *Building in Research and Evaluation: Human Inquiry for Living Systems* (all Left Coast Press, San Francisco, 2011). She is an Adjunct Professor, RMIT University; Hon. Principal Fellow, University of Melbourne; Fellow of the Australasian Evaluation Society and Distinguished Fellow of the Action Research Center, University of Cincinnati. She is a past president and life member of the Action Learning, Action Research Association.

Lesley Wood

Lesley Wood, DEd, MA, BA, BASS, PGCHE is a Research Professor, Faculty of Education Sciences, North-West University, South Africa. Previously a social worker, Lesley is committed to helping educational stakeholders address the social disadvantages they face within contexts of poverty and specifically with reference to HIV and AIDS. Lesley has more than 40 accredited publications and is rated by the National Research Foundation (NRF). She is an Editor of the journal, *Educational Research for Social Change* (www.ersc.nmmu.ac.za) and currently holds an NRF community engagement grant to conduct research on how tertiary researchers can better work with communities to generate knowledge that is mutually beneficial and will lead to contextualised and relevant social change. A past president of the Education Association of South Africa, she currently represents that body on the World Education Research Association Council.

TRIBUTES TO ORTRUN ZUBER-SKERRITT

On a cold, wet winter's night in a Dandenong Mountains' restaurant, Ortrun and I were discussing our action research on using video in higher education. We had just delivered a conference paper. Nowadays, everyone uses screen imagery *in*, or even *as*, the classroom (witness the explosion of MOOCs), and action research is practised worldwide. But back then, in 1988, colleagues simply ignored the educational possibilities of these new technologies and methodologies. Yet Ortrun is both visionary and problem-oriented. She never gives up. On that very night, Ortrun decided that action learning and action research (ALAR) must have its own platform and she conceptualised the first ALAR world symposium, held in 1988. She followed this with biennial world conferences. It is no wonder that she is now pre-eminent in the field, with numerous publications and an international network of peers and students. Congratulations on a stellar career, dear colleague, dear friend.

Mary Farquhar, Emeritus Professor, Sydney

A Google search for 'Ortrun Zuber-Skerritt' reveals a women of influence, intellect and integrity with extraordinary professional achievements. She has been awarded multiple titles in Australia and internationally – from Adjunct Professor at Griffith University, Brisbane, Australia to Professor Extraordinaire, Tshwane University of Technology, Pretoria, South Africa; four doctoral degrees – PhD in Literature (University of Queensland), PhD in Higher Education (Deakin University), DLitt in Management Education (International Management Centres Association), and Honorary Doctor of Professional Studies (GULL). She is a prodigious author of books, book chapters, journal articles, conference papers and videos across a range of topics that centre on her work in action research and action learning. But no Google search will reveal Ortrun Zuber-Skerritt, the friend, colleague and mentor who I have come to know and love through the work we have done together over the past decade. Ortrun is generous and wise – and a force to be reckoned with when a deadline is due! We have laughed and learned with heart and mind, drawing on our action research principles to nurture our friendship and professional work when times were challenging. Her relentless enthusiasm and energy for work parallels her dedication and commitment to her friends and family. Ortrun remains a source of inspiration to many. I feel grateful and privileged to have in my life Ortrun Zuber-Skerritt, a great teacher and true friend.

Margaret Fletcher, Brisbane

Ortrun Zuber-Skerritt is a quintessential international scholar. I have been stimulated by her work for decades, interacting frequently through manuscript reviews and e-mail. I have read the bulk of her work to my benefit, but we have never met in person. Judging from the reflections of others who know her personally, not having met her is my loss. But I am moved to reflect that the ability to be colleagues at a distance affirms the value of publications and the interactions they stimulate. There is, or can be, an international community of action researchers despite distances. This is about more than technology. Ortrun is a networker who encourages our communications by sharing work and maintaining contacts regularly. Consistent with her diverse body of work, she ranges across intellectual, regional, and practice traditions while linking the study of organisations, communities, and pedagogies to create fairer, healthier, and more sustainable organisations.

Davydd J. Greenwood, Goldwin Smith Professor of Anthropology, Cornell University, USA

ORTRUN IS PASSION ...
Passion for her work: Whenever/wherever I have met Ortrun in Austria, Germany or Australia she is always on fire with enthusiasm: bubbling over with ideas for her next book, explaining the concept of her last workshop, planning a stream on action learning and action research at the next world congress ... Not only is she infected with this special virus, but she 'infects' her environment as well – it's nearly impossible not to be beguiled by her passion.

Passion for her mission: 'Make the world a better place' – maybe it is due to her family background and the values learned through her education, to her status as wise woman or, finally, to her role as grandmother. Ortrun worries about the big challenges for humankind – and still works extremely hard to make her contributions for a better world.

Passion for her students: Contrary to some other colleagues, Ortrun loves her students (and vice versa!). She encourages and promotes them with extraordinary commitment and 'blistering patience' (P. Neruda), one reason why the University of Innsbruck awarded her honorary citizenship.

Passion for people and networking: 'Do you know my friend [...] (Liesl, Ernstl, Nancy, Ingrid, Bob, Zbich, Judith, Maureen, Marilyn, Mary, Margaret, Richard, Ron, Chris, Ina etc.)? Whatever your plans might be, you must meet him/her. He/she is a fantastic colleague/person/friend. His/her work would be most valuable for you ...!' You can hardly escape – and typically she is right.

Passion for hospitality: Did you ever have the chance to experience and enjoy Ortrun's hospitality? I did. And my whole family did. I remember wonderful spontaneous meals, enjoyable breakfasts full of laughter, one or another bottle of Chardonnay. I remember Bribie Island, Broadwater Road, Eight Mile Plains etc. And I/we remember a wonderful and most generous host ...

Passion for Tyrol: In her twenties, Ortrun came to Innsbruck studying sport. It was the beginning of an everlasting love. Here, Ortrun learned that people go skiing whatever the weather, whatever the risk of avalanches and whatever their physical shape – even with a damaged knee or two … And again she infected other people with this virus.

People merely exist through reason; they live through their passion. Take care of your passions, dear Ortrun.

Stephan Laske, Professor Emeritus, Innsbruck, Austria

Like honey pot to bees, Ortrun draws people to her. So with me, when participating in a leadership development program that Ortrun facilitated in Pretoria in 1999. Immediately I felt connection with her, particularly her work ethic. Ortrun so clearly wants – and tries hard – to improve and empower people around her. She motivated me to continue studying for my Masters and Doctoral degrees and still offers professional support by encouraging me to publish. I have learned so much through observation; Ortrun truly practises what she preaches in all of her life. Not surprising, then, that on safaris with Ortrun we've sat around the fire, glass in hand, reflecting on a program recently completed while coming to new understanding. As Ortrun observes, 'we worked hard and we play hard', with a few for the road. My road has been extended and enriched by the professional support and camaraderie of our generous colleague and friend, Ortrun Zuber-Skerritt. Qualitatively so! Deep thanks, Ortrun.

Ina Louw, Education Consultant, University of Pretoria, South Africa (and Boen, her good-natured husband, driver, ranger and braai master)

Ortrun is a role model, mentor and coach *par excellence*. She is an embodiment of what Action Research and Action Learning is. From the first day I attended a workshop she was facilitating, I did not want to miss an opportunity to draw out more and learn from her accumulated wealth of wisdom. I find Ortrun extremely resourceful and generous, happily connecting you to her personal networks for your own enrichment and growth. She openly shares her personal strategies that have led to her many accomplishments and makes the tasks ahead all sound so doable. Her persistent work supporting women in higher education is highly commendable, a special contribution to celebrate and cherish dearly. Ortrun is empathetic, deeply caring of the people with whom she interacts, and is such an inspiration. It is a great honour to learn from her and a pleasure to enjoy her friendship over the years.

Matete Madiba, Director Student Affairs, University of Pretoria, South Africa

Professor Ortrun Zuber-Skerritt is one of the best known educational experts in the areas of action learning and action research, and the scholarship of learning and teaching. She has published extensively in these areas, following her earlier scholarship on Australian playwrights, and has received a number of large grants. Professor Zuber-Skerritt continues to deliver keynote addresses both nationally and internationally and is in great demand on the international lecture circuit. Her contribution to learning and teaching scholarship is outstanding, with at my last count 36 books, 45 book chapters, and over 160 research and professional papers and educational programs, and these numbers increase each year. She holds adjunct and honorary positions at a number of universities and continues to teach by invitation in Europe, Australia and South Africa. From a personal point of view, I have worked with Ortrun in a number of universities and have also participated in overseas research programs with her. She is a very caring, talented professional who very generously mentors the next generation of scholars and researchers – a true model as a friend and colleague.

Marilyn McMeniman, Professor Emeritus AM, Griffith University, Brisbane

Ortrun and I have been friends for over 40 years and colleagues for part of that time, albeit in different universities. Over these years Ortrun's enthusiasm and passion for her research and projects has not waned. But of course she has matured in that in later years she has actively mentored less experienced researchers, sought active collaboration with a range of colleagues and nurtured those participating in her action learning/action research workshops in the community. She was entrepreneurial before universities encouraged this – in the German Department of the University of Queensland, in the Centre for the Advancement of Learning and Teaching at Griffith University, and in particular in organising the first World Congress on Action Learning and Action Research and finding sponsors, which was pretty much unheard of in those days. She has always been generous with her time, her ideas and her hospitality. Her humour is infectious. People want to be with her and work with her. Congratulations, dear Ortrun. We love and honour you.

Ingrid Moses, Emeritus Professor, Chancellor of University of Canberra

Ortrun has been a stalwart of the action research community in Australia for many years, and her contributions to our work have been extensive. From her publications to her organisational work, she is recognised for the energy and enthusiasm she injects into her work, and is often responsible for energising those around her. Her international work has been particularly effective, and her ability to marshal the ideas of colleagues and students exemplary. Many thanks, Ortrun, for your contribution to my own and to others' work.

Ernie Stringer, Research Consultant, Fremantle, Australia

Professor Zuber-Skerritt, Ortrun, Otti ... I feel very fortunate to be your friend for quarter of a century. While not a former student or learned colleague, I've enjoyed so many hours of conversation and laughter with you on your beloved Bribie Island. With a glass of wine or two, we've also shared valuable learnings along the way. I've always admired your ability to meet and mix with a diverse range of people with the same respect you afford your peers, and your enthusiasm for what you learn through your interactions. You are extremely generous with your time, resources and ideas. Your passion for action, embraced in Action Learning and Action Research, is infectious. No wonder you are loved and respected by family, colleagues and other friends near and far. Congratulations, Ortrun, on your professional and personal success. Thank you for the bounty of care and compassion, love and laughter, warmth and wisdom you give to us.

Dian Stroud, Brisbane

Ortrun has been a close friend and colleague of mine for many years. She has made an outstanding contribution to the field of action research and to education more generally. She is one of the best teachers I have ever learned from and she has been an extraordinary mentor to colleagues and students. She has contributed to education internationally, not only in Germany and Australia but also in South Africa. Her publication record is amazing and she continues to write and encourage others at full pace. Her personal qualities of loyalty, generosity, affection, sparkling good humour and resilience in the face of setbacks are admirable. We are fortunate to have her as a good friend and colleague.

Nancy Viviani AO, Emeritus Professor, Brisbane

JUDITH KEARNEY

1. FESTSCHRIFT FOR ORTRUN ZUBER-SKERRITT

INTRODUCTION

This book is a Festschrift for Ortrun Zuber-Skerritt. A 'Festschrift', borrowing from German, is a celebratory publication, literally a 'feast-script', to honour a respected person, especially an academic. Publication and celebration are particularly fitting here. Both are vitally important to Ortrun's understanding and practice of scholarship, as an academic oriented to creating knowledge through solving real-life problems. Publication is a staple in Ortrun's career, since central to her epistemology is the understanding that knowledge created through research should be made public for all to share. Celebration is also a staple, since Ortrun actively – joyfully – upholds the importance of publicly acknowledging, sharing the lessons and pleasures, and further encouraging the success of research and learning through efforts and achievements of collaborators, students, colleagues and others.

The chapters in this book shed light on Ortrun's bounty of contributions to knowledge and learning, for and with individuals, organisations, and communities large and small, continuously in pursuit of a better world for all. In this way the book pays tribute to Ortrun's life and endless work. I say 'endless' as Ortrun has never accepted that retirement might mean the end of work. As Ortrun herself explains, 'For me, retirement means doing only what I enjoy most: teaching, coaching, giving seminars and workshops, or generally, helping other people in their learning' (Zuber-Skerritt, 2009, p. 193). I am privileged to be one of the many whom Ortrun has helped in their learning and I am honoured to introduce this Festschrift for her.

ORTRUN ZUBER-SKERRITT: AN ACADEMIC LIFE OF ACTION

Ortrun's undergraduate and early postgraduate studies were at the University of Kiel, Germany, where she gained a broad education including philosophy, languages, literature and culture with a major in human movement studies. When reflecting on her experiences in Germany as a young person, Ortrun has often described herself as 'an action girl' who loved her skiing, cycling, swimming and mountain climbing. A combination of action and learning through recreational pursuits and training and work as a physical education teacher defined who she was. After arriving in Australia in 1971, Ortrun worked briefly as a high school teacher before tutoring in the German Department at the University of Queensland. It was then that Ortrun completed a PhD from the University of Queensland researching Australian drama

J. Kearney & M. Todhunter (Eds), Lifelong Action Learning and Research: A Tribute to the Life and Pioneering Work of Ortrun Zuber-Skerritt, 1–8.

to which she had actively turned her passions. Ortrun further pursued her interest in this field through a collection of interviews with Australia's leading playwrights of the time, which she had made into videos that are now a very valuable contribution to historical record. This was the first of four doctoral qualifications, with the other awards being a PhD in Higher Education from Deakin University, Australia; a Doctor of Letters (DLitt) in Management from the International Management Centre, in the United Kingdom; and an Honorary Doctorate from the Global University for Lifelong Learning.

In 1974, Ortrun was appointed as a lecturer in the Centre for the Advancement of Learning and Teaching at Griffith University in Brisbane. Across the four decades since this watershed move to Higher Education, Ortrun has built a career as a respected academic and contributed many exciting ideas and innovations to learning and scholarship for and through Higher Education. Her contributions are not just to learning and scholarship since Ortrun is a practical hands-on person of action and her research orientation is always to solving real problems in a sustainable way for others to benefit, as well as to the practical and conceptual lessons through that process. The chapters that follow illustrate how.

FESTSCHRIFT CONTRIBUTIONS

People from various strands in Ortrun's life have contributed to this Festschrift. Carsten Zuber, Ortrun's son, has provided the foreword and suggested the striking painting by Ortrun's brother Wolfram for the book's front cover. Brief tributes from some of Ortrun's colleagues, friends and mentees follow Carsten's piece. Collectively, these reflections capture Ortrun as a woman of intellect, integrity, vision and action, who is a loyal and generous friend as well as a dedicated academic.

The rest of the book comprises chapters written by some of Ortrun's colleagues and friends from around the world. Each helps to illustrate Ortrun's seminal role in the evolving paradigm of Action Learning and Action Research (ALAR). ALAR, more recently explicitly identifying its participatory nature as PALAR, is the methodology, approach and worldview by which Ortrun not only researches but lives her life to the fullest, while co-creating knowledge and helping to develop the ability to create knowledge through problem solving among people across the world. In each chapter, authors trace the development of aspects of ALAR relating to their own work, and discuss linkages with Ortrun's work. These linkages interweave with the book's unifying theme of 'change for a better world', consistent with Ortrun's use of this theme in recent publications (2009, 2011, 2012, 2013, 2015). The Festschrift concludes with reflections from Maureen Todhunter, co-editor of this book.

The following 12 chapters are sequenced in four parts that relate to areas of focus for Ortrun's work and interests over the last 30 years. Part I is *Higher Education*, the site for most of Ortrun's work experience since 1974 when she joined Griffith University. Part II, *Organisations*, is a context in which Ortrun has actively explored processes of learning, leadership and development in management education. Part III is *Communities of Practice*, which have characterised Ortrun's work throughout her career as evidenced particularly in her work involving PALAR in higher education and communities. Part IV is *Futures*, an interest that focusses much of Ortrun's recent writing where she advocates for ALAR/PALAR as a flexible and effective methodology for responding to or even pre-empting challenges associated with rapid change.

Higher Education

Ortrun worked for 23 years in the higher education sector, in full-time positions at Griffith University, University of Queensland and Southern Cross University. Since 1997 she has been an Adjunct Professor at Griffith University and, more recently, a Professor Extraordinaire at Tshwane University of Technology (Pretoria) and at North-West University (Potchefstroom) in South Africa. Universities worldwide have sought Ortrun's expertise. As an example, Ortrun was a regular Visiting Professor for 15 years at the University of Innsbruck in Austria, teaching and coaching groups of doctoral students in the social sciences. In recognition for Ortrun's achievements in research and postgraduate teaching, she was awarded an 'Honorary Citizen of the University of Innsbruck' in 2003.

Ortrun's international reputation in the fields of higher education and action research was recognised when her second doctoral thesis, a PhD in Higher Education from Deakin University in 1987, was published in two companion books: *Professional Development in Higher Education: A Theoretical Framework for Action Research* and *Action Research in Higher Education: Examples and Reflections* (both by Kogan Page, London, 1992). Since then Ortrun has published regularly on issues affecting higher education with a very strong focus on postgraduate education. Ortrun's CV reveals she has published what I estimate to be 38 books and almost 100 book chapters or refereed journal articles. Several colleagues have acted as critical friends for her writing. They include Mary Brydon-Miller of the United States and David Coghlan of the United Kingdom, who have co-authored Chapter 2 in this volume, 'Mirror, mirror: Action research takes a hard look at higher education'.

Mary and David acknowledge Ortrun's contribution in promoting Action Learning and Action Research (ALAR) to improve teaching and learning practice through professional development. They share with Ortrun a concern that higher education institutions now and in the future must critically consider how the instrumental rationality paradigm that dominates higher education is neither ethically sound nor effective for embracing local and global challenges in positive ways. The authors propose that action research and lifelong action learning strategies, as discussed in Ortrun's 2013 publication with Richard Teare, provide a way forward in reconsidering learning environments within universities, community engagement practices and research agendas and protocols. As Mary and David conclude, this shift in thinking and action 'offers a more positive and generative image of higher education' in line with Ortrun's quest for a better world.

Chapter 3, 'An action learning approach to writing scholarly journal articles', is written by Chris Kapp. Chris first read Ortrun's work in the late 1980s, but did not meet her until 1996. This meeting began Ortrun's long association with South Africa. Since 1997, higher education institutions in Stellenbosch, Pretoria, Bloemfontein, Cape Town, Johannesburg, Port Elizabeth and Potchefstroom have invited Ortrun to facilitate workshops and present leadership programs. Many of these invitations involved presentations with Chris, and as a result of these visits, Ortrun developed a deep love for South Africa, its landscapes and its animals. Indeed, Ortrun has often followed an intensive week of university work with a safari, a tradition underpinned by her belief in the importance of both 'work and play' and their mutual benefits.

Ortrun clearly has a special place in her heart for the people of South Africa, and has been a treasured mentor for several female academics from South African universities. Between 2000 and 2002, she secured a national competitive grant from AusAID for an international development program on 'Leadership Development for Women Academics in South Africa'. In 2007, she obtained another AusAID grant that funded a leadership development program through action learning and action research for teams from six African countries.

This project involved a partnership between Griffith University and the University of Stellenbosch. It gave me the opportunity to work with Ortrun for the first time and to witness the rich professional relationship she shared with Chris Kapp in action.

Chris's chapter explains how action learning principles and processes are embedded in his approach to promoting scholarly writing. Chris and his team have used this approach with South African academics for ten years with 150 workshops and 3,000 participants. Chris begins the chapter with an explanations of the South African academic context. He explains the philosophical underpinnings of his action learning approach to the writing of journal articles, describes the design of the workshop elements, and provides an analysis of participant feedback. The chapter concludes with a reflection on future strategies to sustain the approach. Chris acknowledges the inspiration, enthusiasm and collegiality of Ortrun in conceptualising his action learning approach to scholarly writing.

Doris Santos from Colombia has authored Chapter 4, the final chapter in Part I. She is one of the many female academics who has benefitted from Ortrun's mentorship and boundless kindness. Their meeting was inevitable as both women shared an interest in action research as a process to enhance learning in a higher education context. Doris's chapter, 'Weaving together: Ortrun Zuber-Skerritt's legacy to PAR from a Colombian female academic's perspective', shares three stories. Collectively, the stories demonstrate Ortruns' inspirational contribution to PAR communities through publishing collaborations and networking activities. Each of the stories emphasises Ortrun's 'generosity, joy, hard work and solidarity' as the threads she uses to weave a web of relationships to move us towards a better world.

Organisations

Part II on Organisations comprises Chapters 5, 6 and 7. Shankar Sankaran, who has lived in a number of countries, has written the first of these, 'Achieving synergy through combining action learning and action research'. He discusses the differences and similarities between action learning and action research as processes, and explains their synergy and practicality when combined, using the example of a model proposed by Ortrun and her colleague, Chad Perry. Shankar applied this model in his doctoral studies and has since used it with postgraduate students to generate research outcomes in the context of organisations. He argues that ALAR is a pragmatic approach for doctoral students seeking both organisational change and rigorous research. Shankar concludes by acknowledging Ortrun's enthusiasm and valuable contribution to his own scholarly journey and to ALAR communities worldwide.

In Chapter 6, Ron Passfield from Australia explains Ortrun as 'The "practical visionary"', who not only describes a vision for a better world but works actively to make it happen while inspiring others to contribute. Ron met Ortrun in 1989 when she was organising the International Symposium on Action Research in Industry, Government and Education in Brisbane. The following year, Ortrun convened the First World Congress on Action Learning and Action Research. Ron supported Ortrun in this endeavour and went on to work with her to create the Action Learning, Action Research and Process Management (ALARPM) Association, an initiative that realised Ortrun's vision to bring together practitioners from a variety of practice contexts where they used three different processes – action learning, action research and process management. In the course of these collaborations, Ron noted particular attributes that set Ortrun apart from others. These include the strength of her belief in others and in herself, her drive to contribute to a better world and support others to do this, her ability to establish a network of critical friends, and her openness to their critique as a means of enhancing her own learning and self-improvement and to some extent their own as well.

In Chapter 7, Eileen Piggot-Irvine from New Zealand and now in Canada emphasises Ortrun's transformative influence on her professional and personal life. In 'Collaboration, innovation and evaluation in action research: Life with Ortrun for a better world', Eileen describes Ortrun as 'the key outstanding mentor in my life's work' and a 'deeply caring, loving friend of myself and family'. Eileen illustrates these claims through three areas of interest as an action researcher:

1. the creation of authentic collaboration as the most important underpinning of action research;
2. the introduction of Repertory Grid Technique as an innovative tool for action research; and
3. the evaluation of process and impact of action research via a global 'Evaluative Study of Action Research' (ESAR).

5

She concludes that what Ortrun espouses – authentic collaboration, openness and transparency – is what Ortrun truly practises. Indeed, Ortrun herself continues to remind us that as action researchers we must practise what we preach.

Communities of Practice

Part III, on the various communities where Ortrun has worked, comprises Chapters 8, 9 and 10. Lesley Wood from South Africa provides Chapter 8, 'PALAR for community engagement: the postgraduate voice'. While Ortrun and Lesley have worked collaboratively for fewer than five years, they have developed a strong partnership in that time using Participatory Action Learning and Action Research (PALAR), an approach to engage meaningfully with communities for mutual learning and development. Lesley reflects on a PALAR project involving higher degree research students and their supervisors. She outlines the guiding principles of the PALAR process, explains PALAR's appeal and benefits, identifies its challenges, and offers a response to these challenges. Lesley argues that we need to reconsider traditional approaches to educational research and adopt a participatory and engaged approach if we are to prepare people for life in the twenty-first century. She acknowledges Ortrun's ongoing support to realise this goal in a South African context.

Chapter 9, 'Building national and international action research communities of practice', is by Pip Bruce Ferguson from New Zealand and now in Dublin. Pip traces the development of action research communities of practice in New Zealand and reflects on that experience as an involved member of the New Zealand Action Research Network (NZARN). She notes the support and influence of the Action Learning, Action Research and Process Management (ALARPM) network then active in Australia and shares reflections on that journey by several ALARPM members, including Ortrun. Pip emphasises the importance of relationships in building communities and the significance of networking. She notes Ortrun's capacity to develop positive relationships and to network locally and internationally. Pip also considers how communities of practice develop in international contexts, acknowledging the role of events such as the World Congress to connect participants with each other, and the potential of digitally mediated platforms to sustain and further develop these connections.

Chapter 10, 'Creating world congresses of action learning and action research to network an international community', is by Yoland Wadsworth from Australia. Yoland pays tribute to Ortrun's contribution to the series of world congresses that have brought together the global community of action researchers and action learners to network and share collaboratively. She provides an historical overview of these congresses, acknowledging Ortrun's initiation and convening of the First World Congress on Action Learning, Action Research and Process Management (ALARPM) in Brisbane in 1990. At the Second World Congress in 1992, Ortrun launched the international ALARPM Association, now called ALARA (http://www.alarassociation.org), a worldwide network of innovative consultants and educators in industry, government, education and the community, using action learning processes. We learn that Ortrun was on the Executive Committee for the first seven world congresses, has contributed at all congresses, and has captured the reflections of congress participants in her publications. Yoland identifies the unique characteristics of world congresses, emphasising features such as networking, creative modes of presentation, and participants' diverse contexts and interests.

Futures

The final part of this Festschrift perhaps inevitably turns to the future. In Chapter 11, 'Action learning and action research for a turbulent future', Bob Dick from Australia emphasises the need for responsive and flexible processes to address rapid change in future times. Ortrun's writings frequently identify this need and similarly urge action for sustainable outcomes. Bob claims that both the AL and AR in ALAR – an integration championed by Ortrun some 25 years ago – are ideal processes in managing an uncertain future. Bob points out two features of ALAR that make it a useful approach when responding flexibly to rapid change: the cyclic process that characterises this approach and the nesting of cycles with different time scales and scopes. The future Bob envisages is turbulent, with possible threats to global wellbeing driven by increasing globalisation and the increasing power of technology. Bob reminds us of how these two trends have transformed means of communication and access to information in current times. He calls on us to consider a response where we intervene locally in communities and organisations using ALAR strategies to create a resilient social ecology where individuals collaborate for collective benefit – and thus for a better world.

In Chapter 12, 'Researching plausible futures: managing the process', Richard Bawden of Australia shares Bob Dick's views when contemplating the future. Like Bob, Richard describes the future as 'unpredictable' and 'uncertain' and emphasises the need for capabilities to deal with it. Richard argues for the development of processes that assist us in 'learning how to learn *from* the future, for the future'. He introduces readers to QUEST™ as a process management approach to scenario learning, and distinguishes it from other approaches to scenario planning by its experiential nature, systemic approach, and emphasis on critical self-reflexivity. Richard acknowledges Ortrun's contribution to his current thinking by reference to a writing collaboration in 1990 where she encouraged him to develop a more critical appreciation of process management.

Richard Teare, of the UK, presents the final contribution to this Festschrift in Chapter 13, 'Applying the concept of lifelong action learning: learning and development for a better world.' Since 2008 Ortrun has championed Richard's work through the Global University for Lifelong Learning (GULL), a not-for-profit foundation that promotes holistic lifelong learning using an action learning approach. In this chapter, Richard explains Ortrun's contribution to the concept of Lifelong Action Learning (LAL), and the conceptual framework that underpins the work of GULL. Richard traces Ortrun's practical and theoretical contributions to the GULL network since its inception in 2007, drawing from five of Ortrun's recent publications. His analysis provides a very clear picture of how Ortrun's contributions have helped shape an inclusive approach to learning and community development. Richard acknowledges Ortrun's pre-eminence as a visionary scholar and generous friend.

Following the four parts, the Festschrift concludes with Part V, Concluding Reflection. In Chapter 14, 'A fitting celebration', my co-editor Maureen Todhunter reflects critically on this Festschrift, its contributions to knowledge of Ortrun as an ALAR 'mover and shaker', and so to historical knowledge of the ALAR paradigm.

TO CONCLUDE

I have known Ortrun Zuber-Skerritt as colleague since 2007. This is a much shorter period than the long friendships and professional relationships that most contributors to this Festschrift have shared with Ortrun. However, during the last eight years I have come to know Ortrun also as a valued mentor and caring friend. Ortrun has inspired me – and all who have contributed to this Festschrift – to be better able to reach out to others through reflective, inclusive action. As the narratives in this book convey, her behaviour has modelled for us how to do this. From Ortrun we have learned further how to take informed, democratic action through ALAR/PALAR as we work collectively to build a better world. We and many others have much to be grateful for from Ortrun Zuber-Skerritt.

REFERENCES

Zuber-Skerritt, O. (1992a). *Professional development in higher education: A theoretical framework for action research.* London, UK: Kogan Page.

Zuber-Skerritt, O. (1992b). *Action research in higher education: Examples and reflections.* London, UK: Kogan Page.

Zuber-Skerritt, O. (2009). *Action learning and action research: Songlines through interviews.* Rotterdam, The Netherlands: Sense Publishers.

Zuber-Skerritt, O. (2011). *Action leadership: Towards a participatory paradigm.* Heidelberg, Germany: Springer.

Zuber-Skerritt, O. (Ed.). (2012). *Action research for sustainable development in a turbulent world.* Bingley, UK: Emerald Group Publishing Limited.

Zuber-Skerritt, O., & Teare, R. (2013). *Lifelong action learning for community development: Learning and development for a better world.* Rotterdam, The Netherlands: Sense Publishers.

Zuber-Skerritt, O., Fletcher, M., & Kearney, J. (2015). *Professional learning in higher education communities: Towards a new vision for action research.* London, UK: Palgrave Macmillan.

Judith Kearney
Director of Community Partnerships
School of Education and Professional Studies
Griffith University
Australia

PART I

HIGHER EDUCATION

MARY BRYDON-MILLER AND DAVID COGHLAN

2. MIRROR, MIRROR

Action Research Takes a Hard Look at Higher Education

Queen: Slave in the magic mirror, come from the farthest space, through wind and darkness I summon thee. Speak! Let me see thy face.

Magic Mirror: What wouldst thou know, my Queen?

Queen: Magic Mirror on the wall, who is the fairest one of all?

(From Disney's 1937 film, *Snow White and the Seven Dwarves*)

When the Wicked Queen in the story Snow White asks the magic mirror this question, she expects to get the same answer she always does. 'You, your majesty, are fairest of them all'. But the mirror tells her the truth…

We're used to deceiving ourselves about the impact of university education and research. But if those of us in higher education had a magic mirror and were forced to face the painful truth about our institutions – Do we provide the highest quality education to our students? Do we make the resources of our universities available to our communities? Does our research contribute to positive social change? – the answers we get might be just as difficult to bear as the mirror's observation that Snow White was the more beautiful. It's important that we take a hard look at the current state of higher education, though, if we are to develop new strategies to improve educational opportunities for our students and ensure that the research carried out under the auspices of our institutions makes a positive contribution to society. Action research can serve as this mirror, and at the same time can act as a window onto potential futures, providing us with a view of the kinds of knowledge we will need to address these concerns.

One of Ortrun Zuber-Skerritt's many contributions has been to explore Action Learning and Action Research (ALAR) in higher education (Zuber-Skerritt, 1992). A particular emphasis has been to explore ALAR's role in improving teaching and learning practice through professional development. Our chapter explores how action learning and action research can be used to challenge the basic structures of the contemporary university, through not only its teaching and research but also its very identity. Recent trends toward an increased emphasis on rankings of students, faculty, and institutions and on the commercialisation of knowledge suggest a system that has lost track of its responsibility to contribute to positive change. In this

J. Kearney & M. Todhunter (Eds), Lifelong Action Learning and Research: A Tribute to the Life and Pioneering Work of Ortrun Zuber-Skerritt, 11–20.

chapter we seek to build on Zuber-Skerritt's work to recapture that focus on social responsibility and to suggest ways in which we might draw upon action research strategies to promote institutional change.

In their book, *Lifelong Action Learning for Community Development*, Ortrun Zuber-Skerritt and her colleague Richard Teare (2013, p. 7) describe a process of learning that is 'about encouraging and helping to enable *all* people, especially in the poorest and most disadvantaged communities in our world, to develop their learning potential by discovering their special gifts, cascading their learning, and developing these gifts together with other like-minded people'. While Zuber-Skerritt and Teare make clear that this process is not to be confined to formal educational systems, our contention would be that institutions of higher education must embrace Lifelong Action Learning (LAL), for both ethical and practical reasons. Higher education finds itself at a critical crossroads. As described in the recent report, *An Avalanche is Coming: Higher Education and the Revolution Ahead* (Barber, Donnelly & Rizvi, 2013), current global economic, environmental, and political issues require citizens who are prepared to respond in innovative, collaborative, and ethical ways if we are to address these challenges successfully. In order to do this, 'deep, radical and urgent transformation is required in higher education' (p. 5).

This same theme is reflected in Ronald Barnett's recent book, *Imagining the University*, which raises the question, 'Is it not part of the task of the university to try to do its best to usher in a different and even a better world?' (2013, p. 10). We would argue that this is not simply a part of the task of the university, but *the* ethical imperative of the university. And one which seems to have been left by the wayside in the current move to turn students into customers, faculty into underpaid part-time labourers, and the university itself into a commercial enterprise. Barnett invites readers to imagine the university anew – to create as many 'feasible utopias' as possible with a view toward expanding our vision of the potential of higher education. Action research provides the tools for this process of recreating the university, and we feel a deep responsibility to bring our own experience and expertise to this process.

Action research offers concrete strategies not only for engaging in research to address these issues outside the university setting, but for leading a critical reflection within the academy itself designed to fundamentally change the very nature of higher education. It is only by embracing this opportunity for reinvention that the promise of higher education as a catalyst for positive change can be realised (Brydon-Miller, 2015, in press).

Highlighting the contrast between traditional educational systems and their own proposed approach, Zuber-Skerritt and Teare (2013, p. 17) identify the following elements of lifelong action learning:

- Learner centred;
- Process and project based;
- Interdisciplinary, problem oriented;

- Located in real-life work;
- Inclusive, accessible to all, aimed at social justice;
- Informal, self-directed learning;
- Based on contemporary cultural context;
- Communities of learning, action learning sets;
- Collaboration, cooperation.

Their description echoes the elements that Levin and Greenwood (2008) outline for the university of the future. 'We believe that universities should be reorganised to meet the challenges of redeveloping public support by structuring teaching and research through action research strategies. This means problem selection, analysis, action design, implementation, and evaluation by collaborative multi-disciplinary teams of academics and non-university stakeholders' (p. 211). Moving to such an idea of a university of the future involves challenging the current model of professional education that dominates higher education.

CHALLENGING THE DOMINANT PARADIGM IN HIGHER EDUCATION

Technical or instrumental rationality is a term that describes the dominant paradigm of professional knowledge (Schön, 1983). It is characterised by underlying disciplines of basic science upon which professional practice is built and instrumental problem-solving is conducted rigorously by the application of scientific theory and methods. Schein (1972) describes its components.

- An underlying discipline or basic science upon which practice is developed;
- An applied science from which day-to-day diagnostic procedures and problem solutions are derived;
- A skills and attitudinal component that concerns actual performance of services to clients using the underlying basic and applied science.

This paradigm is embedded in the institutional structures and philosophy of the education of professionals. Professional curriculum begins with science and is followed by an applied component. Students learn the science first. Otherwise they have nothing to apply. Skills are a secondary knowledge.

The outcome of this paradigm is a hierarchy of knowledge. Science is on top and technical skills of day-to-day practice are on the bottom. The nearer one is to basic science, the higher is one's academic status. Academics are superior to practitioners. The corollary is that there is a split between theory and practice, a split that is grounded in positivist philosophy of science.

Schön (1987) presents the counter-position and argues the case for a different focus for professional education.

- Inherent in the practice of professionals is a competence that we can recognise as artistry.
- Artistry is a kind of knowing that is different from the technical rational model.

- Artistry forms a boundary around the practice of applied science and techniques as there is an art to problem framing, an art of implementation, and an art of improvisation that are necessary in the practice of applied science and technique.

Schön's (1992) conclusion is to call for a new epistemology – one that can work with the tacit epistemology of the skilled professional. This tacit epistemology is the professional's knowing-in-action – the spontaneous behaviour of the skilful practitioner that is based on a knowing of more than can be articulated. Uncovering such knowing is attempted through reflection-in-action and reflection-in-practice. With Argyris he framed the notion of action science, which seeks to create a science of action by systematically analysing and documenting patterns of behaviours and the reasoning behind them in order to identify causal links so as to produce actionable knowledge, that is, theories for producing desired outcomes (Argyris & Schön, 1974).

Kinsella (2012) argues that Schön's call for a new epistemology has much in common with Aristotle's notion of *phronesis* because it involves reflection and certain types of judgement. Aristotle describes *phronesis* in terms of the good person whose life is oriented towards value, and not merely satisfaction, and whose courses of action are genuinely good because they are oriented towards values and because they recognise what is required to implement these values in the concrete situation (Eikeland, 2008). What is required, then, is to recreate the academy around this new epistemological and ethical stance.

With this view of a university grounded in reflective practice and action for positive change, we examine three components of the modern university as they currently exist and as they might be reimagined through an action research and lifelong action learning lens: the learning environment within the university, community engagement beyond the university, and research practice that engages broader issues of social change.

The Learning Environment

Visit almost any modern university classroom and you find yourself in a setting that hasn't changed in centuries. Large lecture halls with tiers of seats all focussed on the podium from which a professor delivers lectures to a largely inert audience. Of course, in today's classroom the room will be lit by the tiny oblong lights of cell phone screens held discretely in the laps of distracted students, but otherwise the scene is not much changed from the nineteenth century. Smaller classes still meet in rooms set up in rows of desks all pointing to the front of the room – the technology has changed, but the assumptions regarding who holds knowledge and who wields power in that setting have not. Try to move the furniture to accommodate any other style of learning and you'll be chastised for creating a nuisance for your colleagues. Even in online learning environments the structure and content of learning remain under the control of the professor with their prepared learning modules and sophisticated systems for tracking student participation. Freire's notion of banking education still dominates classrooms, starting with the architecture (both physical and virtual) itself. And these classrooms sit in buildings that sit on campuses largely isolated from the communities around them. Campus security patrols the perimeter and buildings are locked to outsiders, sometimes physically and sometimes virtually through the use of technology that makes information available only to those with the correct password.

Revisiting Zuber-Skerritt and Teare's criteria, we see how antithetical the modern university campus is to the practice of lifelong action learning. Rather than being learner-centred, classrooms and campuses focus attention on the instructor, reinforcing traditional power relationships at all levels. In place of individualised problem-oriented learning, admissions committees and other governing bodies increasingly rely upon the results of standardised tests to determine who gains access to educational opportunities and as a result curricula, from elementary education through graduate training, focus on the acquisition of a prescribed body of knowledge. Cooperation and collaboration, vital components of lifelong action learning, are discouraged in a system designed to encourage competition and a winner-take-all mentality.

If we are to accept Barnett's challenge to imagine the university anew, how might we re-envision what classrooms and campuses look like? In our own experience there are existing models of learning environments that do reflect these values of cooperation, collaboration, accessibility and active student engagement. Interestingly, however, the models that come immediately to mind are not located on university campuses. The current location of the Highlander Research and Education Centre, founded in 1932 by Myles Horton, Don West and Jim Dombrowski, is on the side of a mountain in rural Tennessee (Hale, 2007; Schneider, 2014; Williams, 2014). The main meeting room is surrounded by windows looking out over the landscape and is furnished with a large circle of comfortable wooden rocking chairs, now the symbol of the organisation. It's no wonder, then, that Highlander was founded after Horton visited the Danish folkhighschools in the early 1930s (the original name of the organisation was the Highlander Folk School), because the folkhighschools we've visited in Denmark and Sweden continue to provide learning environments that emphasise collaboration, problem-focussed learning, and a connection to the local community. For example, on a recent visit we found the Ädelfors Folkhighschool in southern Sweden (http://www.adelfors.nu/information/english.aspx) showcasing the work of local artists, and the use of natural materials throughout the buildings with comfortable spaces for meeting, reading and sharing meals was all a conscious part of the learning environment.

Beyond the physical setting, there are also models of teaching and learning processes that engage the values articulated by Zuber-Skerritt and Teare. Van Lier (2006) in his introduction to Beckett and Miller's volume *Project-based Second and Foreign Language Education* cites John Dewey, Maria Montessori, Jean Piaget, and L. S. Vygotsky as important contributors to the development of project-based learning, one of the principles noted in Zuber-Skerritt and Teare's list. Project-based learning 'has the potential to embody the kind of politically engaged, transformative approach to education envisioned by Freire and other critical educators' (Brydon-Miller, 2006, p. 42). At the same time, however, unless projects also reflect the principles of being learner-centred, inclusive, accessible to all, and aimed at social justice, this approach 'runs the very real risk of instead becoming simply another formula for reinforcing existing systems of oppression' (Brydon-Miller, 2006, p. 42). This leads to our second arena for reframing higher education – community engagement.

Community Engagement

Increasingly colleges and universities are using a rhetoric of community engagement and service learning to attempt to make education seem more relevant and meaningful to students. But too often the opportunities provided through such programs are short-term feel-good bungee jumps into communities, which as often as not reinforce negative attitudes toward the recipients of these efforts rather than encouraging more sustained and critical engagement with issues of poverty and marginalisation. Locating these learning opportunities in the context of community-based research efforts can provide for the kind of interdisciplinary, problem-oriented learning situated in contemporary cultural contexts and aimed at social justice that Zuber-Skerritt and Teare describe. But this kind of community-based research 'requires that instructors venture outside the comfort zone of more conventional teaching, where they have the luxury of assuming a great deal of control over what is taught, how it is taught, and how learning is assessed' (Strand, Marullo, Cutforth, Stoecker & Donohue, 2003, p. 155).

Here again, action research provides a variety of strategies and exemplars of community-based research that exhibit 'a respect for people and for the knowledge and experience they bring to the research process, a belief in the ability of democratic processes to achieve positive social change, and a commitment to action' (Brydon-Miller, Greenwood & Maguire, 2003, p. 15). These core values of action research suggest an approach to community engagement that unsettles the common model of service learning by bringing students, faculty and community partners together as co-creators of knowledge and co-generators of social action. This new model of community-engaged learning faces many challenges within the traditional academic setting, which breaks education into discrete 16-week-long units with students' attention and time divided among multiple academic subjects. The immersive co-op model of learning, in which students work full-time for an extended period within an organisation or business, provides a better model for community-engaged learning. Here the members of the community organisation, neighbourhood association, school, or other setting serve not as passive recipients of services designed and delivered by outsiders, but rather as the experts whose experience and knowledge work with the support of university faculty to provide a curriculum grounded in the real-life work and contemporary cultural contexts described by Zuber-Skerritt and Teare as critical components of lifelong action learning. At the same time it creates the framework for research practices that are designed to grapple with the complexity of real-life problems and constantly changing social, economic, political and cultural landscapes. But this style of community engagement requires a research practice more closely aligned with the kind of reflection-in-practice outlined by Argyris and Schön.

Research Practice

Within the paradigm of technical rationality outlined above, research is firmly grounded in the domain of the disciplinary scientists who advise policymakers and funders what needs to be researched and how. Gibbons, Limoges, Nowotny, Schwartzman, Scott and Trow (1994) describe this approach as Mode 1 research. This is research that arises from the academic agenda, and that agenda usually takes place within a singular discipline and is accountable to that discipline. The data are context-free and validated by logic, measurement and consistency of prediction and control. The role of the researcher is that of an observer, and the researcher's relationship to the setting is detached and neutral. In many respects, Mode 1 captures the normal meaning of the term *science*, by which is meant that the aim of the research is to produce universal knowledge and to build and test theory within a disciplinary field. The type of knowledge acquired is universal covering law.

In contrast to Mode 1, Mode 2 research has the following characteristics. It is produced in the context of a particular application and so is relevant and useful to practitioners. It is characterised by *trans-disciplinarity*, in that it integrates different skills, multi- or interdisciplinary, depending on the application. It is characterised by *heterogeneity* and *organisational diversity*, in that multidisciplinary teams may be temporary and that members come and go as the situation unfolds and as different skills are required at different stages of the project. It is characterised by *social accountability and reflexivity* where there is accountability to outcomes and to the participants. This involves reflexivity and a sensitivity to the process of the research itself and to, for example, the dynamics of trans-disciplinarity. Finally, it is characterised by a *diverse range of quality controls*, in that unlike Mode 1 where the question of knowledge production is judged from the stance of the discipline, Mode 2 draws on a broader range of interests such as its application, and from the perspective of different stakeholders. As Levin and Greenwood (2008) point out, while Gibbons and his colleagues appear to be unaware of the generations of action research work, their notion of Mode 2 has generated rich discussion central to the debates about the future of higher education. It is our view that the constructs of and subsequent discussions about Mode 2 contribute to our reflection on research practice and support our challenge to the instrumental rationality paradigm.

Action research changes what we take as knowledge. Its aim is to generate practical knowing (Coghlan, 2011), to change practices and social structures that maintain injustice, and unsatisfying forms of existence. It is about creating forms of inquiry that people can use in the conduct of their lives. Underpinning action research is the core value that people are not mere data points but are agents of experiencing, understanding, judging, valuing, deciding and acting. Action research adopts the position that research is *with* people, rather than for or about or on them, and that it is those directly affected by the practical issue who decide what research might be done, how, to what ends, and with what outcomes in mind. Accordingly, communities and organisational members act as co-researchers in the design, implementation and evaluation of the research that seeks to both improve the situation and to cogenerate actionable knowledge, that is, knowledge that is useful for practitioners and robust for scholars. It focusses attention on the research process itself alongside the concern for practical outcomes (Brydon-Miller & Coghlan, 2014). This approach also reflects the elements of lifelong-action research described by Zuber-Skerritt and Teare. Developing research practices that address worthwhile purposes, draw on many ways of knowing, generate knowledge in practice through participation and democracy, and follow an emergent developmental form, is a radical alternative to the Mode 1 paradigm in which higher education is currently locked (Reason & Bradbury, 2008).

CONCLUSIONS

In this chapter we acknowledge Ortrun Zuber-Skerritt's contribution of ALAR to improving teaching and learning in higher education practices. We have sought to build on it to open further exploration of how the foundations and philosophical underpinnings of higher education need to be challenged. At the heart of our exploration is a challenge to the instrumental rationality paradigm that dominates higher education and that finds expression in Mode 1 research. As an alternative we build on Schön's notion of the artistry of the professional where practice is afforded value and that researchers and academics are trained in ALAR and create the learning environment of Lifelong Action Learning (LAL) proposed by Zuber-Skerritt and Teare. Their research is deeply embedded in community engagement and, in the form of action research and Mode 2 research, transforms research practices to address worthwhile purposes through participation and democracy so as to generate knowledge in practice. This shift in the way we understand the fundamental nature of research practice then informs changes in the nature of community engagement and a reconceptualisation of the learning environment itself, offering a more positive and generative image of higher education if only we dare to look in the mirror.

REFERENCES

Argyris, C., & Schön, D. A. (1974). *Theory-in-practice: Increasing professional effectiveness*. San Francisco, CA: Jossey-Bass.

Barber, M., Donnelly, K., & Rizvi, S. (2013). *An avalanche is coming: Higher education and the revolution ahead*. London, UK: Institute for Public Policy Research.

Barnett, R. (2013). *Imagining the university*. London, UK: Routledge.

Brydon-Miller, M. (2006). Photovoice and Freirean critical pedagogy: Providing a liberatory theoretical framework to project-based learning in second language education. In G. H. Beckett & P. C. Miller (Eds.), *Project-based second and foreign language education: Past, present, and future* (pp. 41–53). Greenwich, CT: Information Age Publishing.

Brydon-Miller, M. (2015, In press). Creating a legacy: A reflection on the next 50 years of Sage and action research. In Sage (Ed.), Sage *50ᵗʰ anniversary collection*. Los Angeles: Sage Publications.

Brydon-Miller, M., & Coghlan, D. (2014). The big picture: Implications and imperatives for the action research community from the Sage encyclopaedia of action research. *Action Research, 12*(2), 2124–2233.

Brydon-Miller, M., Greenwood, D., & Maguire, P. (2003). Why action research? *Action Research, 1*(1), 9–28.

Coghlan, D. (2011) Action research: Exploring perspective on a philosophy of practical knowing. *Academy of Management Annals, 5*, 53–87.

Eikeland, O. (2008). *The ways of Aristotle, Aristotelian phronesis, Aristotelian philosophy of dialogue and action research*. Bern, Switzerland: Peter Lang.

Gibbons, M., Limoges, C., Nowotny, H., Schwartzman, S., Scott, P., & Trow, M. (1994). *The new production of knowledge*. London, UK: Sage.

Hale, J. N. (2007). Early pedagogical influences on the Mississippi freedom schools: Myles Horton and critical education in the deep south American (1905–1990). *American Education History Journal, 34*(1–2), 315.

Kinsella, A. E. (2012). Practitioner reflection and judgment as phronesis: A continuum of reflection and consideration for phronetic judgment. In A. E. Kinsella & A. Pitman (Eds.), *Phronesis as professional knowledge*, (pp. 35–52). Rotterdam, The Netherlands: Sense Publishers.

Levin, M., & Greenwood, D. (2008). The future of universities: Action research and the transformation of higher education. In P. Reason & H. Bradbury (Eds.), *The Sage handbook of action research* (2nd ed., pp. 211–226). London, UK: Sage.

Reason, P., & Bradbury, H. (Eds.) (2008). *The Sage handbook of action research* (2nd ed.). London, UK: Sage.

Schein, E. H. (1972). *Professional education*. New York, NY: McGraw-Hill.

Schneider, S. A. (2014). *You can't padlock an idea: Rhetorical education at the Highlander Folk School* (pp. 1932–1961). Columbia, SC: University of South Carolina Press.

Schön, D. A. (1983). *The reflective practitioner*. New York, NY: Basic Books

Schön, D. A. (1987). *Educating the reflective practitioner*. San Francisco, CA: Jossey-Bass.

Schön, D. A. (1992). The theory of inquiry: Dewey's legacy to education. *Curriculum Inquiry, 22*(2), 120–139.

Strand, K., Marullo, S., Cutforth, N., Stoecker, R., & Donohue, P. (2003). *Community-based research and higher education*. San Francisco, CA: Jossey-Bass.

Van Lier, V. (2006). Foreword. In G. H. Beckett & P. C. Miller (Eds.), *Project-based second and foreign language education: Past, present, and future* (pp. xi–xvi). Greenwich, CT: Information Age Publishing.

Williams, S. (2014). Highlander research and education center. In D. Coghlan & M. Brydon-Miller (Eds.), *The Sage encyclopedia of action research* (pp. 412–415). London, UK: Sage.

Zuber-Skerritt, O. (1992). *Professional development in higher education*. London, UK: Kogan-Page.

Zuber-Skerritt, O., & Teare, R. (2013). *Lifelong action learning for community development: Learning and development for a better world*. Rotterdam, The Netherlands: Sense Publishers.

Mary Brydon-Miller
Director, Action Research Center
University of Cincinnati
USA
and
Professor of Educational and Community-based Action Research
College of Education, Criminal Justice, and Human Services
University of Cincinnati
USA

David Coghlan
Fellow Emeritus, Adjunct Professor and Research Scholar
School of Business
Trinity College Dublin
Ireland

CHRIS KAPP

3. AN ACTION LEARNING APPROACH TO WRITING JOURNAL ARTICLES

INTRODUCTION

During my academic career covering 37 years, I was introduced to the writings of Ortrun Zuber-Skerritt in the late 1980s while visiting the Staff Development Unit at the University of Sheffield in the United Kingdom. I met Ortrun for the first time in 1996 while attending a Higher Education Research and Development Society of Australasia (HERDSA) Conference at the University of Western Australia in Perth. Ortrun attended one of my workshops. After the workshop she indicated to me that she would like to come to South Africa and we discussed future cooperation possibilities. This began a long-lasting professional partnership. Ortrun has often visited Stellenbosch University where my academic career was based, and has presented several workshops there, mainly on action research.

Ortrun Zuber-Skerritt is one of three academic colleagues who profoundly influenced my career as an academic. I have learned through and with her about action research and action learning and about postgraduate supervision and academic writing. When I had to retire from the University of Stellenbosch in 2007, I started a new career as a training consultant. I continue the work I had been doing and experiencing at the University of Stellenbosch, but now my 'students' (participants in the workshops) are academics from all over South Africa and Southern Africa. I now specialise in workshops on two particular topics: 1) Writing for Publication, and 2) The Science and the Art of Postgraduate Supervision and Assessment. Both are weeklong action learning workshops and were intrinsically inspired by Ortrun's leadership, coaching, example and enthusiasm.

In this chapter I discuss the Writing for Publication workshop. My colleagues and I have conducted these workshops since 2005. I discuss the background and rationale for the workshop and the action learning philosophy on which the workshop is based. I overview content of the workshop and offer an analysis of participants' responses over the past ten years, drawing from their anonymous feedback. As I acknowledge in every workshop, Ortrun Zuber-Skerritt has had a major influence on their nature and content through introducing me to the theory and practice of action learning and action research and to academics whose work has helped shape my understanding of academic writing workshops and how I facilitate these workshops in practice. It can surely be said that Ortrun's ideas are woven into the invisible tapestry of these workshops.

J. Kearney & M. Todhunter (Eds), Lifelong Action Learning and Research: A Tribute to the Life and Pioneering Work of Ortrun Zuber-Skerritt, 21–33.

ACADEMIC WRITING: A SOUTH AFRICAN CONTEXT

Ability in writing academic articles is not developed overnight. Expertise (subject knowledge and competence) takes a long time to develop. Some argue that it takes 10 years or 10,000 hours of practice (Gladwell, 2008; Wingfield, 2010). Academic articles are paths, the result of a process of not just research, but also the craft of writing. They are the product of a conversation between authors, reviewers and editors (Kingsley, 2007). This conversation is essential to discover the gems amongst academic articles.

'No research is research unless it is published' (Gevers, 2006, p. xiii). This truth is supported by several similar views on the importance of publishing one's research as part of the scholarly responsibility of the academic. Chanson (2007, p. 946) emphasises that sharing the results of one's research with the academic community (of scholars) is a major responsibility of all scholars: 'A research project is only completed when it has been published and shared with the community'. A key scholarly attribute is willingness (and ability) to subject one's work (research) to public scrutiny for verification, validation, discussion, consideration and possible alteration. This is done by subjecting scholarly products to double-blind peer review by experts in the field, with the aim of having the work published in reputable, accredited scholarly journals. Furthermore, scholars are motivated by the urge to know, to find out and to understand the ethic of inquiry. This curiosity – the desire to know, the passion to understand, the urge to discover – is a manifestation of the ethic of inquiry.

Within the South African context, several aspects influence academics' need to publish and consequently their need to have some form of training for writing journal articles. One is prevalence of the myth that if you have completed a PhD you are capable of writing an article. Another is transformation of the South African higher education system that has resulted in the loss of many experienced academics and the emergence of a 'new' generation. Government policies of Broad-Based Black Economic Empowerment have led to experienced academics retiring or being replaced by inexperienced academics, many of whom are women (it is estimated that 44% of instruction and research staff and 62% of support staff are female (Department of Higher Education and Training, 2013, p. 16)) or academics from other African countries (mainly Zimbabwe, Zambia, Uganda and some Francophone countries).

Another influential factor is government payment for published articles to promote and reward this practice among academics. South Africa is one of few countries where the government pays a subsidy – approximately R125,000 or US$11,500 – to authors for every scholarly article they have published in a journal accredited by the Department of Higher Education. This subsidy is provided through the National Funding Formula (Republic of South Africa, 2006) and has led to an increase in publication output since 2006 (Pouris, 2003, 2012). A final factor is associated with transformation of the university system in South Africa from a collegial system to a managed/bureaucratic system characterised by red tape and a system of performance appraisal, amongst other things. The performance appraisal system is used to determine whether academics have 'achieved' the outcomes expected of them. These outcomes are stratified according to level of appointment, and no academic will receive 'tenure' or be considered for appointment or promotion without evidence of their scholarly output in accordance with the performance appraisal system. This scholarly output concerns quantity rather than quality, including, for example, the number of scholarly articles an academic has published in accredited journals.

Much has been written about academic writing. From an international perspective, the writings of Rowena Murray (2005), Dernth (2009), and from an Australian perspective the seminal work of Royce Sadler (2006), are best known. From a South African perspective, the works by Maree (2012), Kapp and Albertyn (2008), Kapp, Albertyn and Frick (2010), and Ligthelm and Koekemoer (2009) are the best known. Several other publications include brief references to or chapters devoted to article writing or academic writing in general.

None of the above-mentioned publications provides a practical approach to the writing of an article. Most academics experience several barriers to writing (Kapp et al., 2010). Some of these barriers can be classified as institutional (workload, lack of time, absence of incentives, inadequate library facilities, limited internet access) and others as personal barriers (poor self-management, lack of research skills, poor writing skills, personality traits, inadequate motivation).

One of the barriers academics often use as an excuse for not publishing articles is lack of time because of heavy workload. Academics are often weighed down by the need to fulfil a multitude of tasks and a greater demand on their available time caused by the increased bureaucratisation of the university as an institution. More administrative duties are cascaded to the desk of the dedicated academic. Yet writing an article requires the full attention of the author; no distractions should interfere with the thinking and writing process. The author needs uninterrupted time to focus on these tasks. Clearly, short sessions of 30 minutes, one hour, or even three hours are not sufficient to produce quality articles.

For academic writing, scholars need an uninterrupted period free from disturbances such as appointments, drop-in visitors, meetings, classes, marking, and personal tasks such as preparing meals, doing laundry, taxi-ing children, helping them with homework, or work commutes of several hours. Therefore a retreat workshop, in an attractive natural setting with no interruptions, seemed to be the logical answer.

Recognising this need, colleagues and I designed a weeklong, writing-retreat workshop for academics. The *purpose* of the workshop is to provide the environment, input, support and guidance on structure to enable participants to complete their 'draft' (70–100% complete) articles. The participants receive from the facilitator input on essay 'parts' (introduction, literature review, methodology, results, discussion, conclusion, abstract). During the workshop, participants' written work, structured into appropriate 'parts', is peer reviewed then read by trained critical readers who are part of the facilitating team. Finally the writing is edited by accredited language editors and fine-tuned to enable authors to submit the paper for publication.

Response to the workshops has been remarkable. Over the past 10 years (2005–2014) 150 of these one-week workshops have been facilitated all over the country as well as in Zimbabwe, Zambia and Malawi. More than 3,000 academics (an average of 20 participants per workshop) have participated in these workshops and at least 50 per cent of the papers completed at the workshops have been accepted for publication.

In the rest of this chapter I explain the theory and philosophy underpinning the approach and the conceptualisation of the workshop. This is followed by an overview of the design and facilitation of the program. I then discuss analysis of feedback received from participants from the last 20 workshops as an indication of how the program works for participants. Finally, I attempt to 'look into the future', and to forecast the future for these workshops after the next two years.

PHILOSOPHICAL AND THEORETICAL FOUNDATIONS OF THIS ACTION LEARNING APPROACH

A fundamental aspect of any staff development activity is the facilitators' view on learning and especially on learning by professional adult learners. For the purposes of this workshop, our view as facilitators is that adult learning is based on the principles and practices described by Knowles (1973), Kolb (1984) and Brookfield (1995). The key principles of adult learning espoused by these authors can be synthesised as follows:

- Professional adult learners have a wealth of knowledge and experience that they carry with them and bring to the workshop. This knowledge and experience has to be utilised during the workshop and used to the benefit of all participants.
- Professional adult learners have a positive self-concept.
- Professional adult learners want to learn something practical that they can apply immediately.

In accordance with these principles, learning has to be viewed as an 'active' phenomenon. *To learn* is a verb, not a noun, therefore learning has to take place by doing. As attributed to Confucius and Confucian scholars, 'What I hear, I forget, what I see, I remember, what I *do*, I understand'. This view is supported by the ancient adage that if you give a man a fish, you feed him for a day; but teach him how to fish and you feed him for a lifetime. This is an understanding that has guided Ortrun's work powerfully, as her books in recent years explain.

One can read many articles or books on writing academic articles, but reading alone will not make one a good writer. An author will become a 'good' writer only through writing, by putting into practice what they have learnt. Writers need to *apply* new learning as soon as possible after 'receiving' the input. Such an approach inevitably leads to active learning (Dick, 2004; Zuber-Skerritt, 1992). This view of learning has to be put into perspective by linking it to training and more specifically to the practice of academic staff development, capacity building and human capital development.

As workshop designers and facilitators, we believe that academic staff development should be from the perspective of continuous or lifelong learning with emphasis on an athletic approach. We accept that all staff are good, but they can be better; there is always room for improvement. In this view of learning, individuals identify their own learning needs for growth and development and decide for themselves, obviously prompted by several triggers, what training they need, how that training should be obtained and when and where it will take place.

Learning therefore is a(n) (voluntary) active process where the active part relates to interaction between the (adult) learner and a variety of possible 'objects'. These objects could be the facilitator, peers/other participants or forms of 'media' such as a text book or course material, a computer screen, or information projected on a screen (PowerPoint or video).

Discussion so far in this section has clarified the concept of *action learning* as applied in the context of a training workshop on 'Academic Writing for Publication'. The process of action learning can best be described by means of the action learning cycle, applied to writing, as illustrated in Figure 3.1.

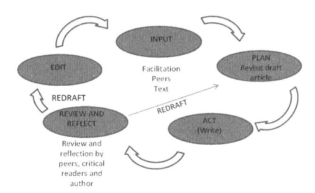

Figure 3.1. The writing cycle (action learning applied to writing)

For every *phase* in writing the article the action learning cycle is applied. Before authors become involved in the writing process, the facilitator offers input on writing an introduction, identifying and explaining its parts using examples in the workbook we provide to participants at the start of the workshop. This is the INPUT part of the action learning cycle regarding the INTRODUCTION. Then all the participants are given time to return to their draft article and to PLAN how they can incorporate or apply their learning, based on the input, to the introduction of their articles. Once their planning is completed, they will ACT by rewriting the introduction to their articles.

Then another part of *interactive* learning becomes operative as the introductions are peer reviewed by at least two peers as well as by a critical reader. During this phase of the writing cycle reflective practice is applied by all the participants. As the authors receive feedback from several sources, they *reflect* on what they have done (their actions) and review their work. During this phase there are two possible outcomes. On the one hand, based on the feedback received during the review process, the author can be requested to *redraft* the introduction. On the other hand, the feedback received from peer reviewers and critical readers or the changes suggested are limited and the draft can be completed and submitted to the language editors without the author having to redraft and resubmit.

This entire process, the action learning cycle, is repeated for each part of the article, namely the body (literature review, methodology, results, discussion), the conclusion and the abstract until all the parts of the article have been through the process of input, plan, write, review and reflect and submitted to the language editors.

CONTENT OF THE WORKSHOP

To do justice to a continuing professional learning opportunity for academic staff, the program has to be designed in a professional way. A thorough needs assessment has to be completed. The program should be designed according to accepted design principles. The clients participating in the learning engagement have to be considered from the outset.

For a program involving action learning, the design, planning and preparation phase is the most important part of the process. This process has to begin *before* the learning encounter/workshop takes place, maximising the benefits of 'action learning' by involving the participants as much as possible. The first step after a participant has *voluntarily* registered for the workshop is to carry out a detailed needs assessment. In the case of the 'Writing for Publication' workshop, we ask all registered participants to complete a *target population* analysis. This is a questionnaire asking eight questions about their paper: its central question, answer, a one-sentence summary, rationale for writing the paper, method, results, contribution to knowledge and practice, and what remains unresolved. We also ask participants to indicate priorities regarding their needs, using a five-point rating scale, for the 28 potential items to be included in the program. The final program is eventually designed based on the outcome of this needs assessment.

All professionally designed action learning programs should be based on a thorough needs assessment. However, although 80 per cent of the content of the program should be based on the *expressed* needs of the target population, the facilitator may contribute 20 per cent to the program based on the 'normative needs' they have experienced and their knowledge of the topic.

The workshop program follows a structured and carefully monitored approach. On the first day participants are introduced to a process of analysing the guidelines for authors of the journal in which they wish to publish. Major errors generally made by authors are identified and the participants are introduced to the characteristics of 'good' writing. The first day of the program culminates in participants writing the introduction of their articles (to be done overnight), which they need to submit to peer reviewers and critical readers.

The focus of the second day is on structuring the body of the article. The facilitator provides input on how to write a literature review, the methodology section, the results section and the discussion, supporting the input with examples included in the workbook. Participants have day two and day three to redraft the body of their paper and to submit this with the redrafted introduction to the critical readers and, once it is accepted by the critical readers, to the language editors.

In the latter part (late afternoon) of day three the focus turns to writing the conclusion. Here the facilitator follows the procedure described in the writing cycle (input, plan, write, review and reflect). Our structured approach uses five 'parts' to explain the writing of the conclusion and makes ample use of examples in the workbook.

On day four, participants are introduced to the writing of an abstract, the selection of a title and authorship. Once again, the action learning cycle is applied. Finally, on day five the emphasis is on fine-tuning the paper and on the process to follow when submitting a paper to a journal to be considered for publication. The facilitator also offers explanation of how to respond to reviewers' comments.

At this stage of the program, the *outcomes* set for the workshop will have been achieved. At least 50 per cent of the papers have been completed and at least 20 per cent of the papers have been copy-edited by the language editors. Continuous support is given to all the participants until their papers have been completed and edited. On completion of the paper and before it is submitted to the journal, the language editors issue a declaration that the paper has been edited by a registered and accredited language editor. Follow-up work is done by the entire team and participants are requested to inform the facilitator once their paper has been accepted for publication. In the next section I describe and analyse workshop results and feedback received from participants, which usefully illustrates how participants engage in the workshops and the learning and publishing results that they achieve.

FEEDBACK AND RESULTS

Over the 10 years we have conducted the writing workshop, we have averaged 15 workshops per year – some months up to three workshops. Over the years, demand has not only been sustained, but has increased in real terms. This attests to the workshop's popularity. The program's success, however, needs to be determined in a more comprehensive way. I therefore use a variety of ways to determine the effectiveness of these workshops.

First, facilitators have sought and received anonymous feedback from every participant at the end of every workshop. We obtain this feedback using a questionnaire that resulted in quantitative as well as qualitative responses. The quantitative feedback obtained ratings using a 5-point Likert-type scale, to evaluate ten key items regarding the workshop. The qualitative feedback was obtained as a response to five open-ended questions.

A *synthesis* of the quantitative feedback received from participants in the workshops conducted during 2013 and 2014 is presented in Table 3.1.

Table 3.1. Quantitative feedback from workshop participants 2013–2014

| Item | Range of ratings | | Average | % |
	Lowest	Highest		
1. General organisation (Chris Kapp & Associates)	4.42	5	4.8	96
2. Organisation (venue)	3.95	4.92	4.34	86.8
3. Personal objectives met	4.02	4.73	4.4	88
4. Relevance	4.57	4.91	4.73	94.6
5. How much I have learned	4.47	4.91	4.67	93.4
6. Facilitator's capability	4.68	4.95	4.83	96.6
7. Peer review	3.75	4.47	4.11	82.2
8. Critical readers	4.07	4.78	4.44	88.8
9. Editors	4.32	4.80	4.6	92
10. Overall evaluation	4.4	4.92	4.69	93.8
AVERAGE	4.4	4.6	4.56	91.2

Notes: Number of participants per workshop: 12–28.
Average number per workshop: 19.

As we can see from an analysis of the summary of these ratings, the participants perceived the workshops to be very successful. The average rating of the workshops was 4.56 on a 5-point scale (91.2%), with a range from 4.4 (88%) to 4.6 (92%). The items that generally received a lower rating were item 3 (the extent to which my personal objectives have been achieved) and item 7 (the value of peer review). There is an explanation for these two lower ratings. Item 3 was generally rated lower because each participant came to the workshop intending to complete their paper. However, despite all the attempts made by the facilitation team to ensure that the participants come to the workshop well prepared with a completed draft paper, some fail to do this. Others, after receiving input on the various stages of the writing cycle, realised both the shortcomings in their early drafts and their need to do much more thinking, planning and rewriting. Also, participants often experience resistance to working with colleagues from other fields who may perceive participants are very junior to themselves.

The explanation for the lower rating of the peer review process is that some participants may not appreciate the rationale for the peer groupings. Participants form into groups of three, with two from the same or similar disciplines and one from a completely different discipline. The rationale is that participants from the same or similar disciplines develop a 'blindness' to their own mistakes. It sometimes requires the input from an 'outsider' for a participant to become aware of possible shortcomings in their writing.

The qualitative feedback that participants have provided in the open-ended questions supports or substantiates the ratings they have given in the quantitative feedback. Participants are asked five questions. The first four are the following:

If you would be given another opportunity to attend a similar workshop, what would you like to have

- *more* time allocated to;
- *less* time allocated to;
- *left out*; and
- *added?*

The fifth question is an open request for participants to comment, suggest or recommend.

The most common response to the first question normally is an expression of a desire for more writing time. Questions two (what needs less time) and three (what needs to be left out) are hardly ever answered and nothing significant is mentioned. In response to the fourth question (what needs to be added) participants have usually indicated topics related to research methodology, which is not the focus of this workshop on writing academic papers.

Responses to the last (open-ended) question (comments, suggestions, recommendations) provide eloquent testimony to participants' satisfaction, gratitude and appreciation for the value of the workshop, in comments such as the following:

- 'Thank you for a wonderful workshop and the opportunity brought by the retreat. I feel that I know more and I am confident to start writing more articles. Article writing is not as daunting anymore'.
- 'Exceptional exposure to knowledge. As a young academic much knowledge was gained on how to write journal articles'.
- 'I would advise any researcher/scientist to attend this workshop (irrespective of their experience) at least once every two years'.
- 'Thank you for the expert way in which the workshop was presented. Such a privilege to have been able to attend another benchmark publication workshop. Be blessed! What a brilliant team'.
- 'Wish I had this opportunity ten years ago'.
- 'Well done, you have made me a better writer'.
- 'The workshop was brilliant, an eye opener and very useful one on writing for publication'.

- 'Great workshop, very valuable, great presenter'.
- 'Keep it up. Most valuable workshop ever attended. Thank you!'.
- 'Great workshop. I will attend your retreat workshop next time'.
- 'Thank you for a fantastic workshop. The value of the learning to my career development is immense!'.

In 2009 we did some follow-up research questioning the participants in two cohorts of workshops (2005–2006 and 2007–2008) about their publication performance. Figure 3.2 indicates the percentages of their articles accepted outright (26%), accepted after revision (48%), rejected after revision (9%) and rejected outright (17%).

There has also been an increase in the number of participants who *completed* their papers as well as the number of participants who *submitted* their papers to journals, as reported in Table 3.2.

We are in the process of completing a follow-up survey of the 2009–2014 groups/ cohorts. The results of this survey will be available in June 2015 and our analysis will be published as appropriate. However, based on the experience of the facilitation team, the following outcomes are anticipated:

Demand for the workshop has *increased*, not only from South African universities but also from universities in other countries in southern Africa. More institutions/organisations are requesting workshops for their institutions or faculties at an institution. Also, the quality of participants' articles has improved since we introduced an extended target population analysis and requested responses to the eight questions mentioned earlier.

It is estimated that at least 50 per cent of all participants in the workshops complete their articles within a reasonable time, most during the workshop and the rest within six months after the workshop. An increase of up to 80 per cent of completed articles was achieved at those institutions where the participants were from the same faculty, where participants' contributions (draft articles) were screened by a panel of reviewers, and where a 'gatekeeper' or a 'champion' was made responsible for keeping track of writing/publishing progress and in fact contracted with the participants to complete their articles and submit them to a journal.

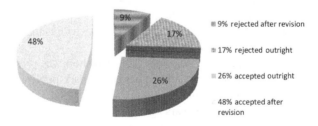

Figure 3.2. Outcomes of papers submitted for publication

Table 3.2. Completed and submitted papers

Workshop group cohort	Completed	Submitted
2005–2006	59%	42%
2007–2008	69%	94%

THE FUTURE OF THE 'WRITING FOR PUBLICATION' WORKSHOPS

Its interactive nature and application of the action learning writing cycle have been the backbone and the strength of this workshop. Having an experienced team with combined experience of nearly 300 years of involvement in higher education (the complete team consists of eight members and each has experience of research and writing in higher education ranging from 30 years to 45 years, with an average of 37 years), we are all considering final retirement in two years (December, 2016). The question is: what will happen to this writing workshop that so many academics have found valuable? Who will continue with the work? What is to happen to the intellectual capital, the crystallised intelligence, the tacit knowledge, wisdom and experience shared by this team?

There are some options. One option is to transform the workshop into a web-based modular course with step-by-step guidance to individual subscribers. This is a potential option, but will need some serious thinking and planning. A second option, and maybe this is not an option, but a requirement: the material used in the workshops will be published in e-book format and be made commercially available in 2017.

CONCLUSION

In this chapter paying tribute to the academic contributions of Ortrun Zuber-Skerritt, I have focussed on the 'Writing for Publication' workshop that I have been closely involved in over the past decade. The workshop aims to empower novice and advanced beginner authors with knowledge, skills and confidence to write a scholarly article for an academic journal that is properly peer reviewed and is accredited by the Department of Higher Education in South Africa. Action learning provides the theoretical underpinning of these workshops, as manifest in the specific design principles I have illustrated such as conducting needs assessment and evaluating through participant feedback. Ortrun's influence upon this workshop has penetrated deeply, through both theory and practice.

The 'Writing for Publication' workshop has made a positive difference in the careers of a significant number of South African academics as well as some academics from elsewhere in Africa. The workshop enables young and novice academics to bring publishing into their career at a much younger age than was the case in earlier years by enhancing their ability to learn, write and engage in mutually supportive work with colleagues, their understanding of the publication process, and importantly their confidence in their own ability as academic authors. Others in South Africa have tried to run academic publishing workshops but these have been shorter and shallower than ours, without the comprehensive approach and action learning philosophy that distinguishes our workshops as active and interactive. As my analysis of participant evaluations reveals, South African academics very much appreciate the worth of participating in our 'Writing for Publication' workshop and having their research published, with built-in benefits for their institutions.

As a personal concluding reflection, I acknowledge that Ortrun's role in influencing, coaching and motivating me in my professional practice cannot be underestimated. It reaches well beyond her place in the 'invisible tapestry' of our academic writing workshops. Ortrun introduced me to the theory and practice of action learning and action research and the writings of its eminent scholars/practitioners. She was instrumental in arranging meetings for me with Australian academics who made significant contributions to my field of practice. She introduced me to the biennial Quality in Postgraduate Research Conference in Adelaide. Beyond my personal sphere, Ortrun was instrumental in establishing the South African ALAR group. And through the cascade effects of teaching, publishing and workshop facilitation, her influence is also apparent in the research of postgraduate students who have used ALAR in their own learning and research. To her great credit, Ortrun's quest for a better world through learning, research and action has inspired, enabled and empowered many in South Africa to pursue likewise and achieve satisfying results.

REFERENCES

Brookfield, S. (1995). *Becoming a critically reflective teacher*. San Francisco, CA: Jossey Bass.

Chanson, H. (2007) Research quality, publications and impact in civil engineering into the 21st century: publish or perish, commercial versus open access, internet versus libraries? *Canadian Journal of Civil Engineering, 34*, 946–951.

Department of Higher Education and Training, Republic of South Africa. (2013). *Post-school education and training in South Africa: Report for 2010.*

Dernth, M. (2009, September). *Basics of research paper writing and publishing* (Unpublished manuscript). Vienna, Austria: University of Vienna.

Dick, B. (2004). Action research literature: Themes and trends. *Action Research, 2,* 425–444.

Gevers, W. (2006). Introduction and background. *Report on a strategic approach to research publishing in South Africa*. Pretoria, South Africa: Academy of Science of South Africa.

Gladwell, M. (2008). *Outliers: The story of success*. New York, NY: Little Brown and Company.

Kapp, C. A., & Albertyn, R. M. (2008). Accepted or rejected: Editors' perspectives of common errors. *Acta Academica, 40*(4), 66–83.

Kapp, C. A., Albertyn, R. M., & Frick, B. L. (2010). Writing for publication: An intervention to overcome barriers to scholarly writing. *South African Journal of Higher Education, 24*(3), 761–779.

Kingsley, D. (2007). The journal is dead, long live the journal. *On the Horizon, 15*(4), 211–221.

Knowles, M. (1973). *The adult learner: A neglected species*. Houston, TX: Gulf Publishing Co.

Kolb, D. A. (1984). *Experimental learning: Experience as the source of learning and development*. Upper Saddle River, NJ: Prentice Hall.

Ligthelm, A. A., & Koekemoer, E. M. (2009). Academic publishing; Lessons learnt from the Southern African business review. *Southern African Business Review*, *13*(3), 28–50.

Maree, J. G. (2012). *First steps in journal article writing*. Cape Town, South Africa: Juta.

Murray, R. (2005). *Writing for academic journals*. Maidenhead, England: Open University Press.

Pouris, A. (2003). South Africa's research publication record: The last ten years. *South African Journal of Science*, *99*(September/October), 425–428.

Pouris, A. (2012). Science in South Africa: The dawn of a renaissance? *South African Journal of Science*, *108*(7/8), 1–6.

Republic of South Africa. (2006). *Statement on higher education funding: 2004/05 to 2006/07*. Retrieved from www.gov.za

Sadler, R. (2006). *Up the publication road: Green guide*. Higher Education Research and Development Society of Australasia, Australia: University of New South Wales.

Wingfield, B. (2010). How long does it take to get a PhD? *South African Journal of Science*, *106*(11/12), 469.

Zuber-Skerritt, O. (1992). *Professional development in higher education: A theoretical framework for action learning*. London, UK: Kogan Page.

Chris Kapp
Emeritus Professor in Higher Education
University of Stellenbosch
South Africa

DORIS SANTOS

4. WEAVING TOGETHER

Ortrun Zuber-Skerritt's Legacy to PAR from a
Colombian Female Academic's Perspective

INTRODUCTION

My 30-year story as a Participatory Action Research (PAR) practitioner is one of the vast swathe of stories linked to the life and work of Ortrun Zuber-Skerritt, whom I have the honour and pleasure to acknowledge here. Her influence on my professional learning process started in 1994 when I was looking for a book about action research in higher education, and found one written by Ortrun in one of the most important bookstores in London. Since then, the potential contribution of PAR to higher education has been my main concern, to the extent that I wrote my PhD thesis about this from my experiences as an academic in Colombia. I will refer to some excerpts from the second part of my thesis to achieve my main objective in this chapter: to highlight what I believe is one of Ortrun's main contributions to the field of PAR. It is, politically speaking, her gift of weaving the web of human relationships that holds PAR together. I discuss some of the challenges that we, PAR practitioners and advocates, have to face when weaving the web of human relationships that exists wherever human beings live together, and my attempts to face some of these challenges hand in hand with Ortrun. I conclude with some reflections on weaving commonalities between non-Western and Western views of bringing about a better world through PAR and Ortrun's contribution to bridging these trans-cultural encounters.

Literature reviews in the field of PAR can serve well to help us understand their practitioners' political commitment to both the communities with which they work and the broader society to which they belong (Santos, 2013). Yet sometimes these reviews lack anecdotal stories that illustrate what this commitment implies. These stories may be missing from the literature because of academics' attempts to meet standardised requirements and expectations for publishing in an ever more competitive higher education system. Due to the importance of making relevant what can be considered irrelevant in present day publications (Santos, 2012b), I use storytelling in this chapter to illustrate what this political commitment can look like. From this perspective, the short stories I tell here concern how Ortrun's life and work have inspired me to weave the fragile web of relationships underlying

J. Kearney & M. Todhunter (Eds), Lifelong Action Learning and Research: A Tribute to the Life and Pioneering Work of Ortrun Zuber-Skerritt, 35–44.

the politics of PAR as I have experienced it. To start, I present in the following section some excerpts about Colombian Indigenous ways to represent the weaving of relationships in one particular handcraft (Santos, 2012a). These excerpts serve to introduce the sort of 'weaving together' that I refer to in this tribute to the life and work of Professor Ortrun Zuber-Skerritt.

WEAVING THE INVISIBLE THREADS OF PAR

At the start of my PhD journey when I was preparing for my trip to Australia in 2009, I considered what gift I might bring for my principal supervisor to express my gratitude. I did not hesitate about what it should be: an Arhuaca mochila bag. The Arhuacos are one of several descendant peoples of the Tayrona Indigenous civilisation, which inhabited the world's highest snow mountain chain closest to the sea. After Spanish conquerors arrived on the northern coast of Colombia in the fifteenth century, they forced the Arhuacos to live in the uppermost areas of this mountain chain, where all the climate zones possible in the tropics can be found. The 5,700 metres high Sierra Nevada de Santa Marta (the Snowy Mountain Range of Saint Martha) represents the entire spiritual world for the Arhuacos. Although all Arhuaco community members are involved in the production of the mochila bag, only Arhuaco women (*Wati*) can weave it. Arhuaco men use three bags according to tradition: one to save personal belongings (*Chige kwanu*), another to carry coca leaves (*Zizhu*) and the third to store food or travel items. Arhuaco women carry one called *Tutu gawa*. When a man and a woman are to marry, the future wife weaves two bags, one for her and one for her future husband, to symbolise the love of the couple.

I always wanted to have an Arhuaca mochila bag but I could never afford one. Not long before leaving for Australia, I was given one by my younger sister, who had been in the region the Arhuacos inhabit. She bought one of these bags for herself, but learning how much I appreciate them, she did not hesitate to give it to me so I could take it with me to Australia, to use myself. Arhuaca mochila bags are one of the most acknowledged handicrafts a tourist can buy when visiting my homeland. However, very few tourists really understand the wisdom they are taking with them; they do not know how to read the knowledge woven into these beautiful objects. This was one of the main concerns of one of my former Indigenous students, who was also a participant in the university's PAR programs I led. He does not belong to the Arhuacos but to the Wayuú people, and he has been really saddened by the inability of the Wayuú people attending universities in Bogotá to read their own Wayuú mochila bags. He laments that many of the new generation of Wayuú people can hardly recognise their own knowledge even when they have the Wayuú mochila bags with them.

The Arhuacos say that they weave each bag based on their most profound thoughts and feelings about their daily life relationships with all that surrounds them: other human beings, nature and the spiritual world. Each mochila bag is unique in this sense; it deals with a particular human being's way of understanding and living in the world. That is why each Arhuaca mochila bag is so valuable and so much appreciated in my homeland, especially by those who know about this woven knowledge. Each Arhuaco keeps all the personal mochila bags that they make throughout their lives as a treasure.

The first image that comes to my mind to describe my weaving experience in PAR is a spiral; this image can represent my weaving experience as a PAR practitioner in general terms. However, it is not the same spiral that PAR practitioners are accustomed to talking about, one of the many spirals concerning the epistemology of PAR. The spiral I am thinking about is one connected mainly to the Arhuaca mochila bag cosmogony: a spiral that exists because of our relationships with those with whom we inhabit this world, and that brings about new realities with these relationships.

According to Barragán (2006), the spiral weaving of the Arhuaca mochila bags is a reference to the creation of the Arhuaco cosmos, that is, the physical and spiritual world that the Arhuacos have inhabited for many centuries. Because this weaving is nurtured with their cultural knowledge, which is represented by one or several of the geometric figures forming their cosmos, it entails a profound reflection of their interrelationships with people and nature. For the Arhuaco people, the mochila bag is the freest symbol of the creation of life, namely, the Universal Mother's womb. This is why the image of a female weaving mochilas is endowed with the power and spirit of fertility in the Arhuaco community. The colours and designs of each mochila bag among the Arhuaco people are the means of introducing each of them to the community – a way for each Arhuaco person to express their identity, and their belonging to the community at the same time. Nowadays the mochilas are also woven for sale but even as saleable items they are still woven in keeping with this cosmogony. Weaving each bag takes time. It is time that the weaver takes to renew their commitment to preserving their relationships with all that surrounds them and, in this way, to renewing Arhuaco spiritual life.

This Colombian Indigenous view of living life together well is quite close to what PAR is aimed at. However, the political spiral of PAR has some other elements concerning the weaving of relationships. These elements are relations among people who have worldviews, interests and ideas that differ from those of PAR about what the common good can or should be.

WEAVING THROUGH PUBLISHING

In 1994, I completed a postgraduate course in teacher education and project management in London. This was part of the strategy of a bi-national project run by the Colombian and British governments to enhance the making of a policy for teaching English language in Colombia. I was part of one of five groups of Colombian academics who attended postgraduate courses to write specific documents aimed at achieving this objective. Before leaving London, I wanted to buy some books about action research in higher education. I was particularly surprised to find almost no pertinent literature at that time. I found just one book – a 130-page small, light yellow volume entitled *Action Research in Higher Education: Examples and Reflections*. As an early career researcher, this was my first encounter with Ortrun. Thanks to her book, not only could I learn about the first working definition of action research jointly authored by the participants of the International Symposium on Action Research held in Brisbane, Australia, in 1989 (Zuber-Skerritt, 1992, p. 14), which provided useful food for conceptual thought and action. I could also confirm one of my suspicions: that while action research had been introduced successfully at the primary and secondary levels, this was not really so in tertiary education (Zuber-Skerritt, 1992, p. 15). I found especially meaningful the book's examples of how action research may be helpful for fostering undergraduate and postgraduate students' learning processes, as well as academic staff professional development, in the midst of increasing pressure for accountability.

When I returned to the private university where I worked at the time in Bogotá, Colombia, I used this book for a while to explore action research with my teacher students. I supervised many action research projects, which, I think, supported my teacher students' professional learning as well as the learning process of their students. Never could I have imagined that I would have the pleasure to meet Ortrun and become one of the many beneficiaries of her teachings and experience at a postgraduate level in my PhD studies.

To reflect here upon the political in publishing, I draw from political theorist Hannah Arendt, who was born in Ortrun's homeland, Germany. Although not usually recognised by practitioners of PAR, Arendt's work has intrinsic conceptual links. Arendt's notion of politics is linked to the human condition of plurality, the condition not only *sine qua non* but *per quam* of all political life. This is so because it is the human condition that corresponds with action, the only activity that goes on directly between human beings without the intermediary of things or matter, as it happens to work and labour, respectively (Arendt, 1998, p. 7). The human condition of plurality is 'the condition of human action because we are all the same, that is, human, in such a way that nobody is ever the same as anyone else who ever lived, lives, or will live' (Arendt, 1998, p. 8). On this basis, Arendt claims that political events, like aesthetic objects, cannot be judged with reference to an external purpose or principle (Disch, 1993, p. 683). She suggests a significantly different ground of validity for political judgement. This ground is '*publicity*': 'the testing that arises from contact with other people's thinking' (Arendt, 1992, p. 42). The type of story Arendt invites us to tell is therefore one that invites 'the reader to "go visiting", asking "how would the world look to *you* if you saw it from this perspective?"' (Disch, 1993, p. 687). In this sense, to serve their political task, PAR stories should 'stir people to think about what they are doing' by inviting readers to try to figure out how the world would look if approached from perspectives different from their own (Santos, 2012b, p. 116). Ortrun's prolific publishing history has been stirring PAR practitioners to think about what we have been doing. In my case, since 1994 her stories have been inviting me to go visiting her way of understanding how the world looks and how it could look through PAR.

It is important to acknowledge that although Ortrun's publishing history has been mainly in the English language, her mother tongue is German. She has made English her own in her urge to widely communicate her perspective of the world. Indeed she has reached beyond the English language domains. In 2007 when preparing a tribute to the esteemed life and work of our mutual colleague and friend Orlando Fals Borda (a story I present in the following section), I suggested interviewing Ortrun in English by email for a text I could translate into Spanish, to be published in a journal special issue dedicated to Orlando Fals Borda before the tribute event. We were then weaving together our explorations of not only how to make this tribute real but also how to reach a Spanish-language readership that Ortrun until then had not yet reached (Santos, 2007a). By putting this idea into action with her, I started another stage of my academic life: I entered the world of academic publishing in English language. Ortrun suggested I publish in English the ideas I presented in the interview-based article in Spanish, first, in an article in the journal of the Action Learning and Action Research Association (ALARA) (Santos, 2007b), and then we could adapt it as a chapter for inclusion in a book of interviews about ALAR that Ortrun was then preparing (Zuber-Skerritt & Santos, 2009). This initiation into the international publishing world was particularly significant for my academic career, and came alongside another very meaningful experience for me also associated with the tribute we were organising for Orlando Fals Borda.

While planning this celebratory event, Ortrun told me about the Festschrift tradition in Germany. Thinking carefully about Ortrun's suggestion, I recognised this as a tradition we could incorporate in our Latin American academic context. Thus, I accepted the challenge to co-edit a Festschrift for Orlando Fals Borda with Maureen Todhunter, a person whose generous hands, mind and heart have meant a lot to me as well as to Ortrun, I'm sure. I needed to invite contributions from Orlando's colleagues, academics from Australia, England, Brazil and Colombia, who were advocates and practitioners of different action research approaches. All were keen to contribute to the Festschrift volume. The result was a double-sided book, where each contributor wrote in Spanish or English as they felt more comfortable (Santos & Todhunter, 2007).

This interweaving of academic work and ideas from different traditions and latitudes through publishing them in various languages in one publication can be appreciated in the context of the geopolitics of academic writing, a notion coined by English as a Second Language teacher from Sri Lanka, Suresh Canagarajah. He has aimed his work at widening the context of academic literacy by locating the place of academic/scientific publications in the intellectual and material inequalities between the *centre* (referred as the West) and periphery (typically communities colonised by Europeans, referred as the Third World) (Canagarajah, 2002, p. 7). He suggests that periphery scholars use centre publications to resist the centre's dominance. This is important, he says, to 'challenge mainstream knowledge, disseminating periphery knowledge effectively, and, eventually, contributing to the enrichment and democratisation of international relations' (Canagarajah, 2002, p. 12). Ortrun and I are both committed to promoting publications like this, prepared jointly by scholars from different latitudes and contexts. We appreciate the contribution of these publications to the democratisation of knowledge between scholars from the centre and from the periphery, in Canagarajah's terms, or to the convergence of scholars from the North and from the South, in Fals Borda's words (Fals Borda, 2006, pp. 357–358). In many ways, Ortrun has contributed to triggering a ripple effect through publishing of PAR. Through her publications and those she has supported, Ortrun has promoted the 'go visiting' the world from various perspectives that Arendt claims is necessary to validate political judgement.

WEAVING NODES THROUGH BRIDGING

In 2006 I received an email from Ortrun asking me to contact Orlando Fals Borda to transmit, on behalf of the Organising Committee of the Action Learning and Action Research Association (ALARA), an invitation to be the keynote speaker at the ALARA conference to be held in Groningen, The Netherlands, that year. I had just started working as a part-time lecturer at the same university as Orlando, the Universidad Nacional de Colombia, and had not yet met him since we worked in different departments. When I contacted him through his wife, sociologist María Cristina Salazar, and transmitted the invitation, he answered regretfully that his doctor had advised him to avoid travelling. I conveyed this to Ortrun, apologising for the unfortunately negative reply to the invitation. Considering Orlando's health condition, I asked Ortrun if she would come to Bogotá to participate in an event to pay tribute to his life and work from PAR practitioners in the field of education. She immediately replied positively. I started writing a proposal for the event to be presented to the Rector of a private university where I then worked as a part-time lecturer in a Masters degree program in education. I exchanged several emails with Ortrun to work through several academic and practical matters. As a result, several PAR advocates and practitioners who had never all been together in a Latin American country confirmed their agreement to participate as keynote speakers. Among others including Ortrun, Stephen Kemmis, Robin McTaggart, Shirley Grundy, John Elliott and his wife Christine O'Hanlon, Paulo Freire disciple Joao Francisco de Souza, and former Jesuit Carlos Eduardo Vasco who has promoted critical pedagogy through PAR, were happy to attend – even in spite of Australian and British government warnings not to visit Colombia. Orlando Fals Borda accepted the tribute a couple of months before his wife passed away. He used to tell me that he would live just to wait for his PAR friends. And so he did. One year after the tribute, he died, his life celebration drawing over 300 PAR practitioners from almost all Latin American countries and outside the continent, as well as across Colombia.

Networking, as weaving different nodes of various webs of human relationships, is something Ortrun knows in depth how to do. Not only has she always thought of ways to bring people together to talk about – and then take action for – the common good, she has also been generous in serving as a bridge to pass on her knowledge and experience to others. She engages actively in organising events here and there, now and then, introducing scholars to one another locally, nationally and internationally. The nodes of the webs she has helped to weave remain in her mind and her heart, as well as in the minds and hearts of those who have had the pleasure to be part of her life and work. For me the following story exemplifies this so clearly.

WEAVING THROUGH SOLIDARITY

In 2005 I had the pleasure to meet Professor Stephen Kemmis in Amsterdam. He had been a keynote speaker with Professor Wilfred Carr in the Collaborative Action Research Network (CARN) Annual Conference in Utrecht, The Netherlands. After the conference, I had planned to apply for a place at the University of Amsterdam to pursue a PhD in Argumentation. I happened to stay at the same hotel as Professor Kemmis. He recognised me when we met at the hotel since, as he told me then, I had said something in the evaluation session of the conference that had triggered the beginning of the 'Pedagogy, Education and Praxis' (PEP) network. At the end of our talks in Amsterdam, he suggested I apply for a scholarship to do my PhD under his supervision in Australia – at a university in an outback country town. Though at the time PAR in education was close to my heart, the suggestion sounded like a crazy idea because of the remote location of the university. The Dutch government offered me an option for my PhD studies that better met my needs as a divorced mother. But life has its ways; my academic career and personal life were both moving along paths I'd not expected. I first received the offer of an Australian award to do my PhD studies and needed to make a decision since the Dutch scholarship was uncertain. I organised family plans for a three-year learning adventure on the other side of the planet in July 2009.

The networking with Australian scholars that started with the tribute to Orlando Fals Borda in 2007 became the web of relationships that would embrace and sustain me through one of the hardest times of my life far from home. It was certainly challenging to continue pursuing my personal project to do a PhD as a female academic, while a divorced mother of a teenager. But I recognised the valuable opportunity for my son to gain from the experience of living in a smaller community and speaking English. Through agreement with his father I prepared every minute detail to receive my son in Australia in July 2010, so facing the end of 2009 I found myself half way through the first year of my PhD studies, alone during the university holidays, on the other side of the planet. Ortrun knew about this and without a second thought sent me a ticket to fly from Wagga Wagga in New South Wales to Brisbane in Queensland. She wanted me not to be on my own during the Christmas/New Year season.

This is the type of person Ortrun is. She received me into her home, her family and her circle, ensuring I felt embraced by them all while so far from my own. My heart is forever laden with gratitude for this gesture. When returning to Wagga Wagga via Sydney, I was informed that my son would not come to Australia as planned. I felt broken hearted and powerless. Of the several beautiful human beings who comforted me while coping with that new reality, Ortrun in particular inspired me. Her personal story gave me strength and personal will to continue. Her never-failing self confidence, strong discipline at all levels, endless joy for life, profound love for her family and friends, her inquisitive smartness and her deep conviction that a better world is possible if we do our best to achieve it, became the example for me of what is possible for a female academic in contemporary higher education.

Ortrun's support for me at this time was not only at a personal level. She also shared her academic and other professional knowledge and experience to support my learning process as PhD student. What I had read in 1994 in her 130-page small yellow book made sense 15 years later in a meaningful way. During my PhD program in Australia, I also had the opportunity to learn from her ways of approaching thesis writing while we shared informal daily routines during a couple of visits I made to Brisbane. I felt so privileged to have great supervision at university and such helpful support from beyond as well.

CONCLUSIONS

As illustrated above, the spiral of PAR incorporates views of the Arhuaco people about weaving our relationships with the natural and social worlds and also learns from the challenges that emerge when different worldviews come together in searching for the common good. Most PAR practitioners in my stories introduced themselves as a politically committed, action oriented group of researchers, seeking to help solve problems of injustice that derive from colliding contemporary perspectives about what it means to live together well. As the beneficiary of a blend of non-Western and Western heritages, I have found the commonalities of these two traditions encouraging. The Arhuacos' understanding of the importance of relationships in the world that human beings inhabit seems to me especially aligned with the thought of German political theorist Hannah Arendt. My PAR experiences provide clear views of the creative ways to weave the web of relationships such as those I have shared with Ortrun.

Based on my understanding of encounters between traditions, in political terms I can describe my PAR experience as one spiral in a set of interconnected spirals (that is, the various PAR projects and programs in which I have been engaged). Every spiral has a living centre (the community in which the PAR practitioner is engaged), which is woven with threads from a variety of sources. Like the starting point of the spiral weaving of the base of the Arhuaca mochila bag, the living centre of the spiral of PAR is a reminder of the creative power of those who weave their actions, ideas and stories. This living centre in PAR needs to be strong enough to keep safe everything that is valuable. It needs to be formed by tight and caring ties, whose forms can be as different as the threads and stitches that constitute them. The power coming from this creative living centre allows the spiral weaving to broaden its scope to form the base of the bag – a scope determined by the weaver. From that moment on, the base of the bag defines the second stage of the spiral weaving: one that is aimed at defining the capacity of the Arhuaca mochila bag. It is at this stage that the Arhuaco weaver creates the geometric figures that contain Arhuaco knowledge. This spiral weaving ends when the weaver finishes the geometric figures. The weaver has then determined the capacity of the bag and so attaches the woven rope to ready the bag for carrying.

I have presented in this chapter several stories about my weaving together with Ortrun, initially as a reader of the books where she invites us to look at the world from her perspective, later as a co-author of writings in Spanish and English to bridge traditions and languages, and later still as a female academic pursuing professional goals in hard social realities. This weaving has gained texture, colour and form, has built strength and purpose by the unexpected circumstances involving us – fortunate generous encounters, as well as coincidences in our shared views of the meaning of being and becoming female academics in higher education in the twenty-first century. Despite hard times in ever more competitive universities, we are called together to keep on bringing about new realities through teaching, learning and research to create a better world. We draw in creatively the broken threads and knots in the webs of relationships we are intended to weave with others, entwining strays and loose threads, but mostly working with colourful threads that enable us to weave new figures, designs and outcomes (Santos, 2012a).

Ortrun continues to strengthen and expand these webs in creative ways, always with generosity, joy, hard work, solidarity and conviction. Because so, the webs of relationships, research and learning she has been engaged with in PAR reach across the oceans, across cultures, across years. They have links with universities and communities in virtually every continent. I see these webs like the spider webs in outback Australia on windy, sunny days, moving through the air 'until they find where to take hold, where they fit comfortably' (Santos, 2012a, p. 205). Ortrun, for who you are and all you have done to our weaving as PAR practitioners to co-create a better world, thank you.

REFERENCES

Arendt, H. (1992). *Lectures on Kant's political philosophy*. Chicago, IL: The University of Chicago Press.
Arendt, H. (1998). *The human condition*. Chicago, IL: University of Chicago Press.
Barragán, J. (2006, June 24). La mochila arhuaca. *Semana*. Colombia.

Canagarajah, S. (2002). *A geopolitics of academic writing*. Pittsburgh, PA: University of Pittsburgh Press.

Disch, L. (1993). More truth than fact: Storytelling as critical understanding in the writings of Hannah Arendt. *Political Theory, 21*(4), 665–694.

Fals Borda, O. (2006). The North–South convergence: 30-year first-person assessment of PAR. *Action Research, 4*(3), 351–358.

Santos, D. (2007a). Desarrollo profesional y del liderazgo en Educación Superior a través del Aprendizaje en la Acción (Action Learning) y de la Investigación Acción. Entrevista con Ortrun Zuber Skerritt. *Revista Internacional Magisteri., 26*, 30–33.

Santos, D. (2007b). Professional and leadership development in higher education through action learning and action research: An interview with Ortrun Zuber-Skerritt. *ALAR Action Learning and Action Research Journal: Special Pre-conference Edition, 12*(1), 113–141.

Santos, D. (2012a). *On new beginnings: Natality and (participatory) action research in higher education* (PhD). Charles Sturt University, Wagga Wagga, New South Wales, Australia.

Santos, D. (2012b). The politics of storytelling: unfolding the multiple layers of politics in (P)AR publications. *Educational Action Research, 20*(1), 113–128.

Santos, D. (2013). (Participatory) Action research and the political realm. In B. Dennis, L. Carspecken, & P. F. Carspecken (Eds.), *Qualitative research: A reader in philosophy, core concepts, and practice* (pp. 492–514). New York, NY: Peter Lang Publishing Inc.

Santos, D., & Todhunter, M. (Eds.). (2007). *Action research and education in contexts of poverty: A tribute to the life and work of Professor Orlando Fals Borda*. Bogota, Colombia: Universidad de La Salle.

Zuber-Skerritt, O. (1992). *Action research in higher education. Examples and reflections*. London, UK: Kogan Page Limited.

Zuber-Skerritt, O., & Santos, D. (2009). Professional and leadership development in higher education. In *Action learning and action research: Songlines through interviews* (pp. 105–128). Rotterdam, The Netherlands: Sense Publishers.

Doris Santos
Department of Linguistics
Universidad Nacional de Colombia
Colombia

PART II

ORGANISATIONS

SHANKAR SANKARAN

5. ACHIEVING SYNERGY THROUGH COMBINING ACTION LEARNING AND ACTION RESEARCH

INTRODUCTION

Today the complementarity between action learning and action research has achieved form in the concept of ALAR: Action Learning and Action Research. The synergy between these two has been built since the formation of ALARPM (Action Learning, Action Research and Process Management) in Brisbane in 1991, through the insight and action of a number of scholars influenced by the work of Ortrun Zuber-Skerritt. Ortrun has championed this unison of 'Action' through her scholarship and her personal efforts to draw together people, ideas and purposes, as her instrumental role in formation of the Action Learning and Action Research Association (ALARA) attests. In this chapter I therefore pay tribute to Ortrun's contributions to knowledge and professional development not just through action learning and action research but also through her quest to achieve the synergy between learning and research through her writings and work. As evidence of Ortrun's influence, I offer my personal experience of effectively combining action learning and action research in a workplace project to meet the real challenges I faced as senior manager in a Japanese company in Singapore simultaneously needing to satisfy the requirements of my doctoral thesis at an Australian university. This experience reveals not just the influence of Ortrun's scholarship on my learning and research but also the trans-cultural flexibility of the action learning–action research combination at a time when globalisation makes this quality not just useful but necessary for solving real problems (Sankaran & Kumar, 2010).

The chapter is organised as follows. First, I briefly review action learning and action research and their usefulness in producing actionable and rigorous outcomes. I then discuss similarities and differences between action learning and action research, and then explain how they can be combined in university doctoral programs to help produce management and research outcomes. I conclude with discussion of why I think doctoral researchers who are interested in improving their workplace as an outcome of their research can find it useful to consider combining action learning and action research.

J. Kearney & M. Todhunter (Eds), Lifelong Action Learning and Research: A Tribute to the Life and Pioneering Work of Ortrun Zuber-Skerritt, 47–63.

BRIEF REVIEW OF ACTION LEARNING AND ACTION RESEARCH

In this section I briefly review action learning and action research and their similarities and differences before I discuss how they can be combined. As these two topics are very broad I confine the discussion to some key thoughts about them. For each, I begin with the ideas of originator of the concept and then provide current, generally accepted definitions from what I consider as reliable sources. I then present ideas from other authors, including Ortrun, whose works informed my thinking and research. These helped in my journey to make sense of these two approaches as I tried to meld them to maximise their utility, as I became an action researcher-cum-learner while employed as a senior manager. I incorporate Ortrun's views on both concepts in these discussions, revealing the amplifier effect of her influence in the field – upon myself as researcher and manager, upon research students I have supervised and guided at doctoral and masters level, and upon many others through my research and publications.

Action Learning

Reg Revans is considered the father of action learning, a process he discovered by observing how reputed scientists working in the Cambridge University Laboratory in the 1940s learnt from each other. In one of his early writings about action learning (Revans, 1983, p. 43), he came close to explaining what it is by stating: 'Action learning, by encouraging men of practice to clarify to each other (not to P-men, the experts) what they believe their problems to be, including their own selves as part of the nightmare, and what they think ought to be done about them, provides an effective workshop for examining, sharpening and testing their managerial weapons – above all, their judgement of the unseen and of the unknown'. He adds (Revans, 1983, p. 43) that these practitioners should use the following steps to carry out action learning to solve their problems:

1. By contact with responsibility and reality, facing honesty of expression from start to finish;
2. The constant interpretation by equal comrades of what one is seen to be doing and saying; and
3. Reciprocally offering one's own advice, criticism and support back to those very same comrades.

Revans noted that these three characteristics of action learning differentiated it from all other forms of management education.

The International Foundation of Action Learning in the UK (http://ifal.org.uk/action-learning/), which was established on the principles Revans proclaimed, further elaborates his description of action learning:

Action Learning involves working on real problems, focussing on learning and actually implementing solutions. It is a form of learning by doing. Pioneered by Professor Reg Revans and developed worldwide since the late 1940s, it provides a well-tried method of accelerating learning, which enables people to handle complex issues more effectively.

Action Learning is based on a radical concept: $L = P + Q$. Learning requires Programmed knowledge (i.e., knowledge in current use) plus Questioning insight. It also uses a small group to provide challenge and support: individuals learn best with and from one another as they each tackle their own problem and go on to actually implement their own solution.

The process integrates: research (into what is obscure); learning (about what is unknown); and action (to resolve a problem) into a single activity and develops an attitude of questioning and reflection to help individuals and organisations change themselves in a rapidly changing world.

Revans emphasised that 'Q' is the most important part of the learning equation, stating that 'the search for Q is the mission of action learning, and it is pursued in a *learning community*' (Revans, 1983, p. 41).

Mike Pedler, the Revans Professorial Fellow at Salford University who has also republished Revans's books, explains that Revans may have resisted defining action learning clearly (Pedler, 1997a, p. xxx) because he felt it was a 'philosophy', thus preventing it from being adopted as a management technique. This disposition is reflected in what Revans writes about the 'philosophy of action learning', where he states, 'Action Learning is the Aristotelian manifestation of all managers' jobs: they learn as they manage; and they manage because they have learned – and go on learning' (Revans, 1998, p. 73).

Pedler, however, ventures to offer his own definition to help newcomers learn the essence of action learning.

Action learning couples the development of people in work organizations with action on their difficult problems. It is based on the premise that there is no learning without action and no sober and deliberate action without learning. This contrasts with the principles underlying most of our formal education. Action learning makes the task the vehicle for learning and has three main components – *people,* who accept the responsibility for action on a particular task or issue; *problems* or the tasks which are acted on; and the *set* of six or so colleagues who meet regularly to support and challenge each other to take action and to learn. Action Learning implies both organizational development and self-development – action on a problem changes both the problems and the actor. (Pedler, 1997a, p. xxx)

As you can observe, this definition helps to differentiate action learning more clearly from other forms of management development by elaborating on its main components.

In my early days as an action learner, Mike Pedler's book *Action Learning in Practice* (1997b) came in very handy to set up an action learning set in my organisation. Pedler was also involved in setting up the journal *Action Learning: Research and Practice*, which publishes refereed papers and accounts of practice.

In spite of Pedler's caution, over the years action learning has become a tool for management consultants in management development work. It has also found wide application in large organisations like General Electric, Prudential, Astra Zeneca and Sandvik, which indicates that it works in practice.

Attempts were also made to introduce action learning in management education programs, using it as a way of teaching instead of lecturing. A recent study by Pedler, Burgoyne and Brook (2014, p. 65), however, concludes that 'business school education remains dominated by the traditional lecturing and case studies and that action learning is not widely used nor are business school staff generally skilled in it'. However, interestingly their research found that action learning has been developed from being a method to being an ethos (Pedler et al., 2014, p. 58), 'a general approach to learning from experience through engaging with actual work challenges rather than the ones described (case studies) or simulated (business-gaming, role-playing) in classroom situations'. They also found new variants of action learning such as Critical AL, Auto AL, Action mentoring, online and remote action learning, self-managed AL and Business-Driven AL.

Pedler and Burgoyne (2008, p. 321) sampled practitioners in the United Kingdom to identify the essential features of action learning that are commonly used, and produced the following list:

1. Sets have about six people.
2. Action is on real tasks or problems at work.
3. Tasks/problems are individual rather than collective.
4. Questioning is the main way to help participants proceed with their tasks and problems.
5. Facilitators are used in the AL process.
6. Tasks/problems are chosen independently by individuals.

Ortrun provides a briefer definition of action learning as 'learning from concrete experience and critical reflection on the experience – through group discussion, trial and error, discovery and learning from each other' (Zuber-Skerritt, 2002a, p. 114). Her definition sets some preconditions that are required to make action learning successful. Through her experience setting up the Queensland University Action Learning Program (QUAL), she stresses that certain values are important for action learning programs to succeed. These include:

1. Collaboration, trust and openness;
2. Team spirit and mutual respect for individual differences, talents and needs; and
3. Tolerance of mistakes, from which we learn (Zuber-Skerritt, 2002a, p. 114).

Can action learning be taught? There are several guides and case studies on how to set up an action learning program (Pedler, 2008), but one often hears the statement that you learn action learning only by doing it and experiencing it. This is what happened when as part of my doctoral research I first started to set up an action learning program in the organisation where I worked as senior manager in Singapore. While the task seemed simple, it took us some time to learn about and practise action learning properly. We learnt about it through organising an action learning workshop and learning by ourselves, with each other, how to do it. I then sought some help from a consultant.

In my search for materials about action learning I came across a very practical book by Scott Inglis (1994), *Making the Most of Action Learning,* which I liked for its simple and practical explanation. We were starting an action learning set in Singapore and did not have the funds to invite Inglis from the UK to conduct a start-up workshop. So we wrote to him and he was kind enough to send all his slides to help us conduct a start-up workshop that we found very useful.

Often action learning guides also advocate the use of a facilitator (or set adviser) to keep the set honest in following the principles of action learning. However, we decided to take on the role of the set adviser ourselves, which often happens when action learning sets mature and become self-sustaining. We found very useful the fish-bowl exercise recommended by McGill and Beatty (2001) to practise 'insightful questioning'. As managers we had been ready to rush forward towards solutions in our set meetings, instead of going through the process of 'peeling the onion' to understand the problem we were facing using an insightful questioning process. Once we mastered this, it was smooth sailing with the set.

When we were trying to make sense of action learning, a workshop conducted by Ron Passfield from Brisbane in Australia helped me to better appreciate and adopt in our action learning set some essential features and values based on Passfield's own doctoral research (Passfield, 1996, p. 19):

Artefacts
set: work teams, mixed teams, inter-organisational teams
problem: projects, placements, personal challenges
people: teachers, educators, trainers, students, street kids, managers, housewives, executives, nurses, academics
field of action: immediate work area, unrelated area, different organisation, the street

Norms
advice, challenge and support
challenging assumptions
questioning insight
treating each other as peers
admitting what we do not know and what is not working well

taking a system perspective
accepting responsibility for own actions and learning

Values
inclusiveness and respect for diversity
honesty and integrity
collaboration
relationships are important

Assumptions
L = P + Q (learning equals programmed knowledge plus questioning insight).
Current knowledge and skill are born of lived experiences in a previous time
and space and, in that sense, are environmentally relative.

Past experience can generate misconceptions, not only because our perceptual
capacity is limited, but also because the past is different from the present and
the future.

Learning can be defined as 'our ability to adapt and change with such readiness
that we are seen to change'. (Revans, 1981, p. 136)

People learn with and from each other when they acknowledge their common
ignorance and vulnerability.
Learning is a social process involving collaborative reflection on action.

Passfield's explanation of the features summarised above informs us on several aspects
and can be used as a quick guide to set up action learning. Another resource that I found
helpful for setting up action learning to develop younger managers in the organisation
where I worked was Alan Mumford's (1993) book, *How Managers Can Develop
Managers*. Our learning set found it helpful to use the 'task cycle' and 'learning cycle'
used in the book, which is derived from Kolb's learning cycle. The two cycles helped
us to deliberately set learning goals before we undertook a task related to the overall
problem we were working with on a large-scale change initiative. See Figure 5.1.

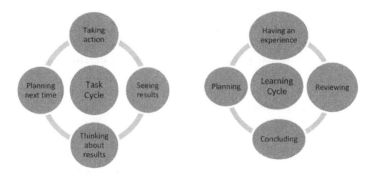

Figure 5.1. Task cycle and learning cycle (Mumford, 1993, p. 50)

In summary, action learning is effective when working on real problems with a group of 'comrades in adversity' to find solutions using insightful questioning that utilises the shared knowledge of group members. Questioning is very important during action learning meetings, as yesterday's knowledge is often not useful to solve today's problems. Questioning should be supportive while also challenging the mental model of the person/s with the problem. Artefacts identified by practitioners that are common in an action learning program can be used to set up the action learning process. However, the group is likely to become self-sufficient once its members learn how to use the artefacts well. Members of our group also knew that within our organisation the 'action learning' meetings acted as a safety net where we could 'discuss the undiscussable' if everyone agreed to keep what happened at the meeting confidential. To be able to do this, an atmosphere of trust needs to be developed within the group.

Action Research

Kurt Lewin is generally credited with coining the term 'action research'. As he explained:

> The research needed for social practice can best be characterized as research for social management or social engineering. It is a type of [*action-research*], a comparative research on the conditions and effects of various forms of social action, and research leading to social action. Research that produces nothing but books will not suffice. (Lewin, 1946 reproduced in Lewin, 1948, pp. 202–203)

His approach involves a spiral of steps, 'each of which is composed of a circle of planning, action and fact-finding about the result of the action' (Lewin, 1948, p. 206). http://infed.org/mobi/kurt-lewin-groups-experiential-learning-and-action-research/

Although Lewin is credited as the founder of action research, Argyris, Putnam and Smith (1987, p. 8) noted that Lewin 'never wrote a systematic statement of his views on action research'. This observation has a connotation similar to Pedler's statement about Revans not defining action learning. However, to be fair to Lewin, he died in 1947 soon after he first used the term 'action research'.

The *Sage Handbook of Action Research* edited by Peter Reason and Hilary Bradbury is a valuable resource for action researchers across the world. Reason and Bradbury (2008, p. 4) define action research as:

> a participatory process concerned with developing practical knowing in the pursuit of worthwhile human purposes. It seeks to bring together action and reflection, theory and practice, in participation with others, in the pursuit of practical solutions to issues of pressing concern to people, and more generally the flourishing of individual persons and their communities.

This definition reflects the development of action research from the initial thoughts of Lewin to its form that has emerged today through the contributions of prominent scholars in the field.

In my doctoral research (Sankaran, 1999) I adopted a simpler definition of action research, given by Bob Dick (2001, p. 21):

> Action research 'pursues both action (change) and research (understanding) outcomes'. It achieves change through a participatory approach, often in conjunction with other change processes. The research is achieved by being responsive to the situation and by searching strenuously for disconfirming evidence. At the heart of AR is a cycle that alternates action and critical reflection.

This worked well for us in the context of the organisational change we were implementing in the company where I worked, which became my doctoral research project. Kemmis and McTaggart's (1988) concept of action research being a spiral of self-reflective cycles of Planning, Acting and Observing, Reflecting and Replanning also helped me to set up my action research process in stages.

Ortrun developed the CRASP (critical, reflective, accountable, self-evaluating and participative) model of action research for use in higher education, based on grounded theory developed from case studies (Zuber-Skerritt, 1991, p. 2). She often uses the working definition of action research developed with her colleagues during the First International Symposium on Action Research in Higher Education, Government and Industry held in Brisbane in 1989. During my doctoral research I found this working definition very useful.

If yours is a situation in which

- people reflect on and improve (or develop) their own work and their own situations
- by tightly inter-linking their reflection and action
- also making their experience public, not only to the participants but also to other persons interested in and concerned about the work and the situation, i.e., their (public) theories and practices of the work and the situation

and if yours is a situation in which there is increasingly

- data gathering by participants themselves (or with the help of others) in relation to their own questions
- participation (in problem posing and in answering questions) in decision making
- power sharing and the relative suspension of hierarchical ways of working towards industrial democracy
- collaboration among members of the group as a 'critical community'
- self-reflection, self-evaluation and self-management by autonomous and responsible persons and groups

- learning progressively (and publicly) by doing and making mistakes in a 'self-reflective spiral' of planning, acting, observing, replanning etc.
- reflection that supports the idea of the '(self-)reflective practitioner'

then

- yours is situation in which ACTION RESEARCH is occurring (Altrichter et al., 1991, p. 8).

We found that our own action research intervention to change our work model to carry out projects reflected on many of the points included in this definition.

Two online courses offered from Australia to teach action research were also very useful in learning about how to set up an action research project. These were Action Research and Evaluation Online (AREOL) (http://www.aral.com.au/areol/areolind.html) facilitated by Bob Dick, and Action Research on the Web (AROW) taught by Ian Hughes. The AROW program is now discontinued and the website is not available.

Similar to action learners, action researchers also adopt some key common values in their work. For Mary Brydon-Miller et al. (2003, p. 15), 'A respect for people and for the knowledge and experience they bring to the research process, a belief in the ability of democratic processes to achieve positive social change, and a commitment to action, these are the basic values which underlie our common practice as action researchers'. For Bob Dick (email 8 January 2015), the values of action research can be thought of as the 'governing variables' of Model II in action science, which is a variant of action research, founded by Chris Argyris. Argyris's (1982) Model I (theory-in-use) and Model II (espoused theory) contrast two sets of values – those we claim to hold (Model II) and those an uninvolved observer would deduce from our actual behaviour (Model I).

Dick (2015) suggests that from this point of view, action researchers would claim to hold such values as stated in Model II:

- valid information
- free and informed choice
- internal commitment to the choice, and
- constant monitoring of the implementation.

A book published recently by Rothwell (2015) states some principles of action research that can be considered to be its values:

Pragmatic: It addresses practical issues and links theory with practice.
Democratic: It involves people and also seeks to empower them to generate their own knowledge.
Extended epistemology: It accommodates many ways of knowing and valuing the experiential, narrative, aesthetic and conceptual.

Value-oriented: It asks how we can contribute to the economic, political, psychological, and spiritual well-being of humans, communities, and the wider ecology.

Developmental: It evolves over time toward a more significant diagnostic model.

In summary, then, as Bob Dick and I explain:

Action research is not a single method or methodology, but refers to a variety of approaches that involves working collaboratively with people who are facing a concern that needs some deliberate action to be taken to address it. Such collaboration creates buy-in for implementing the change that accompanies the action. The group of people who are working together with the action researcher are treated as co-researchers rather than informants. Action research is a cyclic process alternating between action and reflection upon the action to initiate further action converging towards improving the situation of concern. (Sankaran & Dick, 2015, pp. 211–212)

In addition, there are strong values that action researchers adhere to such as participation, equity, justice and the importance of democratic processes.

Similarities and Differences between Action Learning and Action Research

While action learning and action research have several similarities in their features, there are also some critical differences between them. Abraham asks us not to be confused with the two processes even though they both are 'problem-focussed, action oriented and utilise group dynamics' (Abraham, 2012, p. 6). Abraham explains that through Action Learning, Revans was:

more interested in 'questioning insight' than 'solving problems', whereas 'Action Research' was designed as a means by which change could be introduced in problematic situations to bring about a noticeable improvement. Revans places more emphasis on the development of managers, skills and abilities than Lewin, who was more concerned with making a contribution to science, and he accords outside experts a far lesser role.

While this is a useful differentiation, Revans did not support the use of outside experts in action learning because he felt that the knowledge required to solve problems rests within managers and insightful questioning helps to unearth this hidden knowledge.

Pedler and Burgoyne (2008, p. 322) also note the many similarities between action learning and action research, particularly through 'a commitment to action and pragmatism and a reaction against detached research generating abstract knowledge, which is then disseminated through teaching from a position of assumed expertise'. They point out that the differences between the two can be seen in their starting points and development paths. While action learning seems to be dependent on the thought and practice of its founder Revans, action research has moved beyond Lewin's original conception of it. They also observe, 'Another apparently obvious difference is in the name *action learning* versus *action research*; action learning has become a radical alternative to teaching, while action research presents a striking juxtaposition to passive traditions of research, both positivist and interpretivist' (p. 322). Pedler and Burgoyne (2008, p. 323) also contend that action research has become a more developed field 'both in practice and theory, and has been developed and taken forward by a wider community of scholars than action learning'.

Joe Raelin (1997, p. 21) pointed out the common basis of 'action technologies' (a term coined by Brooks and Watkins in 2002 to cover action learning, action research and action science). He sees it 'is that knowledge is to be produced in action. As opposed to "positivist" models that were designed to develop theories purposely separated from practice in order to predict truth, action research applied theory directly to the field with scholars and practitioners collaborating'. Raelin also claimed that action learning and action science evolved from action research (this may be contested by action learning scholars) and that action learning 'is based on the straightforward pedagogical notion that people learn most effectively when working on real-time problems occurring in their work setting'.

Ortrun also considers action learning and action research as 'linked-integrated' concepts located in the social sciences. In her view (Zuber-Skerritt, 2009, p. 6), '"Action Learning" means learning from and through action or concrete experience, as well as taking action as a result of this learning. Similarly "Action Research" is a cyclical iterative process of action and reflection on and in action'. Ortrun differentiates between action learning and action research by stating that while 'both include active learning, searching, problem solving and systematic inquiry ... Action Research is more systematic, rigorous, scrutinisable, verifiable, and always public (in verifiable or published written/electronic forms)'.

My own experience of using action learning and action research indicates that there are more similarities than differences between the two. This agrees with Bob Dick's views published by the Action Learning and Action Research Association in Australia (http://www.alarassociation.org/pages/al-and-ar/action-learning):

> I used to think that action research was the umbrella term, and action learning was an application of it. Some of my colleagues, I found, argue that action learning is the umbrella term. On reflection, I don't think it's worth debating.

> As they were previously practised, I think a useful distinction could be made. In action learning, each participant drew different learning from different experience. In action research a team of people drew collective learning from a collective experience.

> More recently, the advent of in-company action learning programs has begun to change this. The use of a team with a common project or problem leads to an action learning program which looks remarkably like action research.

There were also some differences, on average, in field of application. Action learning was more often used in organisational settings. Action research is more common in community and educational settings. This distinction, too, is beginning to blur.

I now wonder if the distinction is worth preserving.

I want to conclude this brief review with a question. If action learning and action research are similar in many respects, do people who practise these have common values? Apparently they do according to the Action Learning and Action Research Associations. See http://www.alarassociation.org/pages/al-and-ar/ alara-al_ar-principles

COMBINING ACTION LEARNING AND ACTION RESEARCH

Due to their similarities and common principles it is not difficult to combine action learning and action research to deliver management and research outcomes. As I noted above, my doctoral research used a combination of action research and action learning based on an elegant model proposed by Perry and Zuber-Skerritt (1992, p. 76) for doctoral programs. Although their model, shown in Figure 5.2, uses action research for the '(core) intervention projects' and 'thesis writing', we used 'action learning' for the 'intervention projects' as it suited our environment. In this workplace in Singapore, the Japanese corporation's policy was to encourage *kaizen* or continuous improvement in the organisation.

There are three cyclical processes used in this model.

The thesis action research represents the setting up of a (doctoral) research project where the perceived research problem leads to taking some action. This action could be a number of core projects that contribute to the observations required to collect data for the research. This data is analysed using critical reflection that could lead to further improvement to the research plan and how it is adjusted to be emergent and responsive.

The core projects follow a similar cycle but their main motivation is action with less emphasis on research, focussing on the task to be done. Refinements are made through a cyclical process using the steps shown in Figure 5.2.

New understandings developed through the reflections carried out in the thesis action research project help to set up the writing up of the project and its results for publication (usually a thesis, but also possibly journal articles or book). These steps may also be set up as a cyclical process within the project.

The combination of action research and action learning worked for us because there were two main aims for the project that we undertook.

1. Action research, naturally, suited my professional aims as project manager. There was a PhD thesis to be submitted. I aimed to write and submit a PhD thesis based on the intervention that was carried out to change the nature of project

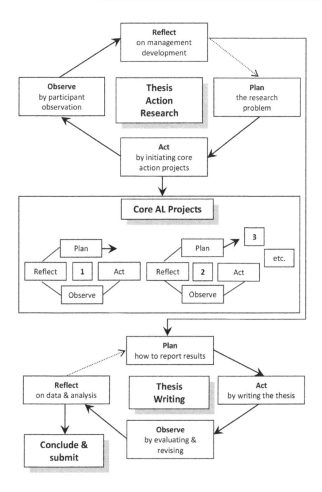

Figure 5.2. Combining action research and action learning in a doctoral thesis (Perry and Zuber-Skerritt, 1992, p. 76)

management in the organisation. The research had to be rigorously carried out, analysed and reported, and published making a contribution to knowledge.
2. Action learning best suited the purpose of the organisational change projects – developing in the organisation younger managers who would take on senior positions once the change project was completed. It also matched the political climate of the organisation, a Japanese company with *kaizen* or continuous improvement as its management philosophy.

As well as her scholarly contributions to and through ALAR, Ortrun has also developed the PALAR model as a structured action learning program that uses action research as a methodology to address a major organisational problem (Zuber-Skerritt, 2002b, p. 144). The PALAR model consists of eight phases:

1. Problem definition and needs analysis
2. Start-up workshop
3. Project work
4. Midway workshop with specialist input
5. Project work continued
6. Concluding workshop
7. Preparing for presentations and publications
8. Final presentation and celebration

While this model was not adopted in our action research project, it was replicated in the group supervision process adopted by our two Australian supervisors. They used it to supervise as a group four doctoral students in Singapore – of whom I was one – in yearly face-to-face supervision sessions in Singapore. All four students were very effective in timely and successful completion of their doctoral studies (Sankaran et al., 2007).

Other scholars have also supported the use of action research in doctoral research. Dick (2002) states that action research is useful for doctoral research as both action and research can be important to the candidate. The action in action research often takes the form of a change or improvement one wants to implement at the workplace. The research helps learning and understanding, and publication of the study contributes to knowledge creation. These were the dual aims of the research that we undertook in our work organisation. Coghlan (2007) explores doing action research in your own organisation, showing how an executive action research doctorate can combine individual activity undertaken by the manager–researcher as first-person inquiry, the collaborative activities carried out by others as second-person inquiry, and the actionable knowledge contributed by the research to the academic and practitioner communities as the third-person contribution.

After I left industry and joined academia in 1999 I started supervising doctoral candidates who used action research as their methodology. One of these candidates, Simon Walker, adopted the Perry and Zuber-Skerritt model combining thesis and core action research projects to implement knowledge management in a large telecommunications company in Europe that had multiple branches across Europe and the United States (Walker & Sankaran, 2014). I have also examined a doctoral thesis that used action research adopting this model.

CONCLUSIONS

Action learning and action research have many similarities despite the differences in their origins and purposes. Both rely on knowledge being produced in action, they are problem-focussed, used in groups, and rely on learning by doing. They can also be used effectively together for management development and postgraduate research. In this chapter I have focussed on the postgraduate research aspect where Ortrun has made a major contribution through her career as an academic worldwide. I have illustrated why using the model proposed by Ortrun and her colleagues was useful in my own research as well as in my supervision of doctoral students. I think combining action learning and action research is a very pragmatic way of carrying out a research project that has the dual aim of producing management outcomes while carrying out the rigorous research expected of a doctoral thesis or dissertation.

Postscript

As a novice action researcher I met Ortrun in the early 1990s in Brisbane, Australia, when I was beginning my doctoral research in Singapore as a manager. She encouraged me to take up action research with enthusiasm when I expressed some concerns about using it in my research due to my positivist background as a scientist and an engineer. After finishing my doctorate as a manager in industry, I joined Southern Cross University in New South Wales to teach in an MBA program. At that time Ortrun had been appointed to help the university become a centre for action research in Australia. After she left the university, I took up that role and established the Southern Cross Institute of Action Research. I have kept in touch with Ortrun through the activities of the Action Learning and Action Research Association (ALARA) of Australia (which she helped establish in 1991) and the Action Research World Congresses where she has taken major responsibilities. I feel privileged to be invited to contribute to a book to recognise the immense and valuable work carried out by Ortrun to promote both action learning and action research around the world.

REFERENCES

Abraham, S. (2012). *Work-applied learning for change.* Adelaide, South Australia: AIB Publications.

Altrichter, H., Kemmis, S., McTaggart, R., & Zuber-Skerritt, O. (1991). Defining, confining or refining action research? In O. Zuber-Skerritt (Ed.), *Action research for change and development* (pp. 13–20). Aldershot, England: Gower.

Argyris, C. (1982). *Reasoning, learning and action: Individual and organisational.* San Francisco, CA: Jossey-Bass.

Argyris, C., Putnam, R., & Smith, D. (1987). *Action science: Concepts, methods, and skills for research and intervention.* San Francisco, CA: Jossey-Bass.

Brydon-Miller, M., Greenwood, D., & McGuire, P. (2003). What is action research? *Action Research, 1*(1), 9–28.

Coghlan, D. (2007). Insider action research doctorates: Generating actionable knowledge. *Higher Education, 54,* 293–306.

Dick, B. (2001), Action research: Action and research. In S. Sankaran, B. Dick, R. Passfield, & P. Swepson (Eds.), *Effective change management using action learning and action research: Concepts, frameworks, processes and applications* (pp. 21–27). Lismore, New South Wales: Southern Cross University Press.

Dick, B. (2002). Postgraduate programs using action research. *The Learning Organization*, 9(4), 159–170.

Dick, B. (2015, January 8). Email communication with author.

Inglis, S. (1994). *Making the most of action learning*. Aldershot, England: Gower.

Kemmis, S., & McTaggart, R. (1988). *The action research planner* (2nd ed.). Geelong, Victoria, Australia: Deakin University Press.

Lewin, K. (1946). Action research and minority problems, *Journal of Social Issues*, 2(4), 34–46.

Lewin, K. (1948). Action research and minority problems (Republished). In G. W. Lewin (Ed.), *Resolving social conflicts: Selected papers on group dynamics* (pp. 201–216). New York, NY: Harper & Row.

McGill, I., & Beatty, L. (2001). *Action learning: A practitioner's guide* (2nd ed.). London, UK: Kogan Page.

Mumford, A. (1993). *How managers can develop managers*. Aldershot, England: Gower.

Passfield, R. (1996). Action learning: A paradigm whose time has come. *Action Learning and Action Research*, 1(2), 14–29.

Pedler, M. (1997a). Introduction by Mike Pedler. In M. Pedler (Ed.), *Action learning in practice* (3rd ed.). Aldershot, England: Gower.

Pedler, M. (Ed.). (1997b). *Action learning in practice* (3rd ed.). Aldershot, England: Gower.

Pedler, M. (2008). *Action learning for managers* (2nd ed.). Aldershot, England: Gower.

Pedler, M., & Burgoyne, J. (2008). Action learning. In P. Reason & H. Bradbury (Eds.), *The Sage handbook of action research* (pp. 319–332). London, UK: Sage.

Pedler, M., Burgoyne, J., & Brook, C. (2014). What has action learning learned to become? *Action Learning: Research and Practice*, 2(1), 49–68.

Perry, C., & Zuber-Skerritt, O. (1992). Action research in graduate management research programs. *Higher Education*, 23, 195–208.

Raelin, J. A. (1997) Action learning and action science: Are they different? *Organizational Dynamics*, 26(1), 21–34.

Reason, P., & Bradbury, H. (2008). Introduction. In P. Reason & H. Bradbury (Eds.), *The Sage handbook of action research* (pp. 1–10). London, UK: Sage.

Revans, R. W. (1981). Management, productivity and risk: The way ahead. *OMEGA International Review of Management Science*, 9(2), 127–137.

Revans, R. (1983). Action learning: Its terms and character. *Management Development*, 21, 39–50.

Revans, R. (1998). *ABC of action learning: Empowering managers to act and learn from action*. The Mike Pedler Library, London, UK: Lemos and Crane.

Rothwell, W. J. (Ed.). (2015). *Organization development fundamentals*. Alexandria, VA: ATD Press.

Sankaran S. (1999). *An action research study of management learning: Developing local engineering managers of a Japanese multinational company in Singapore* (PhD Thesis). Adelaide, South Australia: University of South Australia.

Sankaran, S., & Dick, B. (2015). Linking theory and practice in using action-oriented methods. In B. Pasian (Ed.), *Designs, methods and practices for research of project management* (pp. 211–224). Aldershot, England: Gower.

Sankaran, S., & Kumar, M. R., (2010). *Implementing organizational change using action research, in two Asian cultures*. Proceedings of Project Management Institute, PMI research and education conference 2010 (pp. 1–26). Project Management Institute, Washington, DC.

Sankaran, S., Hase, S., Dick, B., & Davies, A. (2007). Singing different tunes from the same song sheet: Four perspectives of teaching the doing of action research. *Action Research, Special Issue: The Praxis of Teaching Action Research*, 5(3), 30–52.

Walker, S., & Sankaran, S. (2014). A participatory action research study of knowledge management implementation in a large European telecommunication company in their UK office. *Gibaran Journal of Applied Management*, 6(2), 36–63.

Zuber-Skerritt, O. (Ed.). (1991). *Action research for change and development*. Centre for the Advancement of Learning and Teaching, Brisbane: Griffith University.

Zuber-Skerritt, O. (2002a). The concept of action learning. *The Learning Organization*, 9(4), 114–124.

Zuber-Skerritt, O. (2002b). A model for designing action learning and action research programs. *The Learning Organization*, *9*(4), 143–149.

Zuber-Skerritt, O. (2009). Introduction. In O. Zuber-Skerritt & Associates (Eds.), *Action learning and action research: Songlines through interviews* (pp. 1–21). Rotterdam, The Netherlands: Sense Publishers.

Shankar Sankaran
Professor
Organisational Project Management
University of Technology, Sydney
Australia

RON PASSFIELD

6. THE PRACTICAL VISIONARY

INTRODUCTION

I have worked with a number of visionaries over my working life. One thing I have found is that they can see the future so clearly that it already appears real. Typically, however, they do not want to become directly involved in closing the gap between current reality and the perceived future state. They do not want to be bogged down in the detail or the problems of making their envisioned future happen. They prefer to inspire others to create the vision that they espouse. Ortrun is different; she not only paints and promotes her evolving vision but works actively on the ground to make it happen. It is for this reason that I describe her in this chapter as the 'practical visionary'.

INITIATING THE VISION – THE FIRST INTERNATIONAL SYMPOSIUM ON ACTION RESEARCH IN HIGHER EDUCATION, GOVERNMENT AND INDUSTRY (20–23 MARCH 1989)

I first met Ortrun in 1989 when we were members of what was then called The Process Management Association. At the time, Ortrun was working at the Centre for the Advancement of Learning and Teaching (CALT) at Griffith University. I had joined the Faculty of Commerce and Administration at the University on secondment from a senior executive position in the Department of Social Security at the request of the then Dean, Professor Pat Weller.

Ortrun's focus at the time was action research in higher education – an interest she pursued through her PhD study in the Faculty of Education at Deakin University, with Stephen Kemmis as her supervisor. Her newly developed model for teaching, learning and professional development in higher education was refined and explained in two books, *Action Research in Higher Education* (Zuber-Skerritt, 1992a) and *Professional Development in Higher Education* (Zuber-Skerritt, 1992c). I brought to our working relationship a practitioner's approach to Action Learning and Action Research (ALAR) in business and government. My focus on action research was developed in the 1980s through my practice as an internal consultant and my MBA study of organisational change and development with Bob Dick, who was working in the Psychology Department at the University of Queensland (radically introducing participative teaching, learning and assessment much to the horror of the University establishment).

J. Kearney & M. Todhunter (Eds), Lifelong Action Learning and Research: A Tribute to the Life and Pioneering Work of Ortrun Zuber-Skerritt, 65–75.

My collaboration with Ortrun and long term friendship were forged in these early years as we shared our orientations and common commitment to creating a more just and equitable society based on principles of collaboration, trust and participation.

At the time Ortrun was particularly concerned about the parallel development of action research in education and action learning/action research in business/ government. In many senses, it epitomised the divide between the founders of action research (Kurt Lewin) and action learning (Reg Revans), who shared a mutual respect but thought the other's approach was inadequate. Revans was concerned that action research focussed on research at the expense of action; while Lewin thought that action learning sacrificed the rigour of research for the imperative of action and improvement.

In typical Ortrun fashion, she decided to do something about this historical divide. This attests to her vision and action orientation as a practical visionary. Ortrun set about convening the First International Symposium on Action Learning and Action Research at Griffith University in 1989. She used her established network of action researchers in higher education to provide the foundation for this event. Then she set about consolidating and growing her network in business and government to bring the different sectors together. I was invited by Ortrun to join the Symposium as a representative of government/business even though I had just joined Griffith University as an academic on secondment from the Federal Department of Social Security.

The first two days of the Symposium were dedicated to discussions amongst the international leaders at that time in the field of action research in higher education. After much debate, they developed a working definition of action research that they shared with the participants from government and industry on the third day. These later representatives were able confirm the relevance of the definition for application in their own arenas. The process of debate and the working definition of action research is captured in Altrichter, Kemmis, McTaggart and Zuber-Skerritt (1990).

To me, the outstanding achievements of this Symposium were:

- The development of a language that provided a platform for collaboration amongst action researchers in the different arenas (education, business and government)
- Support for the First World Congress on Action Research in Brisbane, to bring together people engaged in action learning, action research and process management in business, government and education.

Ortrun was clearly the primary driver behind both these outcomes, having conceived and convened the Symposium in the first place. The process and output of the Symposium are documented in Ortrun's edited book, *Action Research for Change and Development* (1990).

Having recently had the G20 Summit in my home city of Brisbane, I can only regret that the world's top 20 leaders failed to make a common statement about economic growth and development that recognised their common goals but also acknowledged the critical interdependence between economic growth and social wellbeing. Such a statement would explicitly incorporate the need to develop ways to share economic benefits equitably, rather than in the hands of a few, and would recognise the current reality of global interdependency brought to light in a stark way through the Global Economic Crisis. Such a collaborative statement would have been more in line with the values and aims of action research as reflected in Ortrun's vision and actions.

FIRST WORLD CONGRESS ON ACTION LEARNING AND ACTION RESEARCH

Following the Symposium, Ortrun set about creating the First World Congress on Action Learning and Action Research (Zuber-Skerritt, 1991) and commissioned me to be her right hand man. Ortrun was the Convenor of the Congress and I was the Treasurer. Being relatively inexperienced in the intricacies of conducting an event of this scale we commissioned a conference organiser, UniQuest, to guide us through the process of developing a conference theme, creating mailing lists, designing and seeking expressions of interest, developing a budget, and deciding a venue that could accommodate the conference and overseas delegates. The Congress content and process was developed by a Congress Organising Committee that established a collaborative and fun working ethos developed further by subsequent Congress Committees.

Funding for the Congress was a real issue at the time as we started with a base of zero funds. At Ortrun's insistence, I developed a Sponsorship Program and was able to obtain some funds. Of critical importance was the repayable grant of $3,000 that I obtained from Pat Weller as Dean of my faculty; this served as the essential seeding money to fund the expression of interest document and mailing. In the meantime, Ortrun and I worked for many hours developing mailing lists from our networks and Internet research.

The planning of this Congress brought to the fore yet again Ortrun's vision and absolute determination to overcome any obstacle to achieving it. One of the first such obstacles was from an executive in Ortrun's own Faculty who refused her access to resources and specifically to the fax machine (our lifeblood for instant, global communication at the time). We could only assume that he was threatened by Ortrun's growing influence and demonstrated capacity to make a global impact beyond the narrow confines of her job description. The fact that she was already publishing actively and had achieved two doctorates did not help his growing sense of unease.

Ortrun learned very early on that to survive and gain credibility in the university sector two things were paramount: qualifications and publications. She heeded, to an exceptional degree, the call to 'publish or perish'. As a woman too, she was conscious that this was even more critical for her in what was then a male-dominated university environment. So as usual, Ortrun worked around this problem by accessing the fax machine in my faculty through me. So we met almost daily to send communications, develop strategies and plans, share mailing lists and manage emerging difficulties including the obsessive preoccupation of Griffith's Corporate Communications area who were being prescriptive about the allowable size of the Griffith Logo on the Congress Brochure that acknowledged the University's contribution (a repayable loan). Of course, none of this would have progressed without the absolute dedication and shared vision of other members of the Congress Organising Committee that Ortrun formed to develop the event.

We had just established a contract with UniQuest, when our second major challenge emerged in the form of an attempt to sabotage the fledging conference organisation. Again, a male executive decided to cause mischief by informing my Dean that we had no budget for the Congress and that his $3,000 loan was in jeopardy. I was called up to explain; fortunately we had just developed a budget through our work with UniQuest and were given the go-ahead by Pat Weller who saw the 'sabotage attempt' for what it was. Also, by then, we were able to demonstrate external support through our Sponsorship program. We were especially grateful to Pat Weller for trusting our vision, enthusiasm and energy to make this event happen. It is interesting, on reflection, that UniQuest was our insurance and Pat Weller, despite subscribing to a different paradigm, was our internal supporter.

So after spending many hours in the collaborative planning of the event, in 1990 we were collectively able to hold a World Congress at St John's College in the University of Queensland that attracted 350 delegates. What was very clear at this First World Congress was the very strong divide between academics and 'others', as well as the existing divide between action research and action learning practitioners. However, in line with Ortrun's vision, we were able to take tentative steps towards bridging the gap.

As proved to be the case in the subsequent 25 years, Ortrun was able to inspire others with her vision and engage them in its pursuit. Unlike many visionaries, she was able to identify the need to engage others who could act as translators of the vision and build the processes and systems to make the vision a reality. A clear example of this was the Congress Organising Committee who worked tirelessly and collaboratively to design the Congress, engage their networks, plan the logistics, monitor the funding and conduct the actual Congress.

Like Ortrun, I learned very early on that if you are going to do anything counter-cultural, you need to build an external support base, for validation, credibility and, ultimately, survival. This realisation gave rise to our next collaborative endeavour.

ACTION LEARNING, ACTION RESEARCH AND PROCESS MANAGEMENT (ALARPM) ASSOCIATION

ALARPM was born in an era when the opposition to action learning and action research was quite overt, and driven by people in power who had a vested interest in maintaining the status quo. Kurt Lewin made the point very early on that it is only when you start to change something that you find out what are the forces keeping the present 'reality' in place. People in power define what is real and acceptable and what is 'aberrant' or 'non-conforming' to an existing paradigm that incorporates a fundamental belief system.

So ALARPM arose out of a felt need to gather together people who supported an emergent paradigm and to start building the foundations of that new paradigm – conferences, publications, research and networks.

We were adamant at the time that no organisation would 'own' ALARPM – we were very determined that it would not be positioned within a university as this would only lead to controls being imposed on its development and reach. This proved subsequently to be a wise decision even though there were real costs involved in not having a strong resource base.

With Ortrun's solid encouragement, we set about establishing ALARPM. I used as a guide a template for associations, developed by Queensland University of Technology (QUT), and wrote up a draft constitution. We were under way. The members of the First World Congress Organising Committee formed the foundation of ALARPM, about ten of us who were Brisbane-based.

Behind the vision was the desire to bring together the practitioners of three core processes – action learning, action research and process management – from all arenas – community, business, government and academia. We felt that a group that promoted collaborative processes had itself to model collaboration across the divides of process and different areas of operation.

As a very active member of the Organising Committee for the Second World Congress on Action Learning, Action Research and Process Management, Ortrun chaired a symposium on *Action Research for Building Learning Organisations*, which included presentations by Ortrun, Cliff Bunning, Faith Howell and myself (Bruce & Russell, 1992). This was one of the many symposia that Ortrun has conceived, organised and convened for conferences and world congresses.

Ortrun was a key driver for publication of papers from the *Moving on Conference* by ALARPM at St John's College, The University of Queensland on 29 June 1995 (Pinchen & Passfield, 1995). In addition to providing support to Susan Pinchen and myself in creating and publishing the book, Ortrun wrote a chapter that illustrated her early models of action research (Zuber-Skerritt, 1995) and set the scene for the book. Without her support and inspiration, we would have lost a record of that amazing conference and the post-conference reflections captured throughout this book.

Ortrun continuously contributes to the Action Learning, Action Research Association (ALARA, the new name for ALARPM). She contributes to the development of World Congresses, participates actively in ALARA conversations, provides workshops and presentations at Conferences and Congresses (including Panel presentations), references Congress outputs in her writings, and encourages others to offer their knowledge and expertise to share with network members, either by way of publication and/or by face-to-face engagement.

UNIVERSITY OF QUEENSLAND ACTION LEARNING PROGRAMS

The University of Queensland action learning programs became another arena of collaboration and sharing for Ortrun and me (apart from her involvement as my PhD supervisor). In 1991, I was engaged on a consultancy basis by The Tertiary Education Institute at the University of Queensland to mentor the Program Team developing a University-wide action learning program. My role also involved active participation as a member of the Program Team engaged in the design, facilitation and evaluation of the action learning program.

The primary focus of this initial program was leadership development in concert with organisational innovation. The charter was to create real organisational value in terms of improvements in teaching, learning, research, administration and technical support while developing leaders in these areas. The University funded the first three years of this program, 1991–1993, from a discrete source of funds. The processes, outcomes and evaluations of the first two years of the program, 1991 and 1992, were documented in a monograph published by The Tertiary Education Institute (Dickie & Passfield, 1992).

Ortrun was appointed as an Associate Professor in the Tertiary Education Institute at the University of Queensland in June 1991 with responsibility for professional and organisational development. She immediately set about developing action-learning based development programs primarily focussed on academic staff development and improvements in teaching and learning.

In another example of her boundless energy and capacity to overcome any obstacle, Ortrun obtained funding from the Queensland Department of Employment Education and Training (DEET) for two key programs she initiated: *The Departmental Excellence in University Education (DEUE) Program* and *The Departmental Excellence in Managing Institutional Quality (DEMIQ) Program.* For good measure, Ortrun had also obtained funding for a program aimed at developing women academics as quality teachers and researchers. Her personal reflections on the DEUE Program are encapsulated in her final report (Zuber-Skerritt, 1992b).

Ortrun had focussed on the dual role of the academic – teaching and research – and the tension between the two at a time when University funding was becoming increasingly tied to quality research output. She designed the *DEUE Program* as a solution to the teaching–research tension by enabling academics 'to bring their research skills to bear on developing strategies for learning, not teaching *per se*' (Ryan & Zuber-Skerritt, 1993).

As Ortrun became the Convenor of all action learning programs run by The Tertiary Education Institute, it was decided in 1993 to attempt some form of integration between the four programs operating at the time (the one I was directly involved with and three that Ortrun had developed). So we attempted a joint start-up residential involving participants across the four programs. This design stretched the resources of the program teams and facilitation resources. It also created some confusion in the minds of participants because of the different focus, funding and processes of the four programs. Ortrun, undaunted by the magnitude of the task, had been prepared to attempt the integration at least at the start-up residential stage.

Despite some initial confusion, valuable outcomes were achieved across the four programs and important lessons were learned, which enabled the four programs to be rolled into one on a much smaller scale in subsequent years (Ryan & Zuber-Skerritt, 1993; Passfield, 1995; Timpson & Broadbent, 1995). Following these early developments, the University fully funded the Integrated Action Learning Program (1994–1999), which became known as The Queensland University Action Learning (QUAL) Program.

In a personal explication reflecting on these events and other related activities, Ortrun highlights her thinking and the problems she experienced in developing a new paradigm as well as her progressive move into research and development in management (Zuber-Skerritt, 1993).

A key aspect of Ortrun's commitment to lifelong learning is the way she developed her professional networks and interacted with people in those networks.

NETWORK DEVELOPMENT AND CRITICAL FRIENDS

It is a testament to Ortrun's professionalism that she developed an international network of critical friends to critique pre-publication versions of her books. Ortrun takes reflective practice seriously and seeks the advice and suggestions of her critical friend network with each book she writes.

One of Ortrun's distinctive personal qualities is her lack of defensiveness in the face of professional critique; she has a refreshing openness that enables her to see different perspectives without being constrained by preconceived ideas. I find that Ortrun readily accepts critique and actively seeks out ways to take on board suggestions to improve her books. This focus on continuous improvement contributes substantially to making her the sought-after writer that she is today. Not one to settle for less than perfect, Ortrun also engages a professional copyeditor and proof reader for each of her books.

More recently, I was privileged, along with other critical friends, to provide pre-publication critiques of the following books:

- *Action Leadership: Towards a Participatory Paradigm* (Zuber-Skerritt, 2011)
- *Lifelong Action Learning for Community Development: Learning and Development for a Better World* (Zuber-Skerritt & Teare, 2013)
- *Professional Learning in Higher Education and Community: Towards a New Paradigm for Action Research* (Zuber-Skerritt, Fletcher & Kearney, 2015).

In each case, as a critical friend I focussed on comprehension, consistency and coherence of the text. For example, the challenge for Ortrun in the book co-authored with Richard Teare was to achieve an effective integration between her own writings and conceptual approach and those of Richard who, along with developing a conceptual framework for his own work, was focussed on how the concepts worked on the ground, in the villages with people who lived in a disadvantaged situation. This book represents an integration of their conceptual approach, together with the translation of that integration in practice in challenging situations.

It also epitomises Ortrun's willingness and capacity to support the work of others – in this instance to provide intellectual and emotional support and friendship to Richard in his endeavours on a worldwide basis to create a better world for those who are deprived of equitable access to education. This book illustrates for me how Ortrun has highlighted the work and achievements of others and encouraged them to make explicit their own learning and practice. By using her own visibility, she is able to make more visible the contributions that others like Richard are making to achieve a better world.

THE 'TAP ON THE SHOULDER': HELPING OTHERS EXTEND THEMSELVES

Along with Ortrun's incredible self-belief is her belief in others. She has a happy knack of convincing you that are you are capable of more than you think you are, and then supporting you to move beyond your comfort zone.

Around 1992, Ortrun strongly urged me to undertake a PhD at a time when I was vacillating. I had spent 12 months trying to find a PhD supervisor who was willing and able to assist my doctoral research on a topic that I was interested in – namely, organisational change and development through action learning and action research. After a number of fruitless efforts, I was somewhat discouraged. She encouraged me to publish my ideas from one of the projects I had started (Passfield, 1992) and provided the avenue for that publication (Carr & Zuber-Skerritt, 1992).

Ortrun insisted that I start my doctoral research and told me that I had a PhD inside me that would haunt me if I did not 'get it out'. She suggested that I pursue the nexus between research and practice by focussing on the QUAL Program that I was working on at the time as an external consultant. This was a convincing argument for a practitioner of action learning and action research.

I could see that the doctoral research would help me to improve my practice within the QUAL Program, assist my career and give me an avenue to share my knowledge and experience with others. I was privileged to have Ortrun and Professor David Limerick as my supervisors in this endeavour. The title of my PhD was *Action Learning for Professional and Organisational Development – An Action Research Case Study in Higher Education* (Passfield, 1996).

On one occasion a few years back, I recall sitting down to lunch at one of the ALARA national conferences when Ortrun joined us at the table. After some catch-up conversation, Ortrun suggested to me that I might like to write a chapter for a book she was editing, *Action Research for Sustainable Development in a Turbulent World* (Zuber-Skerritt, 2012). She happened to mention that she needed something on sustainable development in the public sector and that I was the best person to write it. Ortrun mentioned in passing that all the other chapters in the book were already completed and being edited. She wanted only about 8,000 words and I could have two weeks to complete it. When I expressed doubts about my capacity to complete the chapter in such a tight timeframe, along with my ongoing commitments, she convinced me that I could do it. I wrote the chapter in record time (for me).

The chapter enabled me to reflect on my work using action learning and action research for professional and organisational development in the public sector over the previous 20 years. In a lot of ways it helped me to make explicit my learning across three major organisational interventions and enabled me to integrate my thinking about sustainable development within the context of the public sector. The net result was identification of some core strategies for sustainable development, which represent the essence of my approach to achieving real change at the personal and organisational levels within public sector organisations (Passfield, 2012).

My only regret is that I did not take a leaf out of Ortrun's book in the sense of continuous writing to reflect on my experiences, articulate my perspectives, and make explicit my learning while engaging the support of a professional network to sharpen my understanding and contribution.

Our most recent collaborative endeavour was the co-authorship of an article, 'The History and Culture of ALARA: The Action Learning and Action Research Association', for a special issue on action research networks for the journal *Educational Action Research* (Zuber-Skerritt & Passfield, 2015).

CONCLUSIONS/REFLECTIONS

I have never met anyone with the level of self-belief that I have experienced with Ortrun, or with the vision to create a better world in whatever arena she is working. Ortrun has endless capacity for writing as is evidenced in her many books, book chapters, articles and monographs. She has the vision and the ability to engage others in her lifework to create a better world. Ortrun recognises her own limitations, but at the same time has an unshakeable belief in the capacity of others. Through her belief, she helps others to stretch beyond their comfort zone and reach out to an extended self. Underpinning this capacity to contribute to the personal and professional development of others is Ortrun's perspective that obstacles are merely opportunities for mutual learning.

As the practical visionary, Ortrun has created a legacy of how to build a better world; how to develop personal, professional and organisational capacity; and how to overcome every obstacle in the pursuit of this emerging vision. Ortrun is a vibrant example of the power of collaboration and reflective practice in the pursuit of an all-embracing vision – whether it be with colleagues in a university setting, with disadvantaged groups, or with teachers and educators. Ortrun realised very early the power of leverage – leveraging her impact through collaborative endeavour and working with teachers, consultants and educators, who, in turn, influence so many others.

To me, Ortrun encapsulates a real humility, generosity of spirit, endless intellectual curiosity and energy, and a lifelong commitment to make a real difference through her ongoing contribution to articulating a vision for a better world and the means to achieve it. Many people talk about what is possible, Ortrun translates possibility into reality through her collaborative endeavours and encouragement of others to be the best they can be by extending their intellectual and emotional boundaries. I've written elsewhere about three key elements of personal productivity – focus, discipline and leverage. Ortrun has these characteristics to an exceptional degree.

It seems fitting that I am putting the finishing touches to this chapter at Ortrun's apartment in Bingen, Germany, the location for a lot of her writing. The weather has signalled the appropriateness of this event by generating light snow, an uncommon occurrence in Bingen. The chill of the weather has just been offset by the warmth of a phone call from Ortrun in Brisbane that displays once again her generosity in spirit and practice.

REFERENCES

Altrichter, H., Kemmis, K., McTaggart, R., & Zuber-Skerritt, O. (1990). Defining, confining or refining action research? In O. Zuber-Skerritt (Ed.), *Action research for change and development* (pp. 13–20). Brisbane, Queensland: Centre for the Advancement of Learning and Teaching, Griffith University.

Bruce, C., & Russell, A. (Eds.). (1992). *Transforming tomorrow today.* Proceedings of the second world congress on action learning. Upper Mt Gravatt, Brisbane: Action Learning, Action Research and Process Management (ALARPM) Association Incorporated.

Carr, T., & Zuber-Skerritt, O. (Eds.). (1992). *Working together for quality management: Action research in management and education.* Brisbane, Queensland: The Tertiary Education Institute, The University of Queensland.

Dickie, K., & Passfield, R. (1992). *The University of Queensland action learning program, 1991 and 1992: Final report.* Brisbane, Queensland: The Tertiary Education Institute, The University of Queensland.

Passfield, R. (1992). From vicious to virtuous circles: Improving the quality of education through action research. In T. Carr & O. Zuber-Skerritt (Eds.), *Working together for quality management: Action research in management and education* (pp. 29–61). Brisbane, Queensland: The Tertiary Education Institute, The University of Queensland.

Passfield, R. (1995). Action learning and the learning organisation. In W. Timpson and F. Broadbent (Eds.), *Action learning: Experience & promise* (pp. 21–33). Brisbane, Queensland: The Tertiary Education Institute, The University of Queensland.

Passfield, R. (1996). *Action learning for professional and organisational development: An action research case study in higher education* (PhD Thesis). Brisbane, Queensland: Griffith University.

Passfield, R. (2012) Action research strategies for sustainable development in public sector organisations. In O. Zuber-Skerritt (Ed.), *Action research for sustainable development in a turbulent world* (pp. 189–203). Bingley, UK: Emerald Group Publishing Ltd.

Pinchen, S., & Passfield, R. (Eds.). (1995). *Moving on: Creative applications of action learning and action research.* Upper Mt Gravatt, Brisbane: Action Learning, Action Research and Process Management (ALARPM) Association Incorporated.

Ryan, Y., & Zuber-Skerritt, O. (1993). *Departmental Excellence in University Education (DEUE).* Occasional Paper Series, No. 3, Tertiary Education Institute, The University of Queensland, Brisbane.

Timpson, W., & Broadbent, F. (Eds.). (1995). *Action learning: Experience and promise.* Brisbane, Queensland: The Tertiary Education Institute, The University of Queensland.

Zuber-Skerritt, O. (Ed.). (1990). *Action research for change and development.* Brisbane, Queensland: Centre for the Advancement of Learning and Teaching, Griffith University.

Zuber-Skerritt, O. (Ed.). (1991). *Action learning for improved performance: Key contributors to the first world congress on action research and process management*. Brisbane, Queensland: AEBIS Publishing.

Zuber-Skerritt, O. (1992a). *Action research in higher education: Examples and reflections*. London, UK: Kogan Page.

Zuber-Skerritt, O. (1992b). *Final report of the Departmental Excellence in University Education (DEUE) program 1992*. Brisbane, Queensland: The Tertiary Education Institute, The University of Queensland.

Zuber-Skerritt, O. (1992c). *Professional development in higher education: Examples and reflections*. London, UK: Kogan Page.

Zuber-Skerritt, O. (1993). *Research and development in management and higher education: A personal explication*. Occasional Paper Series, No. 2. Tertiary Education Institute, The University of Queensland, Brisbane.

Zuber-Skerritt, O. (1995). Models for action research. In S. Pinchen & R. Passfield (Eds.), *Moving on: Creative applications of action learning and action research* (pp. 2–29). Upper Mt Gravatt, Brisbane, Queensland: Action Learning, Action research and Process Management (ALARPM) Association Incorporated.

Zuber-Skerritt, O. (2011). *Action leadership: Towards a participatory paradigm*. Dordrecht, The Netherlands: Springer International.

Zuber-Skerritt, O. (Ed.). (2012). *Action research for sustainable development in a turbulent world*. Bingley, UK: Emerald Group Publishing Ltd.

Zuber-Skerritt, O., & Teare, R. (2013). *Lifelong action learning for community development: Learning and development for a better world*. Rotterdam, The Netherlands: Sense Publishers.

Zuber-Skerritt, O., & Passfield, R. (2015). The history and culture of ALARA – The action learning and action research association. *Educational Action Research*. London, UK: Routledge.

Zuber-Skerritt, O., Fletcher, M., & Kearney, J. (2015). *Professional learning in higher education and communities: Towards a new vision for action research*. London, UK: Palgrave Macmillan.

Ron Passfield
Director
Merit Solutions Australia
Australia
and
Adjunct Professor
Australian Institute of Business (AIB)
Adelaide
Australia

EILEEN PIGGOT-IRVINE

7. COLLABORATION, INNOVATION AND EVALUATION IN ACTION RESEARCH

Life with Ortrun for a Better World

EARLY 'LIFE WITH ORTRUN'

I begin by briefly backgrounding the early phase of my 'life with Ortrun', a phrase that fully deserves inverted commas because life with Ortrun is always extraordinary. At the beginning of my academic career in the late 1980s I was introduced to action research in a one week course as part of tertiary teacher training. As a committed biologist, at the beginning of the week I was full of initial positivistic scepticism for this approach and was probably the typical painful, critical, questioning adult student who many of us have experienced in teaching. As the week progressed I became more interested and then started reflecting on how this much more humanistic approach to research could interlace with my need not only to be rigorous and show evidence through my research, but also to create collaborative, high ownership, high impact transformation and change through research. I recorded those ideas in my course diary at that time.

A few years passed (young children, busy lives) without my thinking much about action research until the beginning of the 1990s. I was appointed as director of a professional development centre and at my first regional director meeting I noticed that others nationally in New Zealand were strongly recommending action research as a development approach. I dug out my action research course notes and reflections and began to explore further, attending a conference (Second World Congress in Brisbane) where I could connect with key players. Ortrun was one of them – and this connection changed my life! Ortrun swept me up enthusiastically, as only she can do, and encouraged me to focus my upcoming masters' research on exploring the effectiveness of action research as a professional development tool. In particular, she showed me everything she had written on one specific semi-evaluative tool called Repertory Grid Technique (RGT, discussed below) and mentored me in its use. I presented my first conference address (Piggot-Irvine, 1993) as a result of that research on 'The effectiveness of action research as a development tool' and from then on action research has been central to my career.

To list how action research has created a better life for myself (and hopefully the hundreds of others I have encouraged in this approach) in the years between 1992 and the current day would be tedious to even those who love action research …

J. Kearney & M. Todhunter (Eds), Lifelong Action Learning and Research: A Tribute to the Life and Pioneering Work of Ortrun Zuber-Skerritt, 77–89.

including Ortrun. In brief, I: established the New Zealand Action Research Network (NZARN) and coordinated this for 10 years; was Vice President of Action Research Action Learning and Process Management (ALARPM) for a number of years; completed a PhD (Piggot-Irvine, 2001) focussed on an action research approach to overcoming defensiveness; published over 20 journal articles and three books on action research; presented over 20 keynotes on the topic and many more conference sessions as well as hundreds of workshops/seminars; led multiple action research projects; and won five major research contracts based on action research. It hasn't stopped there, however, as the section later in this chapter on my recent evaluative work on action research shows.

None of the latter outcomes would have resulted without Ortrun's initial enthusiasm and support. She has been not only the key outstanding mentor in my life's work, but is also a deeply caring, loving friend of myself and family. No-one in my professional or personal life has given more freely and generously than Ortrun. The rest of this chapter pays homage to that gift by focussing on three areas of my work that Ortrun spurred on, that have created the greatest changes for me personally and those who I have influenced. The first of these is associated with what I consider to be the most important underpinning of action research: the creation of *authentic collaboration*. The second is *introduction of an innovative tool*, Repertory Grid Technique (RGT), that is rarely used in action research yet it initiated my career as an action researcher. The third area is *evaluation* of process and impact of action research. These three examples, typical of the many I could have discussed here, provide insight into Ortrun's far-reaching contributions to knowledge and learning through her influence on, and valuable support for, her circle of colleagues.

AUTHENTIC COLLABORATION

In my view, authentic collaboration is the most important underpinning of action research. I have widely promoted understanding that the interpersonal effectiveness of action research team members working collectively is crucial to the success of action research. While I had alluded to this in multiple publications and presentations, it was Ortrun who keenly urged me to formalise this thinking, which I did in the chapter 'Creating authentic collaboration: A central feature of effectiveness' (Piggot-Irvine, 2012a) in her edited book, *Action Research for Sustainable Development in a Turbulent World* (Zuber-Skerritt, 2012).

The chapter culminated from my long-standing fascination with, and commitment to fostering, open, non-defensive interactions within and beyond research. This approach was the focus of my doctoral study but it arose from and was nurtured by many dialogue sessions with Ortrun. In publications and verbal presentations I have argued that an open, non-defensive approach originating from the work of Argyris (1990, 2003) is central to the collaborative values that are very frequently purported for action research. As stated in Piggot-Irvine and Bartlett (2008, p. 25):

... the advantages to the participants of collaboration in action research are cited as many and various (D'Arcy, 1994; Kemmis & McTaggart, 1990; Tripp, 1990; Wadsworth, 1998). For one thing, it can allow for public testing of private assumptions and reflections; that is, it helps to avoid self-limiting reflection (Schön, 1983). Collaboration can also enhance ownership and commitment to change, and it can leverage the change to a level frequently unattainable through individual reflection alone.

Some researchers (for example, Fengning, 2009; Gajda & Koliba, 2008; Smith, Sydall & Taylor, 2004) have identified difficulties and frustrations associated with collaboration in action research. I have suggested lack of participant skills in creating authentic collaboration as a considerable barrier. In much of my writing I have intended to clarify how understanding and skills associated with collaboration can enhance openness and non-defensive interactions, resulting in mutually informative dialogue and ultimately trust.

I have shown how in interactions that may occur within action research groups, collaboration can range in intensity of challenge from superficial (Level 1) to intensive (Level 5). I urge research participants to strive for Level 5 because it is here that increased awareness links most fully with the openness, trust and creative learning that action research upholds. My colleague Judith McMorland and I (McMorland & Piggot-Irvine, 2000) designed a model of five deepening levels of collaborative learning, which I further adapted in Piggot-Irvine (2012a, p. 93) and present in Table 7.1.

Table 7.1. Levels of challenge

Level 1: *Introduction* (seeking and enjoying exploring commonality, excluding discussion of difference, collaborating in a superficial and task-specific way, and with little demonstration or examination of defensive values or strategies);

Level 2: *Recognition of potential of self and others* (with rising awareness of differential between self and others, waning enthusiasm for exploring commonality, and increasing willingness to entertain multilateral perspectives on reality, but action is usually limited despite personal perceptions of the value of self-contribution, and if doubt arises the response action is likely to be defensive and self-protective);

Level 3: *Gaining an inquiry perspective* (increasing empathy for the perception of others, and coming to genuine acceptance of the validity of another's way of being/ thinking, seeing the world through others' eyes);

Level 4: *Transition to collaboration* (suspending one's own known perceptions and opening up to unknown other perceptions while allowing for exploration of creativity, true inquiry and genuine collaborative action); and

Level 5: *Trust and co-generation* (achieving new levels of awareness of both our own and others' perspectives, emerging as courage is expressed and inquiry leads to action – a process distinguished by spontaneity, synergy and creativity, and leading to openness, trust and learning).

Participants can progressively achieve the deepest level of authentic collaboration leading to mutual trust as they overcome defensive, self-protective values and strategies, but that happens only with a great deal of skill development. Defensiveness surfaces easily while developing skills, and dealing with it is a first step towards authentic collaboration. Understanding that defensiveness is the tendency to protect ourselves and others from potential threat and embarrassment (Argyris, 2003) and that avoidance, power and control (striving to win) are core defensive tendencies is important. People display these tendencies in strategies like withholding vital information or evidence, bypassing threatening conversations, and being indirect by giving mixed rather than clear messages.

Many authors (Argyris, 2003; Cardno, 2001; Dick & Dalmau, 1999; Edmondson, 1996; Senge, Cambron-McCabe, Lucas, Smith, Dutton & Kleiner, 2000) promote shifting to an orientation that is 'productive' and 'more consensual, more open to change' (Dick & Dalmau, 1999, p. 47). Here bilateral (considering two sides) and multilateral (considering multiple sides) checking and understanding of others' perspectives without prejudgement or assumptions dominate in attempts to overcome defensiveness. Such an 'inquiry' orientation is balanced with openness about our own perspective, it reveals evidence and reasoning behind that perspective, and has an 'advocacy' orientation. The balance results in a 'dialogue' where Preskill and Torres (1999) suggest: 'individuals seek to inquire, share meanings, understand complex issues, and uncover assumptions', which facilitates 'learning processes of reflection, asking questions, and identifying and clarifying values, beliefs, assumptions and knowledge' (p. 53).

Dialogue is far removed from a lock-step process because the change from defensive to productive orientation 'requires significant, profound shifts involving exposure, examination and alteration of defensive values at a deeply personal level, which is both cognitively and emotionally difficult and is a lengthy process. … The reason for this is that the approach requires rethinking and altering our underlying value systems' (Piggot-Irvine & Doyle, 2010, p. 61). Such difficulty can be overwhelming for newcomers to this orientation and, in my experience, they are often helped greatly by using a simple heuristic as a reminder of what is important. In Piggot-Irvine (2012a), I summarised and adapted the work of previous authors (Cardno, 1994; Robinson, Absolum, Cardno & Steele, 1990) in creating such a heuristic of elements of dialogue, as shown in Table 7.2 (Piggot-Irvine, 2012a, p. 100).

The values underpinning this approach are as, if not more, important than any steps in dialogue. Honesty, openness, authenticity, non-judgementalism, democracy, rigour and respect are core values. Also important are engaging in both reflection *in* action and reflection *on* action (Argyris & Schön, 1974), and double loop learning featuring examining and changing foundation beliefs and governing values as well as actions (Cardno & Reynolds, 2009).

In summary, I believe the authentic collaboration described in Piggot-Irvine (2012a) is critical to action research that transforms participants, community, organisations and society. In all of my years of association with Ortrun I have seen her not only espouse this ideal, but also practise such collaboration at every level of interaction I have had with her. She is unafraid to express her position with clarity ('advocacy'), yet she always offers her position in a way that opens up response and checking. She is never afraid to move her position or to explore alternative thinking based on this response of others ('inquiry'). She always strives to understand how plausible solutions can be both created and facilitated. I consider that this significant modelling by Ortrun has transformed many of my own and others' ways of interaction.

Table 7.2. Elements of dialogue in productive reasoning

1.	State your perception in a hypothetical way, i.e., be open for challenge and checking.
2.	Provide evidence for your perception.
3.	Outline your reasoning and rationale for your perception. Collectively Steps 1, 2 and 3 are often referred to as 'Advocacy' Steps.
4.	Seek responses (check what others think, feel and perceive) without being defensive. This step is often referred to as the 'Inquiry'.
5.	Summarise shared understanding or the need for more information and determine if there is an espousal–practice gap.
6.	Repeat steps 1 – 5 if necessary before moving on.
7.	Jointly suggest and evaluate solutions.
8.	Decide together on a solution(s).

INTRODUCTION OF REPERTORY GRID TECHNIQUE (RGT)

The second piece of my work that Ortrun has influenced is the little known RGT evaluative tool for action research. I have chosen RGT because I think this tool, though not new, is innovative and encourages (in its final phase) the sort of authentic collaboration and dialogue I have discussed above. Ortrun introduced me to the tool when she urged me to use it in my Masters degree study in determining effectiveness of action research as a development tool (Piggot-Irvine, 1993). As an evaluative tool, RGT has been pivotal in opening up my obsession with evaluating action research (the third area I discuss later in this chapter).

RGT is explained by Ortrun herself in Chapter 2 in *Evaluating Action Research* (Piggot-Irvine & Bartlett, 2008) where she provides definition and explanation, description of purpose and application. RGT derives from Personal Construct Theory, PCT (Kelly, 1955), which recognises people as 'personal scientists' who construct their own versions of reality. The goal in RGT is to help respondents make their implicit and complex views (personal constructs) explicit and then to engage in dialogue about those constructs to identify and better understand them. In both my own early work using RGT (Piggot-Irvine, 1993) and that of Ortrun herself

(Diamond & Zuber-Skerritt, 1986; Zuber-Skerritt & Roche, 2004) our focus has been on eliciting personal constructs of action research attributes and the effectiveness of this approach as a way of evaluating action research.

In Ortrun's typically methodical way she has offered (Zuber-Skerritt, Figure 2.2 in Piggot-Irvine & Bartlett, 2008) clear instructions for eliciting constructs, with an example and detailed instructions that I have condensed in Table 7.3. This example of use of RGT was designed to elicit a participant's views about action researchers (including self).

Table 7.3. Instructions for eliciting constructs in RGT

1.	Elements (action researchers) are chosen and labelled, e.g., E1 = an ideal action researcher, E2 = me as an action researcher, etc.
2.	Ordered comparison of the 'elements' (action researchers) occurs by using a Repertory Grid Elicitation Form.
3.	Consideration is made of how two 'elements' are similar and different from the third and record made of the most distinguishing characteristic that the two action researchers have in common (recorded as *Emergent Constructs* in up to three words).
4.	A record made, as *Implicit Constructs*, of the characteristic or attribute that distinguishes the third action researcher from the other two.
5.	Repeating the process with the next lines of 'elements'.

In both Ortrun's practice and my own, we have followed the process of elicitation with instructions for rating each action researcher (element) on a 5-point scale against the constructs developed (1 = *most like the construct, 5 = least like the construct)*. A following task in the process is to rate each element on overall effectiveness and to analyse the ratings manually (it can be done digitally) to show what participants believe makes for effective action research. Next, participants are asked to rate themselves compared to an ideal action researcher and to note their strengths and needs for further development. Finally, to complete the elicitation and rating, participants dialogue with each other to compare and discuss their own ratings. We both feel that the last dialogue step is probably the most important in the process.

In outlining RGT, both Ortrun and I discuss the advantages and disadvantages of this method. The advantage of the researcher not influencing participants is important. Though replicable, the method provides a snapshot that allows for comparison both over time and between respondents. Such comparison can lead to enhanced awareness of one's own and others' constructs that enables dialogue leading to further improvement of practice. The method's complexity is noted as a disadvantage but this can be reduced with practice and/or with computer analysis. Both of us have emphasised the importance of the interpretation and dialogue component with or without computer analysis. Dialogue at the authentic collaboration level, which I have discussed above, therefore emerges as an essential element in using RGT as an evaluative tool in action research, reinforcing my belief that such collaboration is a critical underpinning.

The discussion so far of authentic collaboration and of RGT as an innovative evaluative tool leads to the third area of my work and life where I acknowledge Ortrun's influence, that is, evaluation.

EVALUATION AND 'LIFE WITH ORTRUN'

Above I have talked briefly about the book, *Evaluating Action Research*. Here I want to step back a little to reflect upon its inception, triggered at the 2003 World Congress in Pretoria, South Africa. I attended many incredible sessions at that Congress (including a keynote by Ortrun) but the more significant impact on me personally was being in the beautiful South African landscape, alongside the breathtaking rhythm created through drumming in Congress breaks. As a lover of dance and rhythm I was deeply affected by this milieu. I was also impacted by my little room in the Congress accommodation: a room with four padlocks on the door, in a building with mammoth security, within a compound fenced with barbed wire. The powerful dissonance in this juxtapositioning of beauty and arts alongside prison-like conditions triggered my deep thinking; I spent hours reflecting and writing. My thinking focussed on how often I heard about the significant impacts of action research on the lives, community and workplaces of people, yet equally I heard about how poorly the approach was viewed by other researchers.

I made a commitment at the end of that Congress to explore how we might demonstrate more rigorously the impact of action research. In the following year I formalised my exploration a little more and identified what appeared to be a gap in the literature around rigorous evaluation of process and impact of action research. In a way this shift was returning me to my research roots because employing RGT as the first research tool in my Masters degree could also be seen as evaluation. My exploration of the gap in the literature led me to start planning a book on evaluating action research. I decided to share this with Ortrun, and her predictable enthusiastic response resulted in key action researchers contributing to *Evaluating Action Research* that I co-edited with Brendan Bartlett.

This book focusses on evaluation *of* action research, rather than evaluation *in* it. Evaluation *of* is associated with worthiness, quality and value overall, keeping in mind action research's purpose that the cycles of research and action build together in informed transformations of practice. An introductory chapter outlined our definitions of evaluating action research, theoretical underpinnings, and the key literature and previous research associated with evaluating impact. Our literature review confirmed that at that time little evaluative study of the impact of action research had been conducted. Acknowledgement of this deficiency in turn opened up the opportunity of offering considerably eclectic approaches to evaluating action research through applying diverse evaluation tools (including RGT discussed above).

Subsequent chapters of this book showcased examples of diversity by authors such as Zuber-Skerritt, Cardno and Marrat, Bartlett, Fletcher, Piggot-Irvine and Stringer. Each illustrated an approach to demonstrate action research worthiness, quality, authenticity, relevance, involvement, methodological rigour, practical improvement and transformation (understanding, learning, development and personal growth). Draft criteria that I established in Chapter 6 attempted to capture some of these elements.

My obsession with exploring how to show the worth and impact of action research did not end with the evaluation book. Once again Ortrun strongly supported the progress of my work. In late 2011 in Brisbane, I called together a small group of action researchers (Shankar Sankaran from University of Technology Sydney, Judith Kearney from Griffith University, and Wendy Rowe from Royal Roads University) to plan a global 'Evaluative Study of Action Research' (ESAR) over five years. Ortrun was nominated as external reviewer for the study. In 2012 we won a national Canadian grant to collaboratively formalise planning for the project and Lesley Ferkins (Unitec New Zealand), Phil Cady and Deborah Zornes (both Royal Roads University) joined the team. The final section of this chapter outlines our intent and progress with the ESAR to date.

The first step of the ESAR has been to update the previous Piggot-Irvine and Bartlett (2008) literature review on evaluation of action research. We have summarised many widely acknowledged points, including that action research, as a developmental methodology with rigorous data collection ('research') and positive change ('action') elements (Piggot-Irvine et al., 2011), typically has espoused claims of personal, team, organisation and community improvement and transformation. It has also been widely promoted as an effective framework of empowerment and emancipation to improve a social situation or condition (Reason and Bradbury, 2001; Stringer, 2007): an intent that has appealed to leaders wishing to create improvement, particularly in low socio-economic and disadvantaged communities. We have noted, however, that validity of such espousals has been substantially under-explored and, as previously reported in Piggot-Irvine and Bartlett (2008), where evaluations have been conducted they have focussed more on process than impact.

A consequence of this under-exploration has been a dubious reputation for action research as a weak form of research, particularly on methodology (E. Koshy, V. Koshy & Waterman, 2011). Winter (1987), for example, reported that action research has been 'dismissed as muddled science' (p. 2), Dick (2004) identified labelling as 'sloppy research' (p. 16), and Cardno (2003) reported commentary deriding action research as a 'messy and weak form of research because it has been practised without appropriate rigour' (p. vii). Brooker and Macpherson (1999) noted the reporting of action research was 'little more than picturesque journeys of self-indulgent descriptions', and that much action research was 'little more than a systematic way of getting things done' (p. 210). Unfortunately such critique has prevailed because little evaluative data has been collected to demonstrate whether the ideals espoused for action research are widely realised. We affirmed this observation in Piggot-Irvine and Bartlett (2008), acknowledging that while a great deal of literature discusses or identifies what constitutes 'good' AR, there is very little evaluation of AR outcomes or impact. The literature review for the ESAR revealed no change in this situation and the research proposed in the ESAR is designed to address this gap.

The second step of the ESAR was to create the study design. We began by clarifying our research objective, which we would pursue via an examination of process and outcomes of approximately 200 action research projects implemented in varied contexts globally. We would (1) explore whether and how the often-touted espousals of action research impacting upon individuals, communities, organisations, and/or societies are actually realised; and (2) advance knowledge and understanding of the elements of action research enhancing outputs, outcomes and impact. We chose a mixed-method methodology (Creswell, 2009; Ivankova, Creswell & Stick, 2006) under an Evaluative Action Research, EvAR (Piggot-Irvine, 2012b) framework to address the under-exploration of action research outputs, outcomes and impact.

The rationale for using a mixed-method design was based on the assumption that neither quantitative (Qn) nor qualitative (Ql) approaches alone are sufficient; Qn and Ql approaches complement each other and when pursued together they enable more robust analysis (Youngs and Piggot-Irvine, 2011, 2014). The EvAR is a meta-action research approach where 'meta' implies action research *on* action research – here the use of an action research model to evaluate multiple action research projects. The EvAR framework, like all action research, emphasises pursuit of positive transformation or change. It intends that researchers follow a phased cyclic, iterative process that sometimes has 'spin-off' (McNiff, 1988), or slightly divergent cycles. Like non-meta action research, the EvAR framework follows phases sometimes described as 'reconnaissance' (current state analysis), 'implementation', 'review', and 'reporting' (Piggot-Irvine, 2012b). The EvAR framework is underpinned by principles of authentic dialogue, focusses on process and outcomes, establishing clarity in evaluative indicators, and considering complexity by seeking to understand meaning as well as searching for causality.

The third step of the ESAR was to identify for our study multiple action research projects in several countries and varied contexts. At the close of 2014 we had identified 120 projects that meet our established criteria of having:

1. clear articulation as action research (including participatory action research);
2. a change emphasis arising out of an issue/concern/need;
3. articulation of espousal of improvement/capacity building that may have been, in turn, linked to goals of personal, team, organisation or society improvement;
4. the usual characteristics of collaboration, iterative phases of action and reflection;
5. resultant in publication or reporting dissemination post-2008; and
6. project lead availability, and other team members and stakeholders accessible.

Our intent is to establish a publicly accessible repository that will serve as a directory for the action research project reports and research findings.

The fourth step was to establish indicators for evaluating action research. We identified these indicators using published accounts of precursors, process, outputs, outcomes and impact for example, Bell and Bryman's (2007) indicators for authenticity; Meyer's (2000) consideration of change and knowledge; Piggot-Irvine's (2008) indicators for meta-evaluating action research; and Wadsworth's (2011) indicators for success – along with our own experience as action researchers. We also drew upon indicators profiled in literature on broader evaluation and research impact assessment.

We developed as sub-sections 'Precursors/Preconditions', 'Process and Activities' and 'Post Action Research Outputs, Outcomes and Impacts' to organise indicators. Given our mixed-method design, we have taken care to ensure that quantitative (Qn) statistical analysis could be carried out on many of the indicators. Conscious that the specific standards for outcomes and impacts of sustainable change can vary wildly from context to context, we decided that collecting qualitative (Ql) data is more appropriate for this 'Post-AR' sub-section. A confounding factor for us in developing these indicators lies in the very nature of action research; it is intentionally open-ended. We have thus asked this vital question: Is evaluation possible given that we cannot predict in advance the outcomes of AR? By definition, until some later time, outcomes and end states of complex systems cannot be known with any degree of certainty, only with probability. To be authentic in the ESAR, our analysis of findings will involve looking in hindsight to examine if/how/what kind of coherence is emerging, and how it is positive and/or negative, rather than examining causality alone.

Now that each of the precursor activities noted in the previous four steps have been completed for the ESAR study (a reconnaissance type phase), we are ready for data collection to begin. Our next step is to issue a large scale survey to all project team members. We will follow with conducting ten full case studies, employing documentary analysis, bibliometric analysis, interviews, focus groups, and goal attainment scaling. A final phase of the project will involve evaluating the effectiveness of the EvAR framework itself.

In summary, the ESAR will be a systematic inquiry analysing intended and unintended outcomes (Owens & Aiken, 2006) and impacts, and an examination of precursor and process elements that have contributed to those impacts in action research. A goal of the ESAR is to advance knowledge through making public our findings on impact at the personal through to societal level (in multiple academic and non-academic publications and presentations). We hope that such findings will further clarify validity claims for action research as an approach to bringing about positive change and transformation. We also hope that this will all happen under the critical eye of Ortrun as the external reviewer.

CONCLUSION

In this chapter I have presented examples of extracts of my work in the areas of *collaboration, innovation* and *evaluation.* I would really need to write several books to do justice to the scale of Ortrun's influence on my work and life. Ortrun's urging of *collaborative* practice in action research is far from academic rhetoric. She lives daily the finest example of authentic collaboration as I have described it earlier in this chapter. She is courageously open and transparent, has no hesitation in being explicit about her own position, and always backing her position with evidence. In other words, she operates from a position of high advocacy. That could of itself appear highly controlling if it weren't for the openness and humility Ortrun also shows to inviting challenge, to listening deeply and critically to alternative perspectives, and to mindfully seeking options for moving forward to meet all needs. She also, therefore, equally applies an inquiring, dialogical stance in her interactions, but she combines that with her hallmark spontaneity and creativity. It is through such openness that she creates *trust and co-generation* – the deepest, Level 5 collaboration (Piggot-Irvine, 2012a, p. 93) through which she enables new levels of awareness of both her own and others' perspectives to emerge.

In terms of *innovation and evaluation* (both of which critically require the aforementioned authentic collaboration as an underpinning), it was Ortrun introducing RGT to me that instigated my 20 year journey exploring worth, quality and value overall of action research. Such evaluation is, I believe, the next frontier of maturity in action research. It is well overdue if the approach is to maintain validity and reputation for transformational change at individual through to global level. With Ortrun at our back in the ESAR, we feel assured that in this work we will be encouraged to ensure our findings help to inform the creation of positive change, and perhaps build the bones for transformation, for a better world for all.

REFERENCES

Argyris, C. (1990). *Overcoming organizational defenses: Facilitating organizational learning.* Needham Heights, MA: Allyn and Bacon.

Argyris, C. (2003). A life full of learning. *Organization Studies, 24*(7), 1178–1192.

Argyris, C., & Schön, D. A. (1974). *Theory in practice: Increasing professional effectiveness.* San Francisco, CA: Jossey Bass.

Bell, E., & Bryman, A. (2007) *Business research methods* (2nd ed.). Oxford, UK: Oxford University Press.

Brooker, R., & Macpherson, I. (1999). Communicating the processes and outcomes of practitioner research: An opportunity for self-indulgence or a serious professional responsibility. *Educational Action Research, 7*(2), 207–221.

Cardno, C. E. M. (1994). *Dealing with dilemmas: A critical and collaborative approach to staff appraisal in two schools* (Unpublished PhD thesis). Auckland University, Auckland, New Zealand.

Cardno, C. (2001). Managing dilemmas in appraising performance: An approach for school leaders. In D. Middlewood & C. Cardno (Eds.), *Managing teacher appraisal and performance: A comparative approach* (pp. 143–159). London, UK: Routledge Falmer.

Cardno, C. (2003). *Action research: A developmental approach.* Wellington, New Zealand: New Zealand Council for Educational Research.

Cardno, C., & Reynolds, B. (2009). Resolving leadership dilemmas in New Zealand kindergartens: An action research study. *Journal of Educational Administration, 47*(2), 206–226.

Creswell, J. (2009). *Research design: Qualitative, quantitative and mixed methods approaches* (2nd ed.). Thousand Oaks, CA: Sage.

D'Arcy, P. (1994). On becoming an action researcher – Who qualifies? Plus ca change? *Action Researcher, 1*(Spring), 1–3.

Diamond, P., & Zuber-Skerritt, O. (1986). Postgraduate research: Some changing personal constructs in higher education. *Higher Education Research and Development, 5*(1), 49–59.

Dick, B. (2004). Action research literature: Themes and trends. *Action Research On-Line, 2*, 425–444.

Dick, R., & Dalmau, T. (1999). *Values in action – Applying the ideas of Argyris and Schön* (2nd ed.). Chapel Hill, Brisbane, Australia: Interchange.

Edmondson, A. C. (1996). Three faces of Eden: The persistence of competing theories and multiple diagnoses in organizational intervention research. *Human Relations, 49*(5), 571–595.

Fengning, D. (2009). Building action research teams: A case of struggles and success. *Journal of Cases in Educational Leadership, 12*(2), 8–18.

Gajda, R., & Koliba, C. J. (2008). Delving into teacher collaboration: Untangling problems and solutions for leadership. *NASSP Bulletin, 92*(2), 133–153.

Ivankova, N. V., Creswell, J. W., & Stick, S. L. (2006). Using mixed-methods sequential explanatory design: From theory to practice. *Field Methods, 18*(3), 3–20.

Kelly, G. A. (1955). *The psychology of personal constructs.* New York, NY: Norton.

Kemmis, S., & McTaggart, R. (Eds.). (1990). *Action research reader.* Geelong, Australia: Deakin University Press.

Koshy, E., Koshy, V., & Waterman, H. (2011). *Action research in healthcare.* London, UK: Sage Publications.

McMorland, J., & Piggot-Irvine, E. (2000). Facilitation as midwifery: Facilitation and praxis in group learning. *Systematic Practice and Action, 13*(2), 121–127.

McNiff, J. (1988). *Action research: Principles and practice.* Hampshire, UK: Macmillan Education Ltd.

Meyer, J. (2000). Evaluating action research. *Age and Aging, 29*, 8–10.

Owens, J., & Aiken, M. (2006). *Program evaluation: Forms and approaches* (3rd ed.). New York, NY: The Guildford Press.

Piggot-Irvine, E. (1993). *The effectiveness of action research as a development tool.* Paper presented to the National Staff Developers' Conference, Dunedin.

Piggot-Irvine, E. (2001). *Appraisal: Reducing control, enhancing effectiveness* (Unpublished PhD thesis). New Zealand: Massey University.

Piggot-Irvine, E. (2008). Meta-evaluation of action research in a school leadership Programme. In E. Piggot-Irvine & B. Bartlett (Eds.), *Evaluating action research* (pp. 147–166). Wellington, New Zealand: NZCER.

Piggot-Irvine, E. (2012a). Creating authentic collaboration: A central feature of effectiveness. In O. Zuber-Skerritt (Ed.), *Action research for sustainable development in a turbulent world* (pp. 89–107). Bingley, UK: Emerald.

Piggot-Irvine, E. (2012b, October). *Evaluation using a collaborative action research approach.* Presentation to British Columbia Canadian Evaluation Society AGM, Vancouver.

Piggot-Irvine, E., & Bartlett, B. (2008). *Evaluating action research.* Wellington, New Zealand: NZCER.

Piggott-Irvine, E., & Doyle, L. (2010). Organizational learning 'in use'. *Journal of Educational Leadership and Policy, 25*(2), 55–72.

Piggot-Irvine, E., Connelly, D., Curry, R., Hanna, J., Moodie, M., Palmer, M., … Thompson, A. (2011). Building leadership capacity – sustainable leadership. *Action Research Action Learning Association (ALARA): Monograph Series, 2*, 1–40.

Preskill, H., & Torres, R. (1999). *Evaluative inquiry for learning in organizations.* Thousand Oaks, CA: Sage.

Reason, P., & Bradbury, H. (2001). Introduction: Inquiry and participation in search of a world worthy of human aspiration. In P. Reason & H. Bradbury (Eds.), *Handbook of action research*. Thousand Oaks, CA: Sage.

Robinson, V., Absolum, M., Cardno, C., & Steele, T. (1990). *The leadership of tomorrow's schools*. Report to the ministry of education on a collaborative action research project. Auckland, New Zealand: Auckland University.

Schön, D. (1983). *The reflective practitioner: How professionals think in action*. New York, NY: Basic Books.

Senge, P., Cambron-McCabe, N., Lucas, T., Smith, B., Dutton, J., & Kleiner, A. (2000). A primer to the five disciplines. In *Schools that learn* (pp. 59–98). New York, NY: Doubleday.

Smith, R., Sydall, L., & Taylor, R. (2004). *Overcoming the PBRF agenda: Fostering a collaborative partnership with academic-practitioners*. Paper presented to the New Zealand Association for Research in Education (NZARE) Conference, Wellington, New Zealand.

Stringer, E. T. (2007). *Action research* (3rd ed.). Thousand Oaks, CA: Sage Publications.

Tripp, D. (1990). Socially critical action research. *Theory into Practice, XXIX*(3), 158–166.

Wadsworth, Y. (1998). *What is participatory action research?* Retrieved from http://elmo.scu.edu.au/schools/sawd/ari/ari-wadsworth.html

Wadsworth, Y. (2011). *Building in research and evaluation: Human inquiry for living systems*. Walnut Creek, Australia: Left Coast Press.

Winter, R. (1987). Managers, spectators, and citizens: Where does theory come from in action research? *Educational Action Research, 6*(3), 361–376.

Youngs, H., & Piggot-Irvine, E. (2011). Evaluating a multiphase triangulation approach to mixed methods: The research of an aspiring school principal development program. *Journal of Mixed Methods Research, 6*(3), 184–198. doi: 10.1177/1558689811420696

Youngs, H., & Piggot-Irvine, E. (2014). The merits of triangulation: The evaluation of a New Zealand school leadership development program using mixed methods research. *Method in Action Case Studies: Sage Research Methods Cases*. doi: http://dx.doi.org/10.1177/1558689811420696

Zuber-Skerritt, O. (2012). *Action research for sustainable development in a turbulent world*. Bingley, UK: Emerald.

Zuber-Skerritt, O., & Roche, V. (2004). A constructivist model for evaluating postgraduate supervision: A case study. *Quality Assurance in Education, 12*(2), 82–93.

Eileen Piggot-Irvine
Professor of Leadership
Royal Roads University
Victoria BC
Canada

PART III

COMMUNITIES OF PRACTICE

LESLEY WOOD

8. PALAR FOR COMMUNITY ENGAGEMENT

The Postgraduate Voice

INTRODUCTION

I first met Ortrun via an electronic introduction in 2011 by a fellow action researcher who thought we might work well together. I duly contacted her and asked her if she would like to come out to South Africa to do some workshops at the university where I was then employed, but funding proved to be a bit of a stumbling block. However, Ortrun is not the type of person to be dissuaded by something as trivial as money and promptly gave me a lead for funding. With her help as critical reader, within weeks I had designed a project and submitted a successful funding proposal. I soon found myself having to organise a week-long start-up workshop for the project, which provided sufficient funds to bring Ortrun and her team (who happen to be the editors of this book) out to South Africa. And so began our collaboration to develop the capacity of South African academics to engage meaningfully with communities for mutual learning and development. On the basis of this initial project, I then applied for a large-scale community engagement grant, which enabled our continuing collaboration. The purpose of this on-going Participatory Action Learning and Action Research (PALAR) project is to explore the perceptions, needs and challenges of academic researchers and community members as they collaborate to promote psycho-social wellness in education communities. The project ultimately aims to produce theoretical, philosophical and conceptual orientations of community-based research for community engagement from a higher education perspective.

One of the reasons that I found it so easy to collaborate with Ortrun is our mutual belief in the potential of people to improve their own circumstances. As a researcher in a Faculty of Education, I am dismayed that, after 20 years of democracy in South Africa, the life prospects of the majority of people are still limited by poverty and disease, in particular the consequences of the HIV and AIDS epidemic. I have come to realise that, if we do not direct our research towards the exploration of how the expected fruits of democracy can be more evenly distributed throughout society, we are failing in our moral obligation as academics. As members of the academy, we occupy privileged positions of power (Said, 1994) that permit us to create knowledge that can inform policy and practice and therefore positively (or negatively) influence the lives of many people. Yet, in general, the knowledge produced by the academy

J. Kearney & M. Todhunter (Eds), Lifelong Action Learning and Research: A Tribute to the Life and Pioneering Work of Ortrun Zuber-Skerritt, 93–107.

has had little positive impact on the quality of life or education in our country – the education of the South African child still remains in crisis (Motshekga, 2010).

In this chapter, which draws heavily on the ideas and work of Ortrun, I propose that a PALAR approach to community engagement by tertiary researchers may offer suitable ways to navigate 'new educational pathways suited for improving and sustaining life in the twenty-first century' (Wood, 2014, p. 660). However, applying this humane and participatory approach to research has not been simple or straightforward. Tensions and stumbling blocks have been encountered both within the academic system and in the community setting. I will discuss these tensions and offer suggestions on how they might be minimised, based on empirical findings from the project referred to above. I hope that sharing the experiences of the postgraduate students on this project will add to the international body of knowledge about the usefulness of PALAR as a methodology for creating and sustaining community–university partnerships for mutual benefit. I begin with a brief overview of the PALAR process (Zuber-Skerritt, 2011, 2012; Zuber-Skerritt & Teare, 2013), followed by discussion of empirical evidence gleaned from our South African project.

BASIC PRINCIPLES OF PALAR

With PALAR, Ortrun has managed to combine the elements of various heretofore discrete genres of action research into a unified process that promotes lifelong learning. She has taken the 'good bits' from different conceptualisations of action research and integrated them into a process that promotes critical reflection in and on action (Schön, 1995); develops capacity for deep learning (Argyris, 2002); and foregrounds the 'I' (McNiff, 2013) as the central focus of change while stressing the importance of democratic and authentic collaboration with others (Piggot-Irvine, 2012; Stringer & Beadle, 2012). Thus, participants in a PALAR project do not only reach short-term project outcomes, but also undergo profound epistemological and ontological changes on a personal and professional level. The learning and the research are separate only in theory. In practice they are inextricably interwoven. As participants research a particular issue in a collaborative group, they learn – from their own reflections, from the reflections of others and from critical dialogue within the safe confines of a community of learning, known as the action learning set.

In this particular project, for example, the action learning set comprises six doctoral candidates and three Masters students, with me and my two co-researchers as supervisors of the postgraduate students. We meet regularly to critically reflect on our learning about engaging with communities for mutual benefit and development. Participation in this action learning set also allows students to learn experientially how to run their own action learning sets within their respective community projects. All of the student projects focus on helping various education stakeholders to improve their own psychosocial and educational circumstances through engagement in a PALAR process. Table 8.1 indicates the different projects led by the students.

Table 8.1. Overview of student research projects

Project	Main research question
Life-enhancing values to reduce toxicity in a further education and training environment: a living theory of organisational development	How do I improve my practice and influence those who I work with to improve their practice, so as to bring about personal and institutional healing?
Assisting teachers to deal with the challenges of teaching learners with autistic spectrum disorder: a participatory action research approach	How can teachers be assisted to be better able to cope with the challenges faced by teaching learners diagnosed with autistic spectrum disorders?
Exploring community partnership for service-learning through creative arts education	How can Participatory Action Research (PAR) be used to integrate a meaningful service-learning experience with the community into a creative arts education module?
A collaborative approach to facilitating learner support by teachers in full-service schools	How can learner support by teachers in full-service schools be facilitated in a collaborative way?
Mobilising teachers to develop a support structure for inclusive education in rural secondary schools	How can teachers develop a support structure to overcome the context-specific barriers in the implementation of Inclusive Education (IE) in rural secondary schools?
Engaging alumni in school support: a participatory action research approach	How can alumni function as a support to the school: a participatory action research approach?
A participatory approach to improving the instructional leadership of heads of departments in under-performing schools	How can heads of departments in under-performing schools improve their instructional leadership practice?
Equipping teachers to support learners with psychosocial challenges: a participatory action learning and action research approach	How could a participatory action learning and action research approach help teachers to create a sustainable psychosocial support process?

You will notice from the topics and questions that some of the students are using participatory action research in the title; one study is also more of a practitioner self-inquiry genre. But in the end they are all following the PALAR model of setting up a project team with their participants and following iterative cycles of relationship building, vision setting, asset mapping, project planning, implementation and evaluation as suggested by the figure eight model of project design and management promoted by Ortrun (see Figure 8.1).

*Figure 8.1. Figure eight: The process of project design and management
(Zuber-Skerritt, 2002, p. 145)*

The reason for not explicitly stating PALAR in the title has to do with the tensions inherent in using action research as a methodology for higher degree studies, where some academics still question its validity. Much has been written on participatory action research, making it a more familiar and acceptable term. However, the students have adapted, and are still adapting, the project design and management model to make it more applicable to the context and needs of their particular participants (see, for example, Figure 8.2).

Since PALAR is an action learning process, continual adaptation is not only necessary in different contexts, but also expected as participants learn how to best approach their respective project goals. Similarly, the theoretical framework that underpins PALAR is eclectic and can and should be adapted by researchers to suit their field of study (Zuber-Skerritt, 2015). Theories compatible with PALAR include experiential learning theory, action theory, grounded theory, critical theory, systems theory and personal construct theory (Zuber-Skerritt, 2011, p. 83), as well as complexity theory, living theory, phenomenology and hope theory (Zuber-Skerritt, 2015, pp. 14, 18–24). What they all have in common is a critical orientation that recognises the multiplicity of 'truth' and human reality; the value, potential and interdependence of human life and the need for continual adaptation, growth and development to learn how to flourish in an ever-changing world. PALAR is not meant to be set in stone, but can be adapted as long as it remains true to certain basic characteristics and values that ensure it remains a democratic, inclusive and growth-promoting process – captured in the 7Cs of PALAR (Wood & Zuber-Skerritt, 2013, p. 3). These are: symmetrical and open *communication*, which helps to build *commitment* to the project outcomes and team, who *collaborate* and *compromise* to attain negotiated goals. *Critical reflection*, in and on the process, helps to build *competence*. If all of these characteristics are embodied in participant interaction, then character building is a natural by-product of the research process. The project facilitators act as *coaches* and mentors, learning themselves from their own reflections on the process.

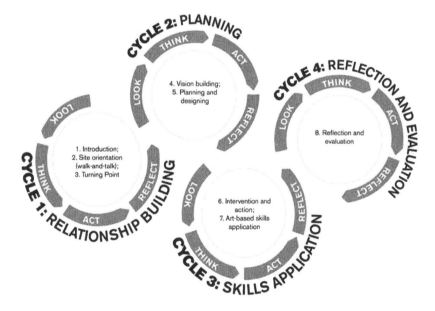

Figure 8.2. Adaptation of PALAR process (Meyer, 2015)

PALAR regards community participants as co-researchers who are knowledgeable and competent. The indigenous knowledge of community participants may be different to that of the academics, but it is vital to the success of the project. Change will not be sustainable without taking local needs, knowledge and networks into consideration. This is only possible when mutually beneficial *relationships* are established between academic and community researchers. The emphasis during the PALAR process is always on people and how they work together for mutual learning and development, rather than on the tasks they set for themselves. Regular critical *reflection* on this process of collaboration helps to ensure that participants attain project goals, as well as develop on personal and professional levels. Another important aspect of PALAR is to give *recognition* to project participants when milestones are reached. Honest self-reflection, feeling valued by others and recognising their value in turn, helps to build and sustain relationships throughout the research process.

A PALAR approach to community engagement thus implies that research is conducted not just *for* social change, but is a process *of* social change in itself. Involving participants as co-researchers foregrounds their indigenous knowledge and experience as important determinants of action for change. It also allows for the development of a more humane scholarship as opposed to a narrow scholasticism (Benson, Harkavy, & Puckett, 1996, p. 206), where knowledge does not really impact on the daily lives of the oppressed and disadvantaged. When knowledge creation remains the sole prerogative of the academy, it actually increases the divide between those who have and those who have not. The appeal of PALAR for me is that it foregrounds the validity of indigenous knowledge and experience, thus positioning participants as co-researchers who learn how to influence change and development to improve their own lives.

THE NEED FOR A DIFFERENT APPROACH TO EDUCATIONAL RESEARCH

Education in South Africa is characterised by stark inequalities, with the majority of children attending schools that lack adequate physical and human resources. However, education will not be improved by the mere provision of resources unless we simultaneously capacitate people to access them and negotiate their use (Sen, 1985). We daily hear stories of how computers are locked up for fear of theft or simply because there is no teacher able to offer computer classes; of how books or science equipment are kept away from children so that they do not get damaged; of how school premises and infrastructure are vandalised by members of the surrounding community; of children who cannot get to school because they have no money for transport, or to buy a uniform; of children who are caring for sick caregivers or acting in *loco parentis* … The stories are never-ending, but they all tell the tale of the fruitlessness of merely providing resources without developing people. Giving more money to the school will not solve the problems in most cases – the inequities and injustices stem from wider social structural conditions. Similarly, conducting research on teachers to come up with recommendations on how they could improve their circumstances does not do much to help them to change their own practices or lead a change process. Change has to come from within, thus the need to involve people in a process of learning about what needs to change, why it needs to change, and how they could exercise agency to realise and sustain that change.

As educational researchers, I believe we should spearhead and facilitate such learning, rather than pursuing an exclusionary and elitist research agenda with little direct benefit for those we are writing about. As I said in an earlier publication (Wood, 2014, p. 664):

This is the paradox – while writing *about* social justice and human rights, we are actually promoting epistemological injustice (Visvanathan, 2001), denying the validity of the knowledge and silencing the voices of those we claim to help. Thus, we hold conferences *about* poverty eradication in a five-star hotel, while those most affected stay safely and quietly in their slums.

Happily, many academics are beginning to acknowledge that human dignity is enhanced by collaborating with others to build better relationships and a better life for all (Odora-Hoppers & Richards, 2011). I agree with Kelly (2006) – we do not need more knowledge *per se*, but should rather focus on creating sustainable relationships among people to work towards improving education and other social practices. This is the essence of PALAR and why I decided to adopt it to guide my educational research in a country where its richest resource – its people – on a daily basis face adversity that tends to disempower them and rob them of hope. But first, before we can help others, we need to start with ourselves and that is why I realised the need to develop grounded theory about how academics can meaningfully engage with communities to generate mutually beneficial knowledge that will help to promote positive social and educational change.

PALAR FOR COMMUNITY ENGAGEMENT BY SOUTH AFRICAN TERTIARY RESEARCHERS: AN EMERGING THEORY

This chapter is premised on the argument that, as academics, we have a moral imperative to develop knowledge that could lead to a better understanding of how to address the 'wicked' (Rittel & Webber, 1973, p. 155) problems we face in education, problems that create a vicious circle of social injustice, thus effectively eradicating any hope of quality education in communities most affected by such social crises. Yet, attempts to shift research paradigms towards a more participatory and thus humane conceptualisation of scholarship often meet with resistance, within both the academy and the community. This project is thus an attempt to generate knowledge to build scholarship in this area. It has been running for 18 months now. All of the students have negotiated entry into their communities and have started to work in a collaborative way with their communities towards attaining their respective research goals. We come together as an action learning set once per month to share reflections on the process and progress of the students' studies. Each student submits a written reflection to the rest of the group beforehand, so that each is aware of what the other is doing, feeling and thinking. These reflections allow the supervisors to pick up on specific issues to focus the group discussion. As part of the ethical considerations, all students gave permission for these reflections to be shared and to be available to all project members to use for research purposes.

The following sections provide evidence in the form of *verbatim* excerpts from the reflections of the learning that has emerged around our experience of using PALAR as a means of community engagement for postgraduate degree purposes. The reflections were the main source of data for this report, along with the transcriptions of the action learning set meetings. I thematically analysed (Creswell, 2003) the written documents, checking the emergent themes with the other project participants to enhance trustworthiness. Much of the knowledge already has been put into the public domain. Therefore, in this chapter I present more of an overview, and refer to specific publications should readers wish to know more about a particular aspect. Where I cite postgraduate students' transcripts, M refers to Masters and PhD to Doctor (PhD) level, followed by the month and year of the reflection.

Theme 1: The Action Learning Set Promotes Development as Action Researchers

Being part of an action learning set has been of great help to the project participants. Sharing, both in person at monthly meetings and via e-mails in between, has helped students in various ways: to develop capacity to reflect on a deep level; to receive much needed emotional support; to gain valuable learning about building and sustaining a relationship with the community participants; and to develop their identity and confidence as action researchers. The interaction with each other, around a productive conversation, has helped them to learn about themselves, their relationships with others and how to facilitate a community-based research process. Through the action learning set, they were able to learn about the importance of *relationship* in the PALAR process:

> What a great feeling to see that the group is becoming closer and more relaxed toward one another. I really think that we are getting to know each other more and more with each meeting. For me this is great because I personally open up much easier to other people if I feel that I know them and that I can trust them. This makes me very excited … By being part of this group, I learnt that every input counts. I may say something that I feel is stupid or common sense, but then I see that someone else understands the concept for the first time … just showing that helping others to understand things by sharing your point of view can make a big difference. The lesson: Nothing is not worth sharing!!! (M 2, 4/2013)

Experiential learning (Kolb, 1984) is one of the theoretical tenets of PALAR, and the action learning set allows the students to learn how to create a relaxed, open and trusting learning space.

> There was no sign of power positions between promoters and students – all were equally allowed to participate, add comments, ask questions and confirm agreements. I think that this is due to the facilitation skills of the supervisors who practise inclusivity as action researchers. (PhD 1, 6/2013)

True to the action learning paradigm, all learning is valuable learning, especially when it stems from a 'mistake'. The enabling of critical *reflection* was a core purpose of the action learning set. (For a more detailed discussion on fostering reflection skills, see Wood, Seobi, Selthare-Meltor & Waddington, 2015). The accepting climate within the action learning set freed students to admit to their struggles and actively seek the feedback of their fellow set members:

> I think the sharing of the reflections with others helps to create, foster and maintain this oneness, supportiveness and loving care. As I reflect back on receiving those reflections my heart warmed to those who were brave enough to spell out their frustrations as it was like looking in a mirror – 'I've been there, am there, etc.'. (PhD 3, 5/2013)

Although critical reflection remains a challenging skill for students to master, the dialectical space created by the group made it an ideal place for each one to learn how to deepen their reflections:

> I am still not very confident in my reflection skills. When I read the other's reflections, it looks so structured, in depth and professional. I am literally sitting here, writing down what is on my mind and what I am feeling. I feel that we can help each other to write better reflections by sharing our thoughts, ideas and knowledge. By reflecting and by reading other's reflections, I am starting to think about my research more. Seeing where others have problems. I can think of ways to limit my problems in that certain aspect. (M 1, 7/2013)

A PhD candidate wrote:

> Reflecting leaves me with uncomfortable feelings, having to sift what is important and what may seem trivial to others. After the meeting I have come to realise that nothing can be considered to be unimportant, or one should have the courage to reflect, considering that it is something that has been on one's mind. I have come to learn that one develops greater perspective within a group set up. I was so insular in thinking that I'm the only one under pressure – I just have to prioritise. I was motivated when I noticed how some group members send their reflections promptly. I am going to make a greater effort not to leave my reflections for the last minute. (PhD 4, 5/2013)

Engagement in a PALAR process aims not only to develop capacity to reach the specific research goals, but also facilitates epistemological and ontological changes that spill over into other aspects of life, as explained by one of the students:

> My reflections are helping me to solidify my thoughts around how I am going to deal with the participants in my own ALS [Action Learning Set]. The inclusiveness, non-judgemental positioning, the participatory approach, the value of all contributions, the openness to respect each other, will all become upper most thoughts when I meet my participants AND when I write any memos, reports etc. in my daily duties as an HRD [human resource development] Manager. (PhD 3, 7/2013)

However, trying to remain true to the principles of PALAR within a bureaucratic, rigid and traditional academic setting was not always easy.

Theme 2: The Challenges of a Participatory Methodology for Postgraduate Studies

When students embark on an action research study, they often have to listen to negative remarks from other academics, which, to a novice researcher, can elicit doubt and anxiety. For example, a visiting professor addressed the newly enrolled postgraduate students at our institution and made some disparaging remarks about action research. Unfortunately, I was not present to engage him in dialogue and soon after at least two students (not on this project) decided to change their methodology. One of the students in this project shared similar feelings:

> I definitely want to do the PhD research and I am so grateful to have a PALAR practitioner/researcher as my promoter, but do I have the strength to convince the experts that this alternative way is empirically valid? I foresee so many questions and challenges when interacting with the experienced researchers. I just want to do my thing and not need to keep justifying it along the way to people who just would not want to understand anyway. I know I am an action person. Sitting and writing and pondering endlessly about the 'why and why not' gets in the way of actually doing, in my opinion. The expansion on that with Zuber-Skerritt's work this year makes me wonder how people can still continue to do 'human' research 'the old way' where they are disconnected from who the research is actually about. (PhD 5, 11/2013)

This student seems to have reinforced her belief in the validity of action research through her reflection, but negative attitudes towards participatory action research still abound, making it more difficult to attract students to this methodology. However, the sheer number of students involved in this project in one faculty is slowly making a difference. Each time I have to go with a student to defend a proposal or convince the ethics board that the research is indeed ethical and valid, it becomes easier as my colleagues are 'educated' about the purpose and process of action research. The need for the student to formulate research aims and questions before even being allowed to meet with participants is not so much a stumbling block as some perceive. The emergent, dynamic and flexible nature of PALAR means that it is easy to justify a change in focus during the process, and so we have learnt to indicate in the proposal that the questions may change in line with community needs. I have found that many of my colleagues are very happy to support this type of research once they realise how scholarly and valid action research is, and also how appropriate it is for engendering educational change in our settings.

Another issue is that building relationships takes time. If students try to rush the process, it often results in losing participants or the study morphing into to a researcher-driven project. Yet, the time lines for completion in a postgraduate study are very tight. At least three of the students on this project struggled initially to get participants to become actively involved on a regular basis, which caused them to panic somewhat. However, by sticking to the guiding principles of PALAR (see Table 8.2) they eventually ended up with very committed and active project teams. One student learnt this the hard way, after her participants exerted their right to withdraw from the study. Many painful discussions later, where I had to explain how she had violated the participatory principles through being too directive and focussing more on her own research agenda than the needs of the participants, she wrote:

> I acquired a great learning from cycle one – an experiential learning, which is a long lasting one, the kind of learning that I acquired is still guiding my steps at the second site. For instance, at the second site participants raised issues that I felt are not what I intended to research on, but since I learnt my lesson, that it is crucial to listen to participants, and let them be equal partners, we are now dealing with those issues and participants are responding positively. (PhD 2, 8/2014)

Used to a more traditional approach to research, defined and directed by academic practices, policies and needs, the students (and academic supervisors) on this project frequently expressed how difficult it was to adopt a more collaborative and democratic approach. I have found the '7Cs' useful as standards of judgement against which students can evaluate their interaction with participants (see Table 8.2).

Table 8.2. The guiding principles of PALAR (Wood & Zuber-Skerritt, 2013) as used to guide students in reflections on their research

The 7 Cs of PALAR for character building	Consider the following questions: How well did I live out these characteristics in my project? What successes/challenges did I encounter? What do I need to change in my thinking, acting? How can I improve these aspects?
Communication	How dialogical, how symmetrical, and how inclusive is my communication?
Commitment	How committed am I to the project, the participants and the outcome?
Competence	As facilitator of the process, and as researcher, what do I need to learn?
Compromise	How willing am I to listen to other points of view and reach mutual agreement?
Critical reflection	How do my feelings, thoughts, motives, and values impact the research process?
Collaboration	How collaborative is the process? What role do I and the participants play? Who holds the power at each stage?
Coaching	How directive am I? How can I improve my mentoring/ facilitation skills?
3 Rs	
Reflection	How can I help participants to reflect on their own learning?
Relationships	How can I improve the research relationships?
Recognition	How do I recognise and value participants' achievements?

Adhering to these principles becomes even more important in our education contexts, when so many teachers are stressed by the challenges inherent in teaching in contexts of poverty and disadvantage. It is understandable that teachers are reluctant to enter into a research process that they perceive as more work and added stress, but we have learnt that if sufficient time is spent on the relationship building and project design stage, then energy levels seem to rise and participant commitment increases. As one student 'complained', 'the participants seem to be taking over now, it is as if they don't need me on MY project' (PhD 6, 8/2014). This was said tongue in cheek, since it was actually a welcome realisation for her. She had struggled for many months to make progress, which taught us another lesson – patience and sustained commitment on the part of the researcher is vitally important to win participant trust. This brings us to the last theme, the often incalculable benefits of the PALAR process.

Theme 3: The Benefits of a PALAR Process for Postgraduate Students

Student reflections attest to the profound effect that engaging in a PALAR process had on them as researchers and as people. Holding themselves accountable to the foundational values and assumptions of PALAR turned out to be a life-enhancing process, helping them to improve their interactions and empathy levels. I let their words speak for themselves:

> It has made me a better person, but I still have issues to work on. I'm patient with other people, but impatient with myself. I used to talk far too much, but in the past year I've been trying to work on that and perhaps have become too reticent. I need to find a balance there. I assume how others feel instead of giving them the opportunity to explain. I should be aware of that during the study, to make sure I get the real picture of how the teachers are responding, without making assumptions about how I would feel in their situations. (M 2, 2/2014)

> Though relatively new to me, PALAR as research methodology has forced me to self-reflect and contemplate how I express myself, my values, language and actions as I research with others. While I was reporting on the first phase of my project, I realised that I was not true to the principles of PALAR. It dawned on me that the terms like leaders, elections, and steering committee were not true to the process of participatory action research. Though the first phase of my project was flawed, it was a valuable learning curve. (PhD 5, 5/2014)

> From my perspective, this grounding of doing action research enriched my learning especially as we are engaged with social beings as partners in the research process. I believe that I have become a better person, I am a better observer of my own and other's behaviour and practice, and I am better at writing up reflections for which I am ever grateful. I am also grateful for the

journey started, new colleagues met and respected, and the learning gained with and through them. (PhD 2, 6/2014)

CONCLUDING REFLECTIONS

As the evidence above shows, there are challenges in using PALAR as a methodology for postgraduate studies. These stem from the tensions that emerge when participatory and engaged forms of research have to comply with policies and procedures that were developed for researcher-driven inquiries. Also, when implementing PALAR in education communities, we have encountered problems that stem from years of 'learned helplessness' under a system that was designed to disempower those at grassroots level. Community members often have expectations of being 'done for', rather than learning to do for themselves. These entrenched ideas are cemented further by current approaches to teacher 'training' and its strong focus on the learning of technical pedagogical skills and content knowledge taught in a contextual vacuum that ignores the harsh reality of working within a mostly dysfunctional education system. Yet, as I have tried to show here, PALAR can offer an alternative pathway to education for sustainable development. First we have to capacitate scholars to develop a body of scholarship and this is what we are trying to do through this project. Through rigorous inquiry into the process, we are generating knowledge of how to develop PALAR as a form of community engagement. We need to adapt PALAR to suit our South African contexts, to make it culturally and practically feasible. We are fortunate that Ortrun is continuing to work with us to do this. Although her physical presence in South Africa is limited to a short annual visit, she has had, and continues to have, an enormous influence on our thinking through her writing and electronic interactions.

To conclude, if we want to prepare people for life in the twenty-first century, then we have to change our approach to educational research. PALAR can help academic researchers to work hand in hand with those at the 'coal face' to find new ways to improve their quality of life and contribute towards sustainable development for the social good. I know that the participants on this project, myself included, would agree that PALAR capacitates academic researchers to engage in a participatory way with community members to develop knowledge that leads to practical, relevant and sustainable change. We are committed to continuing to develop participatory action learning and action research and we can only thank Professor Dr Ortrun Zuber-Skerritt for setting us on this path and collaborating with us to help us to advance.

ACKNOWLEDGEMENTS

A community engagement grant from the National Research Foundation (NRF) enabled the research reported on here. Any findings, opinions, conclusions or recommendations expressed in this material are those of the author and therefore the NRF does not accept any liability thereto.

REFERENCES

Argyris, C. (2002). Double-loop learning, teaching, and research. *Academy of Management Learning & Education, 1*(2), 206–218.

Benson, L., Harkavy, I., & Puckett, J. (1996). Communal participatory action research as a strategy for improving universities and the social sciences: Penn's work with the West Philadelphia Improvement Corps as a case study. *Educational Policy, 10*(2), 202–222.

Creswell, J. W. (2003). *Research design: Qualitative, quantitative and mixed methods approaches* (2nd ed.). Thousand Oaks, CA: Sage Publications.

Kelly, P. (2006). Learning for sustainable futures: One intervention. *Journal of Future Studies, 10*(3), 1–14.

Kolb, D. A. (1984). *Experiential learning: Experience as the source of learning and development.* New Jersey, NJ: Prentice-Hall.

McNiff, J. (2013). *Action research: Principles and practice.* London,UK: Routledge.

Meyer, G. M. (2015). *Exploring community partnership for service-learning through creative arts education* (Unpublished Masters dissertation). Potchefstroom, South Africa: North-West University.

Motshekga, A. (2010). *National council of provinces debate.* Retrieved November 28, 2014, from http://www.gov.za/address-minister-basic-education-mrs-angie-motshekga-mp-national-council-provinces-occasion-debate

Odora-Hoppers, C., & Richards, H. (2011). *Rethinking thinking: Modernity's 'other' and the transformation of the university.* Pretoria, South Africa: UNISA Press.

Piggot-Irvine, E. (2012). Creating authentic collaboration: A central feature of effectiveness. In O. Zuber-Skerritt (Ed.), *Action research for sustainable development in a turbulent world.* Bingley, UK: Emerald Books.

Rittel, H. W. J., & Webber, M. M. (1973). Dilemmas in a general theory of planning. *Policy Sciences, 4*(155), 169.

Said, E. (1994). *Representations of the intellectual: The 1993 Reith lectures.* New York, NY: Pantheon Books.

Schön, D. A. (1995). Knowing-in-action: The new scholarship requires a new epistemology. *Change: The Magazine of Higher Learning, 27*(6), 27–34.

Sen, A. (1985). *Commodities and capabilities.* New York, US: Oxford.

Stringer, E., & Beadle, R. (2012). Tjuluru: Action research for indigenous community development. In O. Zuber-Skerritt (Ed.), *Action research for sustainable development in a turbulent world* (pp. 151–166). Bingley, UK: Emerald Books

Visvanathan, S. (2001, August 18). Durban and the dalit discourse. *Economic and Political Weekly, XXXVI*(33).

Wood, L. (2014). Action research for the 21st century: Exploring new educational pathways. *South African Journal of Higher Education, 28*(2), 660–672.

Wood, L., & Zuber-Skerritt, O. (2013). PALAR as a methodology for community engagement by faculties of education. *South African Journal of Education, 33*(4), 1–15.

Wood, L., Seobi, A., Selthare-Meltor, R., & Waddington, R. (2015, In press). Reflecting on reflecting: Fostering student capacity for critical reflection in an action research project. *Educational Research for Social Change.*

Zuber-Skerritt, O. (2002). A model for designing action learning and action research programmes. *The Learning Organization, 9*(4), 143–149.

Zuber-Skerritt, O. (2011). *Action leadership. Towards a participatory paradigm.* Dordrecht, The Netherlands: Springer.

Zuber-Skerritt, O. (2012). Introduction. In O. Zuber-Skerritt (Ed.), *Action research for sustainable development in a turbulent world.* Bingley, UK: Emerald Books.

Zuber-Skerritt, O. (2015). Conceptual framework. In O. Zuber-Skerritt, M. Fletcher, & J. Kearney, *Professional learning in higher education and communities: Towards a new vision of action research* (pp. 1–37). London, UK: Palgrave Macmillan.

Zuber-Skerritt, O., & Teare, R. (2013). *Lifelong action learning for community development: Learning and development for a better world.* Rotterdam, The Netherlands: Sense Publisher.

Lesley Wood
Faculty of Education Sciences
North-West University
South Africa

PIP BRUCE FERGUSON

9. BUILDING NATIONAL AND INTERNATIONAL ACTION RESEARCH COMMUNITIES OF PRACTICE

INTRODUCTION

Action research has been developing within and across countries for nearly a century now. There is some agreement about its origins, with Adelman (1993) and others attributing its commencement to the work of Kurt Lewin in the 1930s, although McKernan (1991) identifies work dating back to the nineteenth century as influential in the movement. Masters (1995), as well as Zeichner and Noffke (2001) in the United States, also trace its development through the work of Dewey, the Group Dynamics movement, post-war reconstruction and the teacher–researcher work of Stenhouse in the United Kingdom. A useful literature review on the history and development of action research is provided by McLaughlin, Black-Hawkins and McIntyre (2004).

My intention in this chapter is to investigate specifically the ways in which action research communities of practice have been built up both nationally and internationally. As most of my action research practice has been based in New Zealand, the chapter has more of an antipodean flavour, although it alludes to the building of communities elsewhere and suggests some guidelines for such work. Professor Ortrun Zuber-Skerritt, to whose enduring work this book is a tribute, has been active in building communities of practice in her home country Australia and well beyond, so her influence in this kind of community-building is referenced as the chapter progresses. One of the places where Ortrun has been active is in work with African educators, and in a recent book (Zuber-Skerritt, Fletcher & Kearney, 2015) she prefaces her chapters with quotes from Nelson Mandela. Here I repeat the quote that prefaces Chapter 1 of that book. From my dealings with Ortrun I believe this is typical not only of Mandela's thinking, but also of Ortrun's: 'What counts in life is not the mere fact that we have lived. It is what difference we have made to the lives of others that will determine the significance of the life we lead' (Nelson Mandela, 18 May, 2002, in Zuber-Skerritt et al., 2015, p. 1).

As the chapter focusses on international as well as national communities of practice development, I allude below to international concepts of community that demonstrate relevance across cultures and nations. A theme running through the chapter is the importance of relationships in the building of communities. Tying together this importance with the African work that Ortrun and others have engaged in is the African concept of *Ubuntu*, which I first encountered when it was promoted

J. Kearney & M. Todhunter (Eds), Lifelong Action Learning and Research: A Tribute to the Life and Pioneering Work of Ortrun Zuber-Skerritt, 109–121.

by Jack Whitehead, based on the doctoral thesis of Eden Charles (2007). Charles wrote:

> What is Ubuntu? There are many descriptions of Ubuntu. Some see it as 'African group solidarity' (Rwelamila et al., 1999). Most others extract from the embodied notions of solidarity in the Ubuntu way of being and extrapolate it more generally. I like to think of Ubuntu as a clear manifestation of African cosmology. It is popularly thought of as an approach to being in which people recognize their interconnection and interdependency. This is reflected in the phrase 'I am because we are'. (p. 10)

A Māori word with similar meaning, although originally more genealogically linked, is '*whakawhanaungatanga*'. The online Māori dictionary defines it as 'the process of establishing relationships, of relating well to others' (http://www.maoridictionary.co.nz/word/12711, retrieved 14 November, 2014), and it is often used in non-genealogical connections in education and social development work. It is these kinds of interconnection and interdependency that I have observed in the creation and development of action research communities of practice. In-depth work has been done in building relationships, and in establishing connections that are mutually beneficial and respectful. Before considering some of the specific examples of community-building in action research, I discuss some relevant literature on this concept.

WHAT IS A COMMUNITY OF PRACTICE?

The term 'communities of practice' was advanced by Lave and Wenger in 1991. They described the process of situated learning, demonstrating movement from a novice learner status by those not deeply involved in a community, to becoming practitioners deeply embedded in the field who are able to share insights with new arrivals to the community. This is certainly the process by which I became 'enculturated' into the action research community in my part of the world. For Wenger, McDermott and Snyder (2002), 'Communities of practice are groups of people who share a concern, a set of problems, or a passion about a topic and who deepen their knowledge and expertise in this area by interacting on an ongoing basis' (p. 4).

The authors stress the often intermittent interaction of the group, along with its focus on sharing knowledge, helping to solve problems, exploring common issues and insights, and acting as sounding boards. The last-mentioned is, of course, common to the 'critical friend' role that action research espouses. Laidlaw described the role of this person as one who '... has to interpret and listen, to play back what the researcher is trying to reveal, to illuminate where there is any ambiguity, and to challenge where there is any untruth' (Laidlaw, 1997, p. 29). I refer to this kind of critique later in the chapter where I talk about the work of Action Learning, Action Research and Process Management (ALARPM), an action research community of practice. In such groups, personal relationships are built up over time, and often (but not automatically) a common identity is formed. McTaggart (1994) observed action research as 'a broad church', while Ortrun and colleagues describe it as 'a family' (Zuber-Skerritt et al., 2015, p. 104). Communities of practice may have common principles, but not necessarily a strict common identity. Yet this does not preclude the action research approach from being the underlying 'cement' for communities of practice locally and internationally.

As Wenger et al. (2002) noted, communities of practice have always been present. However, with the inception of the internet and faster forms of travel, investigation within and across countries has greatly enhanced the speed with which these communities can become established.

The theory of social constructivism is also pertinent to the development of communities of practice. Social constructivism refers to the development of forms of knowledge as a result of interaction with others, rather than knowledge existing as pre-determined content, although some social constructivists may debate this (see Dupré, 2004, for a science-related interpretation). Accordingly, in social constructivism, the people involved in a community of practice can and do develop forms of knowledge that are emergent. Given the tendency of action research approaches to 'morph' over time, social constructivism also seems to be relevant in the development of action research communities of practice.

The development of the teacher-as-researcher movements in both the UK (Stenhouse and Elliott's work in the 1970s, cited as vital in McNiff, 1988) and the US (Cochran-Smith & Lytle, 1999) are examples of how a previously dominant discourse of reliance on university-based educational research was broadened by the work of teachers investigating their own practice. The work of teachers (and practitioners in other fields) undertaking investigations in their own practice has certainly been evident in my home country of New Zealand, and it is to the development of action research there that the chapter turns next.

ACTION RESEARCH DEVELOPMENT IN NEW ZEALAND

I alluded to my integration into the action research community as a gradual process, where I started as novice 'on the periphery' but have gradually been enculturated into what I perceive as a vibrant community of practice. How did this come about? Interestingly, in light of my comment above on a changing discourse from university-based educational research to practitioner-based investigation, I encountered action research first through a professional development course run by a couple of University of Auckland lecturers. John Jones and Tony Morrison taught an action research course to polytechnic staff wishing to learn about the approach, and through their connections and my own as a staff developer in a polytechnic I met Eileen Piggot-Irvine in the late 1980s. Eileen also attributes to John and Tony her early interest in action research, and sought their advice on forming the New Zealand Action Research Network (NZARN) in 1992. She had support from Judith McMorland and myself.

A conscious decision was taken to develop the group as a network rather than a centralised executive. Subscriptions were held to $10 per annum, remarkably cheap even in those days, and the money was used for printing and postage of newsletters providing short case studies of work being done using action research in a variety of contexts, not just educational ones. The newsletters also advertised snippets from action researchers and groups around the world, as we became aware of these. It is easy to feel 'isolated' academically in New Zealand, and while I believe alot of our practice is exemplary, we do rely on also 'touching base' with developments in other places, perhaps more than in larger countries. The Network relied totally on volunteer support; there were no cash reserves to pay for speakers, travel and so forth, a point that becomes critical in the next section. The Network aimed to appeal to a broad spectrum of practitioners, although these were mainly drawn from the tertiary education sector. Membership continued to be reasonably stable until 2003, when an increase in subscription to $30 deterred some from continuing.

In my perspective, critical to the development and flourishing of this community of practice was (a) the absolute passion and energy of its founder, Eileen; (b) the ongoing support for the work by a cohort of people who totally believed in action research as an appropriate approach for professional development and improvement of practice; (c) the newsletter, which served to maintain connections and knowledge of events in New Zealand and elsewhere; and finally, and most importantly, (d) the annual conferences, which served to attract new members to join the community. In these events our connections to and support from Australian action research colleagues were absolutely critical.

As I earlier mentioned, our network lacked money. We needed to rely on institutional positioning of colleagues, largely staff developers, to have conferences funded or otherwise supported through free provision of conference facilities and/or printing and distribution for publicity materials, or through financial contributions to help with costs of visiting speakers. NZARN held annual conferences at Unitec, Auckland, in 1995; the Waikato Polytechnic (the institution where I worked) in Hamilton in 1996; Waiariki Polytechnic in Rotorua in 1997; Wellington Polytechnic in 1998, with Professor Robin McTaggart as keynote;the University of Auckland in 1999, with Professor Yoland Wadsworthas keynote; Christchurch Polytechnic in the South Island in 2000, with myself as keynote; Manukau Institute of Technology in Auckland in 2001, with Jill Chrisp and TePora Emery as keynotes; and back at Unitec in Auckland in 2003, with Professor Ortrun Zuber-Skerritt as keynote. The last conference of which I am aware was held at Christchurch College of Education in 2004, with Geoff Mills as keynote.

These details reveal the strong institutional support for NZARN conferences, especially from within the polytechnic sector for which both Eileen and I were staff developers. While the bulk of the events were held in the North Island (where most of our members were based), we did our best to move around the country, which was important for those who could not afford large travel expenses. We used local speakers where needed but were *hugely* supported, largely free of charge, by well-known Australian action researchers in Robin, Yoland and Ortrun. NZARN went into recession after 2004, when the annual conferences were no longer held. In recent years we have the formation of a related group, the New Zealand Collaborative Action Research Network (NZCARN), with support and encouragement from CARN in the UK. The latter's leading researcher Bridget Somekh has visited to assist with NZCARN's development. I have been less involved in this group, especially since my move from Waikato to the University of Dublin in 2014. In my last two years at Waikato, however, I attended events 'remotely', and with a South Island member of NZCARN and NZCARN colleagues from my university I co-presented in a symposium at the 2010 Research in Education Conference (Alcorn, Bruce Ferguson & Locke, 2010). Susan Groundwater-Smith from Australia has also been involved with the group and has presented as a keynote. And so the New Zealand action research movement continues its development and connections, both locally and internationally.

CONNECTIONS WITH THE AUSTRALIAN ACTION RESEARCH MOVEMENT

This chapter is not the place to expand on the development of the Australian action research movement, which is not my story to tell. But that development (largely parallel with that in New Zealand in terms of timeline) was critical for New Zealand, with our sense of isolation and need to connect with a wider academic community. Swepson, Dick, Zuber-Skerritt, Passfield, Carroll and Wadsworth (2003) identify as a milestone the International Symposium on Action Research in Education, Government and Industry held in Brisbane in 1989, largely at Ortrun's instigation. Eileen attended that symposium, which developed the definition I use regularly when teaching about action research, a definition reinforced at the 1991 World Congress on Action Learning, Action Research and Process Management (ALARPM) (Altrichter, Kemmis, McTaggart, & Zuber-Skerritt, 1991, p. 8):

If yours is a situation in which

- People reflect on and improve (or develop) their *own* work and their *own* situations by tightly interlinking their reflection and action; and
- Also making their experience public, not only to other participants but also to other persons interested in and concerned about the work and the situation, that is, their (public) theories and practices of the work and the situation;

and if yours is a situation in which there is increasingly

- data-gathering by participants themselves (or with the help of others) in relation to their own questions;
- participation (in problem-posing and in answering questions) in decision-making;

- power-sharing and the relative suspension of hierarchical ways of working toward industrial democracy;
- collaboration among members of the group as a 'critical community';
- self-reflection, self-evaluation, and self-management by autonomous and responsible persons and groups;
- learning progressively (and publicly) by doing and by making mistakes in a 'self-reflective spiral' of planning, acting, observing, reflecting, replanning etc.;
- reflection that supports the idea of the '(self-)reflective practitioner';

then

- Yours is a situation in which ACTION RESEARCH is occurring.

The ongoing ALARPM events in Australia and later internationally (Bath, 1994; Cartagena, 1997; Pretoria, 2003) were significant in building action research communities of practice in Australia, and influencing those communities developing in New Zealand and elsewhere. The narrative account of ALARPM's development (Swepson et al., 2003) provides so many nuggets of wisdom on how to build action research communities of practice that it could almost constitute a 'how to' manual. It draws on interviews with key informants from the Australian ALARPM movement, including Anne-Marie Carroll, Ron Passfield, Yoland Wadsworth, Ortrun Zuber-Skerritt and Bob Dick. Here I briefly summarise some of their ideas since they give helpful pointers on how to develop and maintain sound communities of practice.

- 'Think and act global but act and think local', a concept mentioned by most interviewees.
- Concentrate on similarities between various approaches to action research rather than being hard-line about definition and methodology – be 'non-doctrinaire' as Bob Dick put it.
- Learn from failures instead of being overwhelmed by them (Ron Passfield cited the great example of learning from World Congress 1 for implementing better relationship practice in World Congress 2).
- Use personal networks for 'spreading the word' about the new ALARPM community of practice, and particularly for attracting keynote speakers and financial and 'in kind' support.
- Since raising membership fees deters membership, to maintain a sound membership base and minimise costs, take action to secure the availability and commitment of volunteers to do work where possible, rather than paying for services.
- Make face to face meetings fun as well as business focussed, since most of the work is done by volunteers.
- Ensure the Management Committee remains strong. (This message was clear in ALARPM but less evident in NZARN, where commitment from key individuals rather than a committee structure helped to maintain forward movement).

- Ensure empowerment at local level, not just via the Management Committee.
- Remember the high importance of networks and of maintaining 'networks of networks', recognising that members are involved in other communities of practice as well as ALARPM, and drawing on these strengths and connections.
- Keep the *Action Learning, Action Research* (ALAR) journal non-refereed; it is spreading the word internationally.
- Encourage members to actively introduce and induct new groups to ALARPM. Ortrun illustrated with her example of bringing South African colleagues to the Fifth World Congress in Ballarat in 2000.
- Acquaint new members with the concept of 'critical friend' culture that encourages constructive critique, which is not recognised as personal attack.
- Bring people from the 'periphery' into the group, since this is vital for building communities of practice.

Some interviewees noted institutional barriers, recognising the resistance of many universities to action research and action learning as legitimate research approaches. Ortrun advised the utility of responding to these challenges with ongoing questions rather than with rebuttal and argument. Some acknowledged the critical nature of relationship-building, and Ron Passfield noted the need to build these relationships *prior to* the conferences and Congresses. Ron explained how the group had worked to retain the membership of those attending conferences and Congresses by building a year's membership into the conference fee. Another important factor is to trust and support those who put their hands up to organise conferences, contributing seed funds and sound guidelines to try to ensure success, whilst recognising that sometimes events don't generate sufficient funds to repay the seeding loan.

But the big events were not the only 'glue' holding together people and organisations in communities of practice. Some interviewees noted the importance of maintaining connections and forward movement between big events (such as the World Congresses) by ensuring that smaller local conferences and happenings continued, which was certainly important for us in the NZARN. Interviewees also recognised the importance of being able to draw on an international cohort of executive members, using communication technologies (for instance I was co-secretary from New Zealand at a time when the co-ordinator of new memberships was US-based, and an Assistant Editor of the ALAR journal in South Africa). It was vital that key people built on their networks – Ortrun's 'consummate networking' and 'Euro-international' connections were mentioned by Yoland Wadsworth, who also advocated for a 'networked, nodal, "virtual organisation" resting heavily on a website and e-communication, reflecting and supporting networks of independent, local, face-to-face groups as well as World Congresses' as a way forward (Swepson et al., 2003, p. 279).

It is also an important support for newly developing communities, I believe, to link with existing formal groups. Many of the New Zealanders and Australians were also members of the Higher Education Research and Development Society of

Australasia (HERDSA), of which I was an international Vice-President for some years. This is a well-funded and long-established society, which produces a peer-reviewed journal and holds well-respected annual conferences, which many of our institutions funded us to attend. Most members are based in higher education, and while both NZARN and ALARPM drew on multi-disciplinary fields, the status of HERDSA and its regular conferences in both Australia and New Zealand (and in recent years also Sarawak, Malaysia, in 2004, and Hong Kong in 2014) enabled those interested in action research to connect there as well as in the action research-related conferences. The syntheses between those two groups, and the importance of shared networks, were stressed in one account in Swepson et al. (2003, p. 89), noting the key support of Phil Candy, a strong HERDSA member in a senior position at Queensland University of Technology, in providing secretarial help and seeding money as a loan when the ALARPM 1992 World Congress organisers were wound up as the congress was being planned. It may be wise for groups wanting to start a community of practice in a developing context to 'piggy-back' on the networks and strengths of established, like-minded groups as they grow. Ron Passfield noted:

> I always had the goal that it was a strategic network; i.e., everyone in ALARPM was also in another network, or multiple networks. So ALARPM was to be a connection between the network 'nodes' and a resource and support to them. And I think that's still the challenge for the future. (Swepson et al., 2003, p. 261)

As Bob Dick claimed (Swepson et al., 2003, p. 246), 'You could write a paper just on exploring the networks. Strong networking has been a feature of ALARPM right from the start, or before the start', alluding to connections between institutions and other business, workplace learning and action research networks that had contributed to ALARPM's development. His own AREOL (Action Research and Education Online) free course has also provided connections between and across individuals in different countries.

I now want to move from the largely antipodean exploration of the development of action research communities of practice, looking largely at face-to-face connections, to exploring how action research communities of practice are developing in other international contexts of which I have knowledge or am a part.

DEVELOPING INTERNATIONAL ACTION RESEARCH COMMUNITIES OF PRACTICE

It is evident from the discussion above that the influence of key people within and across countries helps with the development of local variations of action research. Bob Dick, in his interview in Swepson et al. (2003), mentioned various US-based experts and influencers of practice. He also mentioned the importance of the work of Robin McTaggart, an Australian, with Stephen Kemmis, who was originally from the U.K. Ortrun also mentioned those two, and cited other influential authors globally as influencers, as well as connections from the UK and Sweden, the multi-national attendees and keynotes at the various World Congresses, and of course her South African colleagues. The World Congresses held outside Australia also helped with the development of local communities of practice that were action research (or Participatory Action Research (PAR) in the case of the South American event) oriented. I was fortunate to attend the World Congress in Pretoria in 2003 and to meet people engaged in action research work across the globe, including, obviously, on the continent of Africa itself. Some of the connections built up at these Congresses continue to this day, mediated by the ready availability of the internet, Skype and the like.

Yoland Wadsworth, in her comment cited above, anticipated more 'virtual' forms of connection. Bob Dick aluded to the AR-list group that he moderated, later adding the *Action Research International* journal online, of which I am on the editorial board along with colleagues from across the globe, although the journal is currently in recess. These forms of international communication, along with the Joint Information Systems Committee (JISC) practitioner–researcher online group, have provided me with links to, and examples of, the work of colleagues across the globe who are interested in action research. They also enabled me to work on two papers, one with Geof Hill (Australia) discussing who is marginalised in thesis presentation (Hill & Bruce Ferguson, 2002), and one with Paulus Murray (Africa/UK) on interrogating issues of race and oppression using Living Educational Theory. I presented a workshop on our developing ideas to the ALARA[1] annual conference in 2003 (Bruce Ferguson, 2003), and we intended to co-present at the World Congress in Pretoria, but Paulus was unable to be there. However, he wrote a paper about our conversations (Murray, 2003). I had met neither man, but our shared interest in action research enabled us to negotiate shared understandings and respect. I had 'met' Geof through ALARPM links, and Paulus through JISC's practitioner–researcher group, which continues to this day.

Probably the most in-depth action research-related community of practice with which I am engaged is via the *Educational Journal of Living Theories*, http://ejolts.org. This international publication has Editorial Board members, Development Group members and reviewers (I'm in both latter groups) and it uses an open reviewing process to encourage successive iterations of papers in ways that stretch the knowledge of both authors and reviewers. Because the process is open, an equitable and honest exploration of issues and approaches is possible. I have a publication currently 'in press' in which, with submitters with whom I've worked, I investigated possibilities of this group developing transnational, cross-cultural research skills in both reviewers and submitters. One submitter said:

EJOLTS presents a quite remarkable opportunity to contextualize reflection and inquiry in terms of living relationships. I am still deeply moved and inspired by the fact that love can be present and visible in an academic journal and between academics who know one another only as online colleagues.

117

This particular submitter and I are currently negotiating to submit an abstract for the 9th ALARA World Congress to be held back in Pretoria in 2015, although we have never met. Connections are evident and developed not only through the journal itself, but also on the site via the 'EJOLTS community' forum and via a Facebook page. In this way, the journal's Editorial Board and Development Group are striving to build the kinds of connections and relationships internationally that encourage the 'virtual community of practice' to thrive and grow. Members of the Board and the development team frequently use Skype to meet and discuss issues of relevance to this work. While I have met face-to-face most of the folk in the UK via action research events, others, such as colleagues based in Canada, Croatia, India and Japan, I have never met but interact with regularly. Yoland Wadsworth, quoted earlier, suggested digital methods for extending our action research communities. The relatively recent theory of connectivism, promoted by both Siemens (2004) and Downes (2007) and presented and critiqued by Kop and Hill (2008), draws attention to the ways in which digitally mediated connections can lead not only to the development of knowledge, but such development is in ways that 'value add' in a community beyond what is possible by individuals. Kop and Hill (2008) cite Siemens' claim that '… knowledge does not only reside in the mind of an individual, knowledge resides in a distributed manner across a network … learning is the act of recognizing patterns shaped by complex networks' (Siemens, 2006, p. 10, in Kop and Hill, n.p.). These networks are internal, as neural networks, and external, as networks in which we adapt to the world around us (Siemens, 2006, p. 10, in Kop and Hill, n.p.).

I have observed through EJOLTS work that individual perspectives are broadened, and that a real 'community of inquirers' using Living Educational Theory is continuing to develop. This approach requires submitters to be clear about their values, about what motivates their practice, and to what standards they hold themselves to account for working out these values in their practice. 'Critical friends' then provide feedback, which enables submitters to make their accounts more robust and rigorous, and it is all done 'online' and in a public forum.

This kind of knowledge development and 'e-connections' was also advocated by Ortrun Zuber-Skerritt back in 2000, when she participated in a conversation with researcher Jim Murphy (Murphy, 2000, n.p.). Ortrun noted:

> In the next five to ten years action research will become one of the most appropriate methodologies in professional and organisational development, and most relevant to all sectors of society, because of the increasingly rapid change in all spheres of life. Instead of relying on external experts and knowledge in books (too quickly outdated), organisations will have to rely more and more on their own people's collaborative abilities to solve problems fast, to network, to anticipate change and actually to be faster than change.

Action learning and action research have been proven to develop transferable skills and lateral, critical, analytical, creative and innovative thinking, needed in a fast changing and competitive global world.

Later in the interview, and linking closely with the view propounded in Living Educational Theory work, she commented that 'everyone has to develop his or her own theoretical framework and this framework cannot simply be copied or transmitted from one person to another. It depends on and must be founded in our values and worldviews. Everyone builds and lives in a very individual home'.

CONCLUSION

Throughout this chapter I have attempted to show how various networks and organisations, based around action research in the main, have provided data and guidelines that might contribute to the sound development of action research communities of practice, both locally and internationally. The concept of *Ubuntu* – 'I am because we are' – has been demonstrated in the reliance I have described not only on support from colleagues in the same country, but from international connections. Our '*whakawhanaungatanga*' – building of relationships, and seeking to relate well to others – has been facilitated by very generous sharing from those further down the road than we, and also by the ability to advance and respond to positively critical feedback. While some of the pioneers of the action research movements across the globe, including Ortrun herself, are now well on in years, I have confidence that the groundwork laid, and the examples provided, can assist the oncoming generations of action researchers to further grow and develop their work. It must not remain static, or it will ossify, as McNiff warned in a paper she wrote in 1994:

> Are we not then in danger of providing an elitist group within C.A.R.N. [Collaborative Action Research Network] that is actually going to start setting clear parameters as to what constitutes quality action research, or what constitutes action research itself? … Some eminent action researchers – I certainly don't share this view – are quite specific about the kind of criteria they lay down as to what counts as action research. (p. 19)

McNiff was not arguing against standards; indeed, her life work has been focussed around teachers being clear about what constitutes responsible and ethical practice based on sound values, and holding themselves accountable for these. But she was warning about rigidity in the approaches, which would work against the 'broad church' and 'family' observations of McTaggart and Zuber-Skerritt. As this book is a tribute to Ortrun, I wish to conclude the chapter with her words from the interview reported in Swepson et al. (2003):

Hopefully, we'll carry into the future a postpositivist, dynamic, continuously developing vision, belief and strategy – open to new challenges and criticism as well as self-criticism. (p. 256)

NOTE

[1] In the Swepson et al. paper, Ortrun Zuber-Skerritt proposed dropping the 'PM – process-management' side from the acronym. The organisation was subsequently called ALARA – Action Learning and Action Research Association.

REFERENCES

Adelman, C. (1993) Kurt Lewin and the origins of action research. *Educational Action Research, 1*(1), 7–24.

Alcorn, N., Bruce Ferguson, P., & Locke, T. (2010). *A critical overview of action research in New Zealand 1980–2010*. Symposium paper presented at New Zealand Association for Research in Education Conference, Auckland, New Zealand, 6–9 December.

Altrichter, H., Kemmis, S., McTaggart, R., & Zuber-Skerritt, O. (1991). Defining, confining or refining action research? In O. Zuber-Skerritt (Ed.), *Action research for change and development* (pp. 13–20). Aldershot, UK: Power Publishing Company

Bruce Ferguson, P. (2003). *Interrogating issues of race and oppression using living educational theory*. Workshop presented at Learning Partners in Action, Action Learning, Action Research and Process Management 6th and Participatory Action Research 10th World Congress, Pretoria, South Africa, 21–24 September.

Charles, E. (2007). How can I bring Ubuntu as a living standard of judgement into the academy? Moving beyond decolonisation through societal reidentification and guiltless recognition (PhD thesis). University of Bath, UK.

Cochran-Smith, M., & Lytle, S. L. (1999). The teacher research movement: A decade later. *Educational Researcher, 28*(7), 15–25.

Downes, S. (2007) *What connectivism is*. Retrieved November 27, 2014, from http://halfanhour.blogspot.co.uk/2007/02/what-connectivism-is.html

Dupré, J. (2004). What's the fuss about social constructivism? *Episteme, 1*, 73–85.

Hill, G., & Bruce Ferguson, P. (2002). *Conversations around difference in thesis presentation: Who is marginalised?* Refereed paper presented at Quality Conversations, Higher Education Research and Development Society of Australasia Annual International Conference, July 7–10, Perth, Australia.

Kop, R., & Hill, A. (2008). Connectivism: Learning theory of the future or vestige of the past? *The International Review of Research in Open and Distance Learning, 9*(3)(Unpaginated). Retrieved November 19, 2014, from http://www.irrodl.org/index.php/irrodl/article/view/523/1103

Laidlaw, M. (1997). How can I create my own living educational theory as I offer you an account of my educational development? (Unpublished PhD thesis). The University of Bath, UK.

Lave, J., & Wenger, E. (1991). *Situated learning: Legitimate peripheral participation*. Cambridge, MA: Cambridge University Press.

Masters, J. (1995). The history of action research. In I. Hughes (Ed.), *Action research electronic reader*. Sydney, Australia: University of Sydney.

McKernan J. (1991). *Curriculum action research. A handbook of methods and resources for the reflective practitioner*. London, UK: Kogan Page

McLaughlin, C., Black-Hawkins, K., & McIntyre, D. (2004). *Researching teachers, researching schools, researching networks: A review of the literature*. Cambridge, MA: University of Cambridge Faculty of Education.

McNiff, J. (1988). *Action research: Principles and practice*. Hampshire, Shire county, UK: Macmillan Education Ltd.

McNiff, J. (1994). Conversations with action researchers. *Action Researcher, 1*(Spring), 18–19.

McTaggart, R. (1994). Participatory action research: Issues in theory and practice. *Educational Action Research, 2*(3), 313–337.

Murphy, J. (2000). An interview with Ortrun Zuber-Skerritt: A personal perspective. *Action Research International.* Retrieved November 27, 2014, from http://www.aral.com.au/ari/p-jmurphy00.html

Murray, P. (2003). Iraq, utter humiliation and hypocrisy: An educative contribution to the practice of co-enquiring written in the first and third person. Retrieved November 27, 2014, from http://tinyurl.com/lwq3xdr

Siemens, G. (2004). Connectivism: A learning theory for the digital age. Retrieved November 27, 2014, from http://www.elearnspace.org?Articles/connectivism.htm

Siemens, G. (2006). *Connectivism: Learning theory or pastime of the self-amused?* [Elearnspace blog]. Retrieved March 18, 2015, from http://www.elearnspace.org/Articles/connectivism_self-amused.htm

Swepson, P., Dick, B., Zuber-Skerritt, O., Passfield, R., Carroll, A-M., & Wadsworth, Y. (2003, August). A history of the Action Learning, Action Research, and Process Management Association (ALARPM): From Brisbane (Australia) to the world through inclusion and networks. *Systemic Practice and Action Research, 16*(4), 237–281.

Wenger, E., McDermott, R., & Snyder, W. (2002). *Cultivating communities of practice: A guide to managing knowledge.* Boston, Mass: Harvard Business School Publishing.

Zeichner, K., & Noffke, S. (2001). Practitioner research. In V. Richardson (Ed.), *Handbook of research on teaching* (pp. 298–332) (4th ed.). Washington, DC: American Educational Research Association.

Zuber-Skerritt, O., Fletcher, M., & Kearney, J. (2015). *Professional learning in higher education and communities: Towards a new vision for action research.* Basingstoke, UK: Palgrave Macmillan.

Pip Bruce Ferguson
Teaching Enhancement Unit
National Institute for Digital Learning
Dublin City University
Ireland

YOLAND WADSWORTH

10. CREATING WORLD CONGRESSES OF ACTION LEARNING AND ACTION RESEARCH TO NETWORK AN INTERNATIONAL COMMUNITY

Most associations of people dedicated to furthering an area of human endeavour start small and local and build up, possibly over many years, to operate at a larger scale. Not so for Ortrun Zuber-Skerritt! This chapter acknowledges and honours Ortrun's visionary enthusiasm for connecting people and ideas on a large scale – in this instance through her collaboratively establishing an action learning, action research and process management association with a starting aim of conducting world congresses. The range, quality and values maintained by these world congresses are testament to Ortrun's professional network and her powers of networking. We thank Sage Publications Ltd for kind permission to reproduce in this Festschrift the following entry that illuminates Ortrun's significant contribution in this area. An earlier version was published originally as Wadsworth, Y. (2014). World congresses of action research, in D. Coghlan and M. Brydon-Miller (Eds) *Encyclopaedia of action research* (pp. 826–829), London: Sage Publications; and drawing on Wadsworth (2010).

The purpose of the World Congresses is to provide a global forum every two to three years for participants to meet together across disciplinary boundaries and geographical distances to develop and exchange concepts, ideas, experiences and reflections on current thinking and practice, and to explore possibilities for further development of practice, networks and other collaboration.

HISTORY OF FOUNDING

ALARA World congresses were founded by Australia-based Ortrun Zuber-Skerritt and Ron Passfield, both working in the higher education, managerial and organisational learning field in Brisbane in the 1980s and 1990s. They also co-founded the congresses' auspicing organisation: the Action Learning Action Research and Process Management Association (ALARPM), from 2008 renamed the Action Learning Action Research Association (ALARA).

The precursor to the world congresses of action research was the first International Symposium on Action Research organised by Mary Farquhar and Ortrun Zuber-Skerritt in 1988 at the then Queensland Institute of Technology in Brisbane, Australia. This led in 1990 to the inaugural World Congress of Action Learning,

J. Kearney & M. Todhunter (Eds), Lifelong Action Learning and Research: A Tribute to the Life and Pioneering Work of Ortrun Zuber-Skerritt, 123–130.

Action Research and Process Management. From here I refer to the ALARPM/ ALARA World Congresses as the World Congresses.

DETAILS OF MEETINGS

First World Congress 1990 – Griffith University, Brisbane, Australia

Partner organisation:	Australian Institute of Training & Development
Convenor:	Ortrun Zuber-Skerritt
Theme:	'Action Learning for Improved Performance'
Keynotes:	Reg Revans, John Elliott, Sheila Harri-Augstein, Laurie Thomas

Second World Congress 1992 – University of Queensland, Brisbane, Australia

Convenor:	Patricia Weeks
Theme:	'Transforming Tomorrow Today'
Keynotes:	Peter Checkland, Bob Dick and Tim Dalmau, Orlando Fals Borda, Brian Hall, Robin McTaggart, Yoland Wadsworth

Third World Congress 1994 – University of Bath, United Kingdom

Convenors:	Pam Lomax, Jack Whitehead
Administrator:	Moira Laidlaw
Theme:	'Accounting for Ourselves'
Keynotes:	Pam Lomax and Jack Whitehead, Orlando Fals Borda

Fourth World Congress 1997 – Convention Centre, Cartagena, Colombia

Partner organisation:	Eighth World Congress of the International Participatory Action Research (PAR) Network
Coordinator:	Orlando Fals Borda
Theme:	'Convergence in Knowledge, Space and Time'
Keynotes:	Immanuel Wallerstein, Manfred Max-Neef, Agnes Heller, Marja Liisa Swantz, Rajesh Tandon, Robert Chambers, Robert L. Flood, Robin McTaggart, Ted Jackson, Rodolfo Stavenhagen, Anibal Quijano, Peter Reason, Budd Hall, Anisur Rahman, Eduardo Galeano
	Paolo Freire was advertised to be lead keynote but died two months before the World Congress.

Fifth World Congress 2000 – University of Ballarat, Australia

Partner organisation:	Ninth World Congress of the International Participatory Action Research (PAR) Network
Congress Advocate:	Stephen Kemmis
Theme:	'Reconciliation and Renewal – Through Collaborative Learning, Research and Action'
Keynotes:	John Gaventa, Evelyn Scott, Susan Weill, Patricia Maguire, Bob Macadam, Susan Goff, Yvonna Lincoln, Martin von

Hildebrand, Vijay Kanhere, Susan Noffke, Robert Flood, Munawuy Yunipingu, Anisur Rahman, Victoria Marsick, Isaac Prillitensky, Robert Chambers, Deborah Lange

Sixth World Congress 2003 – University of Pretoria, South Africa

Partner organisation: Tenth World Congress of the International Participatory Action Research (PAR) Network, and five South African technical and higher educational institutions
Convenor: Tessie Herbst
Theme: 'Learning Partners in Action'
Keynotes: Ortrun Zuber-Skerritt and Thomas Kalliath, Peter Reason, Cheryl de la Rey, Susan Weil and Danny Burns, Ineke Buskens, Richard Bawden, Tim Dalmau

Seventh World Congress 2006 – University of Groningen, Netherlands

Convenor: Ben Boog
Theme: 'Standards and Ethics in Participatory Research'
Keynotes: Ben Valkenburg, Yoland Wadsworth, Judi Marshall, Michiel Schoemaker, Øyvind Palshaugen, Sandra Schruijer, Naomi Scheman, Julia Preece

Eighth World Congress 2010 – Bayview Eden Hotel, Melbourne, Australia

Partner organisations: Institute for Development Studies, UK; Deakin University
Convenor: Jacques Boulet
Theme: 'Participatory Action Research and Action Learning: Appreciating our Pasts, Comprehending our Presents, Prefiguring our Futures'
Keynotes: Alan Rayner, Budd Hall, Linda Tuhiwai Smith, Yoland Wadsworth

CHARACTERISTICS OF WORLD CONGRESSES

Networking

Networking is a central feature of the World Congresses. Ortrun Zuber-Skerritt's European background and international perspective has brought to these congresses the fields of action learning and process management, and her numerous and extensive personal contacts. Her co-organiser Ron Passfield, a strong local networker and publisher, encouraged diversity and a focus on dissemination of thinking.

Congresses often arise out of partnerships with a related institution or network – most significantly with the international PAR network. Three World Congresses were held in conjunction with those of the older international Participatory Research Network (also called World Congresses: eighth in 1997, ninth in 2000, and tenth in 2003).

An important driver is the common experience by action researchers of isolation in situations where the field may be small and diverse or other methodologies have dominated. As an epistemology of change, action research also endures the paradox of simultaneous popularity and unpopularity as it questions how things are and how they could be otherwise. Networking serves a function of strengthening practitioners' confidence and theory of practice.

Individuals attending have been encouraged to network by different methods adopted at different world congresses. These have included daily-meeting affinity groups, the use of hosts and host groups in advance of the World Congress, the presence of central 'open space/marketplaces', continuous availability of refreshments in 'gathering spaces', extensive bring-and-share tables, poster displays and noticeboards, as well as the formal meeting of named sub networks including the five main 'strands, streams and variants' (see *Diverse contexts*).

Numerous and durable examples of international collaboration, co-research, co-writing and publishing, journal board participation, inter-country visitation and for teaching (including north-south alliances such as Ecuador, Britain, Netherlands, Tanzania, Australia and Bangladesh; or China, USA, Bangladesh, Israel and Norway) have followed from networking at World Congresses.

Diverse Contexts and Different Foci

The multiple 'strands, streams and variants' around which World Congresses have structured their programs have emerged from the social, historic, economic and political contexts in which the characteristics of action learning and action research have proved relevant.

The five key substantive topic streams have been education; agriculture, environment and farming; health, welfare and human services; community development; and business and management. The auspicing organisations also indicate a natural history of the key methodological interests of action learning, action research, process management and systems thinking, as well as the participatory research tradition represented in adult and community education; urban and community development; immigrant settlement; indigenous, consumer and other critical and appreciative movements; the colonised world and the natural environment. Other streams of interest are feminism, evaluation, organisational development, human resources, user-centred design and the climate emergency.

Creative Modes of Presentation

Reflecting the diversity of stakeholders and the methods needed to give voice to people's knowledge, experience, concerns and visions, the World Congresses have experimented with creative, artistic, aesthetic and alternative presentational methods, often in preference to traditional academic methods. World Congresses have pioneered, for example, an informal 'conversation pit', a 'Café of Possibilities', meeting spaces/market places, a 'Garden of Proposals', photographic displays, a video salon, song-writing, narrative-creation, memorabilia, dramatic presentations, and collective artworks. A conference dinner has on occasion enabled table groups to form small learning communities, for example, to create and present micro theatres representing key concepts of the field.

Built-in Evaluation

Each World Congress has developed methods to 'feel its own pulse' by encouraging small self-correcting action inquiry to better understand the nature of the World Congress experience for participants. Methods have included roving reporters, photographic and video narratives, a giant ear 'listening post', check-ins at the end of sessions, reflections by affinity groups/pods at the end of each day, post Congress written feedback, a published evaluation journal article, and follow-up reflection, report-back and sharing sessions by local networks.

Numbers

Typically attendances have ranged between a low of around several hundred and a high of 1,800 at Cartagena in 1997.

Participants in World Congresses

Those attending are employed or self-employed people working in schools, universities, higher education providers, technical and further education, government research departments, training and development agencies, health care, human resource management, consulting firms, NGOs, church organisations or community groups, small and medium size businesses or large corporations, finance, defence, police, agriculture, travel, real estate, architecture and engineering. Particular world congresses have attracted higher numbers than usual of Aboriginal/Indigenous/First Peoples, self-help group members, service-users, health service patients, consumers, residents, members of other communities-of-interest and citizen activists. To some extent the philosophy of co-researching has brought groups and teams of people to the world congresses, crossing boundaries of class and other distinctions.

GOVERNANCE AND AUSPICING ORGANISATION

World Congresses were initially auspiced by the founding group in Brisbane, Australia, but soon began to be hosted in other countries by local groups and institutions. ALARPM formed as a governance vehicle and continues, as ALARA, to be a core contracting, not-for-profit, non-government, community-based association, committed to continuity. ALARA is legally incorporated in Brisbane, Australia. ALARPM/ALARA expanded beyond organising the world congresses to develop an interested membership who meet locally or in state or national network meetings primarily in Australia. It also provides membership (called networking) directories; an online open access journal to circulate practitioners' accounts in accessible written form; and national conferences in Australia in the years between World Congresses.

To ensure the Australian basis of ALARPM did not skew governance of the World Congresses, and assisted by a participatory action research process facilitated by Susan Goff, ALARPM's committee of management became more internationally representative in 2001 with more than 20 members, of whom 17 were from countries outside Australia. An attempt to unite within a self-coordinating world network-of-networks with other national groups has been discussed at several World Congresses without practical result to date.

MANAGEMENT OF CONGRESSES

Various experiments with the continuum between central and local control led eventually to risk-management of potential losses by the ALARA Management Committee by use of a legally robust Memorandum of Understanding and a linked World Congress Policy as the basis for negotiating each local agreement to achieve transparency and equity. The Association's Global Vice President, supported by these two documents, establishes the World Congress Committee or subcommittee and any networked groups to support the Committee's work. Typically there is a local Convenor with the local committee, plus overlapping membership of some kind.

WORLD CONGRESSES AND THE DEVELOPMENT OF THE ACTION RESEARCH FIELD IN WIDER SOCIAL, POLITICAL AND ECONOMIC CONTEXTS

The World Congresses' themes and the nature of their sponsoring contexts illuminate their hermeneutic character in the context of the wider co-creating social, political and economic situations. For example, in 1990 the focus on *performance* reflected the concerns of a worldwide post-recession context. In 1992 a focus on *transformation* reflected introducing the community development and the health and human services streams, which in turn reflected desires for social change and improvement in a post-war era of change from the 1970s, and turbulence after the late 1980s' economic and technological business crash. In 1997 in South America, the focus on '*convergencia*' reflected the hitherto isolated 'strands, streams and variants' beginning to learn about each another in a rapidly globalising world economy.

In 2000 the focus on *reconciliation* in Australia highlighted the historic strengthening of Indigenous voices taking place, while in 2003 the focus on *learning* was situated within a post-reconciliation 'new South Africa'. By 2006 in the Netherlands, a focus on *standards*, with stronger representation of both agriculture and the environment, reflected a maturing field in a business world wanting to see grounded evidence of quality assurance and outcomes. And in 2010, back in Australia, a focus on *stock-taking* indicated the field's growth and consolidation after the long post-war era, its taking a strong local–global perspective on international development, merging with the new systems thinking, and joining the action research epistemology with biological and ecological systemic approaches, to address more deeply the growing imbalances of wealth, power and environmental degradation worldwide.

OTHER INTERNATIONAL CONFERENCES

Over the decades of the World Congresses, a wide range of local, regional and nationally based action research associations, groups and networks has also formed around the world, as well as a growing number of consultancies, academic groups and centres. Only one other of these networks has held regular international conferences. Originally titled the Classroom Action Research Network with a teaching/learning and education focus, the UK-based Collaborative Action Research Network (CARN) broadened to include other professions and disciplines. The World Congresses and CARN remain the only research associations/networks currently offering opportunities for action researchers and those using related methodologies to meet internationally to further the work of the field.

As a steadfast member of CARN, Ortrun has attended and promoted CARN international conferences and held hopes that CARN and ALARA might act in concert to further the complementary aims of each of these pioneering organisations in the future.

CONCLUDING REFLECTION

Ortrun continues to work on a world stage to further the aims of taking action learning and action research to a scale at which innumerable opportunities unfold for further networking and collaboration on knowledge co-creation. Indeed, Ortrun has not only organised key proponents and participants to attend and speak at the world congresses, and attended every World Congress herself, but has also captured people's voices as outcomes of world congresses in her own subsequent writing and publishing projects (e.g., Zuber-Skerritt, 2009, 2012). It is fitting that this Festschrift for Ortrun is presented at the ALARA World Congress in Pretoria, South Africa in 2015, 25 years and nine World Congresses after her commencing them in 1990. We hope an equally fitting continuation of Ortrun's invaluable contribution to the field will be achieved as World Congresses continue in the spirit of international networking and collaboration far into the future.

REFERENCES

Wadsworth, Y. (2010). *Learning from our experience of 20 years of ALAR(PM) world congresses.* Unpublished Presentation to Plenary Symposium – Celebrating 20 years of ALARA: Revisiting the past for present and future. PAR&AL (ALARA) World Congress, Melbourne.

Wadsworth, Y. (2014). World congresses of action research. In D. Coghlan & M. Brydon-Miller (Eds.), *Encyclopaedia of action research* (pp. 826–829). London, UK: Sage Publications.

Zuber-Skerritt, O. (2009). *Action learning and action research: Songlines through interviews.* Rotterdam, The Netherlands: Sense Publishers.

Zuber-Skerritt, O. (Ed.). (2012). *Action research for sustainable development in a turbulent world.* UK: Emerald.

Yoland Wadsworth
Adjunct Professor
RMIT University
Melbourne
Australia
Hon. Principal Fellow
University of Melbourne
Australia
and
Distinguished Fellow of the Action Research Center
University of Cincinnati
USA

PART IV

FUTURES

BOB DICK

11. ACTION LEARNING AND ACTION RESEARCH FOR A TURBULENT FUTURE

INTRODUCTION

Among other things, Ortrun Zuber-Skerritt and I share a birthday. We were born on the same date just one year and half-a-world apart. We share also an interest in the commonalities between action learning and action research, and their applications in education and numerous other settings. Ortrun's many publications include, for example, examinations of action research and action learning in the service of change (e.g., Zuber-Skerritt, 2001), the focus of most of my own work.

In addition we have both explored the future of action learning and action research in the world of increasing complexity and turbulence (Zuber-Skerritt, 2012). Since our births, the world has shrunk enormously to the point where 'global village' is only a mild exaggeration. Partly because of that interconnectivity, we believe the world most probably faces greater turbulence and unpredictability. That, and the combination (and potential contribution) of action learning and action research, is what I wish to address here.

ACTION LEARNING AND ACTION RESEARCH

Action learning and action research have differing provenance, different originators, and initially different literatures that overlapped very little. The development of action learning is attributed to Reg Revans, with earlier seeds in his experience as a physicist at the Cavendish Laboratories. Kurt Lewin is usually credited with the beginning of action research, with earlier threads present in the copious writing of John Dewey (e.g., 1929) and other influences from the work of Paulo Freire (1972). According to Boshyk, Barker and Dilworth (2010) there is no evidence that Revans and Lewin ever even met. I suppose it's no wonder then that I came across action learning and action research in different ways and at different times.

I think I first encountered action learning in 1970. I say 'think' because it wasn't titled action learning. It was known as the productivity group movement, championed by the Department of Labour and National Service (1959), where I was employed as an Industrial Psychologist. A productivity group consisted of senior managers who met regularly in the style of traditional action learning sets. They helped each other to resolve the problems they faced in their businesses. I noted with interest that rural productivity groups seemed to function better than city groups. City productivity

J. Kearney & M. Todhunter (Eds), Lifelong Action Learning and Research: A Tribute to the Life and Pioneering Work of Ortrun Zuber-Skerritt, 133–146.

group members were typically drawn from the same industry. As this wasn't possible in provincial centres the rural group members were more diverse, and usually weren't competitors. It was my perception that the greater diversity and openness enhanced the quality of their discussions. I concluded that the way participants related to each other was therefore important.

My colleague John Damm at the University of Queensland in the mid-1970s introduced me to action research. He used it in his own research and in his community development work. I adopted it in my own practice, initially because it suited my needs better than the quantitative methods I had learned as an undergraduate. It was promising enough in my consulting work to encourage me to continue its use. In my work as an educator I found it even more helpful. It assisted me to bring democracy and experiential learning into the university classroom. There is independent evidence (Johnston, 1984) that class members later found it very relevant to their work as practitioners, which was my intention.

I later explored the literature, curious how much overlap there was between action learning and action research. I found that during the 1970s MCB University Press journals had articles on both, though almost never (as far as I found) in the same article. In other journals, authors such as Malcolm Knowles (e.g., 1972) might occasionally mention both in the same paper. However, the context suggests that the term 'action learning' was then used as a label for experiential approaches generally. That may have been because Revans' influential books on action learning (1980, 1982, 1983) were yet to appear. MCB University Press also published a number of Revan's articles, too many to cite, mostly between the late 1970s and the mid-1980s.

For action research in small group settings, it seemed to me that the processes and principles were extremely similar to those of action learning. I was therefore surprised that action learning and action research had such different and independent origins. Yes, there were different emphases, though they mostly seemed to me to be trivial. It is more usual now for the similarities to be recognised, with action learning and action research generally regarded as part of the same family. Action learning has a prominent presence in the *Sage Encyclopedia of Action Research* (Coghlan & Brydon-Miller, 2014). Joe Raelin (2009) clearly treats them as closely allied members of the 'action modalities', and Carol Cardno and Eileen Piggot-Irvine (1996), for example, regard them (and experiential learning) as related practices that 'aim to narrow the gap between theory and practice' (p. 20).

For me, 1990 marks the year when action learning and action research were integrated. Ortrun Zuber-Skerritt (1990) linked them in a paper about university and management education. In the same year Ortrun was instrumental in setting up the First World Congress on Action Research and Process Management, subtitled *Action Learning for Improved Performance* (Wadsworth, 2014). Reg Revans was a keynote speaker. Arising out of a second Congress two years later, ALARPM (the Action Learning, Action Research and Process Management Association) was formed (Swepson, 2003). By then, I think it could be said, the marriage of action learning and action research was complete.

134

I will later return to action learning and action research. I will then explain the contribution I think they can make to coping with the uncertain future that may confront the world. Before that, however, I will sketch in what the future promises or threatens to be – as far as can be told.

A TURBULENT FUTURE

Some futurists believe that the future can be predicted. Ray Kurzweil (2005), for example, claims that by 2045 machine intelligence will exceed human intelligence, triggering a substantial change – the singularity – in human experience. Other futurists believe that the future is unpredictable, though increasing computing power may improve predictability. Most futurists, however, believe differently. They think that predicting the future is inherently impossible because we lack data from the future. The futurist Herman Kahn (1982, p. 82) sums up the unpredictability of the future by saying that 'The most likely future isn't'. Jim Dator (2002) argues that we can't *predict* the future. However, we can use data from the past and present to *forecast* possible and preferred futures. We can develop strategies that can help to increase the likelihood of the more preferred futures. That is what most futurists now do, and is part of my aim here.

Adam Kahane (2004) provides an encouraging description of the use of futures techniques in the Mont Fleur study, a scenario planning activity. In the early 1990s just before the 1994 post-apartheid South African elections, representatives of South African interest groups met to prepare for the future. They used scenario planning, a common futures technique. When four plausible scenarios had been developed it became clear that only one of the four offered a sufficiently promising future to all South Africans. As a result, many participants abandoned their earlier positions. They began instead to plan how they *might* support the emergence of the most promising of the four scenarios.

Whether or not we use actual futures techniques we can identify present trends that seem likely to continue. We can anticipate their possible effects. Among the many drivers that suggest increasing turbulence, two stand out. One is increasing globalisation. The other is the increasing power of technology. Those two drivers unite in the form of the internet and its supporting communication technologies. If those trends continue we can anticipate some of the effects and prepare for them.

It is easy to forget how much these trends have recently transformed the world. In my youth and for some years afterwards, reaching across the world would have required a physical journey, the sending of a physical letter, or a long-distance telephone call. However, at the time I had no such need. My communication was with those who lived and worked near me. Now I regularly communicate easily and almost instantly by email or Skype with friends and colleagues scattered across the globe. Some I have not met face to face. Similarly, in my younger years access to the literature required a visit to a library or a long wait for a physical copy of a book or article. Now much of the world's literature is available at the tap of my keyboard.

135

To glimpse the extent of technological changes consider Moore's Law. Though not a law in the same sense as a law of physics, it captures well the developments in communication technology miniaturisation. In 1965 Moore (1965/1998) used it to summarise the speed of technological improvement in electronics. He reported that the number of transistors accommodated within an integrated circuit had recently doubled every two years. He projected what would result if the trend continued. Despite suspicions occasionally being voiced (e.g., by Kish, 2002) that the 'law' would eventually collapse, it still holds today. Technological innovation averts each threatened breakdown. Today's electronics can thus be *over a million times smaller* than in 1959. Are you impressed? I certainly am. To illustrate, the smartphone in my pocket has more processing power than the GE225 computer that occupied an entire room in the computer centre at the University of Queensland in the mid-1970s.

That processing power applied to communication technologies has interconnected the world. A global economy has resulted. The increased interconnectivity has come at a cost, however. As connections have increased, so have turbulence and unpredictability. The context in which our organisations and other social systems are obliged to operate is increasingly characterised by volatility, uncertainty, complexity and ambiguity – VUCA in shorthand (Arnold, 1991).

There are organisations and projects that follow current trends to try to look ahead. The Millennium Project is one. Each year since it was founded in 1996, it has tracked global progress on 15 indicators of global wellbeing (Glenn, Gordon & Florescu, 2014). It increases its reach by drawing on information from 50 'nodes' of volunteers around the world.

The 2014 report is able to report some improvements in global wellbeing. Child mortality is falling. Global wealth, education and life expectancy have increased. In many other respects the news is less promising. The environment is suffering, with falling water tables, increasing ocean acidity and growing ocean dead zones. The topsoil of the world is disappearing. Pollution is severe in many parts of the world. Youth unemployment is dangerously high. Civil liberties are being eroded while bribery and corruption are substantial. Socially, the wealth and income gap has increased substantially. As Piketty (2014) has catalogued, wealth and income are increasingly concentrated in the hands of few. In the absence of corrective actions Piketty expects the concentration to increase further.

Much of the corporate world has thrived, becoming globalised to benefit from the global economy. Multinational corporations move to jurisdictions where tax is lowest and labour is cheapest. They manipulate internal charges to minimise their apparent profit. They arrange their financial affairs so that they earn money where it is plentiful but pay taxes elsewhere. No effective system of global governance keeps them in check. As David Korten (1995, 2009) has documented, they thrive at the expense of nation states and citizens. In much of the developed world, governments respond by *supporting* business and curtailing welfare. Governments use free market rhetoric to justify reducing welfare while willingly distorting the market to benefit business. In return, business supports financially those governments that are cooperative, aiding their re-election.

Where might this lead? It seems unlikely to me that it can continue. I agree with Sitrin and Azzellini (2014) that citizens will retaliate as they realise that their governments act mainly in the interests of the rich and powerful. Movements such as Occupy, the Arab Spring, the 'umbrella revolution' in Hong Kong, and the upsurge of local democracy may be the beginnings. On the web there is increasing reference to revolution and to tumbrels, the cart used during the French revolution to take the aristocracy to their appointment with the guillotine. So far, most of the references I have seen are humorous. I recently saw a photo (on Bill Moyers' website http:// billmoyers.com) proclaiming 'The French aristocracy never saw it coming, either'.

It's not that I'm in favour of violent revolution. The excesses of the French revolution provide sufficient warning of the risks involved when the tumbrels roll. Any resulting *liberté*, *egalité* and *fraternité* were short-lived. However, it seems to me that we have lost control of our governments, which corporations have taken over. I am pessimistic about being able to win them back. Instead, my preference is for a quiet and peaceful revolution where we intervene *locally*. We can take back for ourselves those matters that we can decide at local level in communities and organisations. There, action research and action learning can offer some strategies. In particular, I see benefit in the cyclic nature of action research, the nesting of those cycles to increase resilience, and the valuing of participation and equity so that *everyone* can benefit.

THE ACTION RESEARCH CYCLE

Current action research literature identifies the mindset and values of action research as more important than its methods. According to this view, action research is an 'orientation to inquiry' rather than a methodology, as Peter Reason and Hilary Bradbury (2008, p. 1) expressed it in their introduction to the second edition of the *Sage Handbook of Action Research*. Elsewhere, various chapters of the handbook make clear that participation and collaboration are important components of that orientation. Those affected by a decision are involved (in theory, as equals) in decision-making. The benefits can be substantial. The valuing of equality is reinforced. Relevant information is more likely to be available. The involvement of those who have to act on the decisions is more likely to enhance their commitment to the decisions.

I would go further. In my experience the attitude of participants towards each other affects the outcomes of their deliberation. A genuinely collaborative culture improves the quality of listening. When participants can express disagreement in supportive and non-blaming ways they are often able to craft a deeper and more effective agreement from their disagreement. Common dysfunctional behaviours are an obstacle to effective decision-making, as Argyris (2010) has explained. In conventional communication styles, important information – especially about untested assumptions – is suppressed. A culture to overcome such dysfunction is not easily achieved, as Argyris notes. But when Argyris's processes and concepts are integrated within an action research approach, communication effectiveness is improved. More effective collective action can result.

The cyclic process of action research is mentioned often in the action research literature, though less emphasised than in the past. Earlier literature gave it more prominence. Beginning with Lewin (1946, p. 38), action research was described as a 'spiral of steps each ... composed of a circle of planning, action, and fact-finding about the result of the action'. I doubt that Lewin invented this cycle. It is a natural way for me to respond to novel situations. Faced with an unexpected problem I first engage in fact finding, collecting information about the situation. I then devise a strategy for dealing with the problem. I try out my strategy, and notice how well it works (or doesn't). Many or most other people would do the same, I think.

At its simplest the action research cycle is an alternation between action and reflection. Practice and theory are thus integrated within each cycle, as are rigour and relevance (Coghlan & Shani, 2013). This, too, is my approach to my own work and life. I use the action research cycle to build ongoing learning and improvement into my work – as Peter Checkland (1981) did to develop soft systems methodology.

Other writers describe the same cycle with different numbers of steps, differently labelled. For Susman and Evered (1978) the cycle had five steps: diagnosing, action planning, action taking, evaluating and specifying learning. An often-used variation, especially in the educational literature, is the Kemmis and McTaggart (2005) cycle of plan, act and observe, and reflect. There are other variations too, as Geof Hill (2014) has explained. Mike Pedler (2008) describes a cycle specifically for action learning as: action, learning, reflection and re-framing.

The same cycle, again differently labelled, crops up in the experiential learning literature – reasonably enough, as action research and action learning incorporate experiential learning. Learning emerges from experience. Best known is the cycle expounded by David Kolb (1984): active experimentation, concrete experience, reflective observation and abstract generalisation. Again, many variations exist. Palmer (1981) lists, compares and analyses six of them.

Less obviously, the quality management cycle is in effect similar: plan, do, check, act (or sometimes plan, do, study, act). Developed by Shewhart (Best & Neuhauser, 2006), it was further popularised by Deming (1986). In that form, the cycle has particular relevance to the present discussion.

Explicit in much discussion of the Deming cycle (as it is often called) is the goal of continuous improvement. The cycle isn't applied once only. It is instead intended to be a way in which people *continue* to act, modifying and improving their behaviour as their experience accumulates. Less explicitly, in this form of the cycle there is a hint that the 'do' may be a trial action nested within the larger 'act' of continuous improvement. If cycles can be thus nested, and therefore applied at different scales of time and scope, flexibility and usefulness can be much increased.

NESTED CYCLES

Let me illustrate the application of nested cycles over different time scales with an example from my work as educator. At the University of Queensland I facilitated a fourth-year unit in *Advanced Social Consultancy* as an elective within a psychology honours program. I used action research and action learning principles and processes to design and facilitate it. With certain non-negotiable limits it was self-managed. Within it, class members and I together negotiated in turn the course content, the course process and learning activities, and the tasks for which we would each take responsibility. Class members were organised in small self-selected groups that functioned as action learning sets, for collaboration and mutual support (Dick, 1989).

Within the unit the action research cycle was applied at multiple scales, from the whole year to in-the-moment facilitation and reflection:

- At year's end the class met off-campus to evaluate the unit. Responses were captured as two lists of suggestions: (a) to me, about what I could do differently the following year, and (b) to the members of the next class. Both lists were conveyed to those enrolled in the unit the following year. In addition, previous and current class members met face to face near the beginning of each year.
- Mid-year, we set aside about half a day to evaluate the first semester. In the first class of second semester we applied what we had learned from that evaluation. We modified the class content, process and roles accordingly.
- In addition, from time to time during both semesters we set aside brief time, perhaps a couple of hours, to review our progress so far and to make minor adjustments.
- Weekly, most of the classes consisted of experiential workshops (usually two each week) designed and facilitated by small groups of class members (or occasionally by me). Remaining class members were the participants. Each such workshop (including those I facilitated) concluded with an evaluation by the participants.
- Authors accompanied every written assignment with a brief evaluation of what they believed was most and least effective about their work. This was to encourage them to treat all work as work in progress, capable of further improvement. In addition, to encourage critical reflection authors were asked to include a brief account of what they had learned from planning and writing the assignment.
- In all experiential activities, class members were encouraged to pay moment-by-moment attention to what was happening so that they could adjust their plans accordingly. They were also given the opportunity to critique their colleagues' facilitation and my own.

The philosophy exemplified by the approach above accords with a saying attributed to Dwight Eisenhower: 'Planning is everything – the plan is nothing'. A planning process is undertaken to anticipate what might happen. It is not intended to be followed closely no matter what happens. The reflection component of the action research cycle serves the purpose of noticing what worked and what didn't and revising plans accordingly. The more changeable and unpredictable the situation, the greater are the benefits of this approach. In changeable situations, behaviour is preferably a response to what actually happens rather than observance of a pre-determined plan.

I suspect that almost all action researchers subscribe to a similar philosophy. Yet nested cycles are less often mentioned in the action research literature than is the basic action–reflection cycle. There are some exceptions. Dennis List (2006) writes of cycles within cycles in his description of the use of action research in scenario planning. Dawn Buzza and her colleagues (Buzza, Kotsopoulos, Mueller & Johnston, 2013) espouse the advantage of recursive cycles for learning. Mary Edson (2012), drawing some of her inspiration from the ecological work of Gunderson and Holling (2002), remarks that recursive cycles contribute resilience to a project team. Holling (1973) has elsewhere identified recursive cycles as a contribution to the resilience of ecologies, including social ecologies. I return to this topic shortly.

Similar ideas occur in various literatures (including action research) using different terminology. Xavier Deroy and Stewart Clegg (2014) label a similar concept recursive contingency. Jon Dron (2014) refers to a similar approach as tinkering and bricolage. The latter term is increasingly common in the qualitative research literature at least since its use by Denzin and Lincoln (2000) and particularly by Joe Kincheloe (2001, 2005).

For Charles Lindblom (1959, 1979) the equivalent term was 'muddling through'. He explained that this was how *experienced* administrators responded most effectively to complex problems. They avoided the more systematic approach they had been taught and that the literature then recommended. I interpret this to mean that trial and error is most virtuous when the situation is most complex and therefore least predictable. Raymonde Guindon (1990) observed a similar phenomenon in software design. In theory, design was to be top-down using the 'waterfall' method: data collection followed by analysis, solution development and finally implementation. In practice the designers alternated between understanding and solution in a seemingly chaotic fashion, driven by emerging opportunities. For complex problems and situations I conclude that highly structured processes on their own are inadequate.

Let me summarise the preceding sections before addressing practical implications. My intent has been to explain that action research and action learning use iterative cycles, producing an evolving and continuously improving process of trial and error, informed by experience. Applying the cycles recursively, nested within one another and applied at very different time scales and scopes, further amplifies the flexibility and responsiveness. The increasing uncertainty occasioned by globalisation and technological change can therefore be better managed.

The formal origins of action learning and action research may be traceable to the middle of the twentieth century. However, my assumption is that their nested cycles approach has been practised for much longer. I suspect that our species, or at least some of its members, have always responded in like manner to unexpected and problematic situations. Such situations threaten to be more common in the future than they have been in the past.

On current evidence (Davies, 2013) it seems unlikely that governments will respond to an uncertain future with approaches that attempt to meet the needs of all. As those who are disadvantaged react, the result may be resolute but peaceful revolutions that seek to restore local agency – or so I hope. Events accompanying the recent global financial crisis reveal the opposing views of governments and citizens. Most governments supported the banks that triggered the crisis. They financed the bank bail-out by penalising the victims. In response around the world, citizens have voiced their dissatisfaction in social media and/or on the streets. The question becomes, how constructive an outcome is possible? Can action learning and action research contribute to that outcome, and how? As Tony Stevenson (2009, p. 669) framed his corresponding challenge to futurists: 'Do we re-imagine the future; and if so, how do we put new ideas into practice?'

CREATING A RESILIENT SOCIAL ECOLOGY

I recall images on television of the Occupy Wall Street movement in Zuccotti Park, New York, in 2011. Committed to democratic and egalitarian decision-making, the participants adopted procedures that were egalitarian (Calhoun, 2013), but also necessarily cumbersome. Humans are a tribal species, Robin Dunbar (1998) reminds us, that function most effectively in smaller groups. As numbers increase, egalitarian decision-making becomes difficult and inelegant. I don't know if Dunbar's explanation based on brain size is correct. His description of the consequences of growth in numbers accords well with my own experience.

As an action learning team grows beyond three or four participants its efficiency drops, though increased diversity may repay the drop. Thus, Alan Lawlor (1991) reports a preferred learning set size of four to six (though he encourages a willingness to innovate in this regard). Small groups experience a transition from easier to more difficult functioning as they add members. In my own work I've had good results from action learning sets of three participants, encouraging them to co-opt another person or two temporarily into the group for specific information or expertise.

In university classrooms and in public workshops I've found another transition occurs at about 40 participants or a few more. Up to this size, in a one-semester class or in a two-day workshop I find it worthwhile to spend time on building an overall sense of community and collective responsibility. For numbers beyond that it is easier for me to ask participants to form small groups, and to provide relationship building primarily within those groups.

It therefore seems to me that a resilient social ecology is likely to be based on small groups, with as much decision-making and action as possible devolved to them. Above, I mentioned a fourth year university class in social consultancy. It was organised on similar lines. Small groups were given as much autonomy as possible. For whole-class decisions, structured processes were used to encourage equal participation in decision-making. There is good evidence (Emery, 2010) that in organisational settings, relatively high small-group autonomy enhances both performance and satisfaction.

Even in that class, though, class members assumed responsibility only after other outcomes were achieved. We had first to establish a sense of community in the class, and clarify our expectations of one another. Anxieties associated with assessment had to be resolved. I therefore facilitated the first three or four weeks of each class, investing time in building relationships and clarifying the possibilities and the limits.

My consulting experience is similar. When I establish action learning sets I am usually present for the first three meetings. (These learning sets usually consist of diverse project teams with a joint project.) In the first meeting I clarify the project by helping the learning set to define the desired outcomes of their project work. I do relationship building as intense as the learning set willingly permits. We do some preliminary work on deciding the processes used for decision-making. We list absent stakeholders, so that we can take their views and interests into account. At a second meeting, a member of the learning set facilitates. I act as a supportive coach. By the third meeting my hope is that I will seldom need to intervene. Most learning sets by then have shown that they are capable of self-management.

Such experience persuades me that citizens can similarly take local control of aspects of their life and work that are within reach. However, not everything can be done in very small groups. For some issues, coordination is needed between the small groups. In university classes I facilitated whole-class decision-making using very structured processes: defining the purpose, sharing and analysing the relevant information, then making the decision. In both organisational and community settings I have facilitated structured 'visioning' processes (Emery & Purser, 1996) so that the organisation or community selected desired projects. Small groups of volunteers then became learning sets, one for each project, dispersing responsibility more widely.

For coordination I also established one action learning set whose project was to keep learning sets informed about each other's progress and emerging needs. My aim was to create a communication hierarchy that was not a control hierarchy. The coordinating group provided lateral coordination and communication. It had no control over the decisions or actions of the other project teams, which operated within the brief developed by the community in the visioning activity.

These specific designs might or might not work well in different situations. I developed them using action research, continuously improving them until I and others were satisfied with the outcomes they allowed us to achieve. I assume that in seeking to re-establish local control, citizens would similarly use the recursive cyclic process of action research to refine their approach in the light of their experience. Better, then, that they begin if possible from values and principles rather than from 'recipes'. Let me specify some of the principles that have informed my own experimentation.

In 2010, Adam Kahane reflected on his experience of the Mont Fleur study mentioned earlier. He decided that the Mont Fleur processes worked when they achieved a best-of-both-worlds combination of a desire to achieve one's purpose and the drive to form close relationships with others. Similarly, Dee Hock (2005) contemplated the difficult path to success in establishing Visa International collaboratively. He recalled that difficult problems were overcome only when participants were able to achieve both the desire to succeed and the grace to compromise.

I came across these accounts soon after they were published. In reading both of them I was reminded that Anton Zijderveldt (1972) proclaimed that we are both individuals and social beings. In seeking to improve my practice in education and facilitation I found it useful to remember this. There are both constructive and unconstructive outcomes of our individuality and our sociality. For me, in community or organisation, effective processes are those that achieve the constructive forms of both. Individuals contribute their experience and effort for the common good. The communities or organisations value the wellbeing of all, in word and especially in deed.

To achieve this, I think, two components are needed. First, whole-community or whole-organisation decisions take into account the wellbeing of all. This is done by engaging everyone. Leadership is facilitative and engaging rather than controlling. As much decision-making as feasible is devolved as close to the workface or community face as possible. Second, collaborative small groups build and maintain good internal and external relationships. They function with substantial autonomy and shared leadership, making local decisions as they respond to emerging local circumstances. At all levels, common ground and transparency and openness are sought, with attention to both present and likely future imperatives. Shared reflection is common, supporting learning and continuous improvement.

This, then, is my intent and hope for the community and organisational response to a future I expect to be turbulent. Large group decisions will be made effective through the use of skilled facilitation, lateral coordination and well-designed and well-structured processes. But by default, as much as possible of the decisions and responsibility will be devolved to small groups and teams, largely self-managed. There, the nested cycles of collaborative action learning and action research will achieve an appropriate balance between individuality and sociality, for individual and collective benefit.

REFERENCES

Argyris, C. (2010). *Organizational traps: Leadership, culture, organizational design.* Oxford, UK: Oxford University Press.

Arnold, A. V. (1991). *Strategic visioning: What it is and how it's done.* Carlisle, PA: US Army War College.

Best, M., & Neuhauser, D. (2006). Walter A. Shewhart, 1924, and the Hawthorne factory. *Quality and Safety in Health Care, 15*(2), 142–143. doi:10.1136/qshc.2006.018093

Boshyk, Y., Barker, A., & Dilworth, R. (2010). Milestones in the history and worldwide evolution of action learning. In Y. Boshyk & R. Dilworth (Eds.), *Action learning: History and evolution* (pp. 117–204). Basingstoke: Palgrave Macmillan.

Buzza, D., Kotsopoulos, D., Mueller, J., & Johnston, M. (2013). Exploring the relationship between self-regulated learning and reflection in teacher education. *Journal of Teaching and Learning, 9*(1), 1–12. Retrieved from http://ojs.uwindsor.ca/ojs/leddy/index.php/JTL/article/view/3578

Calhoun, C. (2013). Occupy Wall Street in perspective. *British Journal of Sociology, 64*(1), 26–38. doi:10.1111/1468-4446.12001

Cardno, C., & Piggot-Irvine, E. (1996). Incorporating action research in school senior management training. *International Journal of Educational Management, 10*(5), 19–24. doi:10.1108/09513549610146105

Checkland, P. (1981). *Systems thinking, systems practice.* Chichester, England: Wiley.

Coghlan, D., & Brydon-Miller, M. (Eds.). (2014). *Sage encyclopedia of action research.* London, UK: Sage.

Coghlan, D., & Shani, A. B. (2013). Creating action research quality in organization development: Rigorous, reflective and relevant. *Systemic Practice and Action Research, 27*(6), 523–536. doi:10.1007/s11213-013-9311-y

Dator, J. (2002). *Advancing futures: Futures studies in higher education.* Westport, CT: Praeger.

Davies, W. (2013). When is a market not a market?: 'Exemption', 'externality' and 'exception' in the case of European state aid rules. *Theory Culture and Society, 30*(2), 30–59. doi:10.1177/0263276412456567

Deming, W. E. (1986). *Out of the crisis.* Cambridge, MA: MIT Centre for Advanced Engineering Study.

Denzin, N. K., & Lincoln, Y. S. (Eds.). (2000). *Handbook of qualitative research* (2nd ed.). Thousand Oaks, CA: Sage.

Department of Labour and National Service. (1959). *Productivity groups.* Canberra, Australia: Australian Government.

Deroy, X., & Clegg, S. (2014). Back in the USSR: Introducing recursive contingency into institutional theory. *Organization Studies, 36*(1), 73–90. doi:10.1177/0170840614544556

Dewey, J. (1929). *The sources of a science of education.* New York, NY: Liveright.

Dick, B. (1989). *Mechanisms for democracy in learning: Some reflections on continuing experiments on democracy in the tertiary classroom.* Chapel Hill, Queensland, Australia: Interchange.

Dron, J. (2014). *Ten principles for effective tinkering.* In Proceedings of World Conference on E-Learning in Corporate, Government, Healthcare, and Higher Education, 2014 (pp. 505–513). Chesapeake, VA: Association for the Advancement of Computing in Education (AACE). Retrieved from http://www.editlib.org/p/149013/

Dunbar, R. I. M. (1998). The social brain hypothesis. *Evolutionary Anthropology, 6*(5), 178–190. doi:10.1002/(SICI)1520-6505(1998)6:5<178

Edson, M. C. (2012). A complex adaptive systems view of resilience in a project team. *Systems Research and Behavioral Science, 29*(5), 499–516. doi:10.1002/sres.2153

Emery, M. (2010). Refutation of Kira & van Eijnatten's critique of the Emery's open systems theory. *Systems Research and Behavioral Science, 27*(6), 697–712. doi:10.1002/sres1010

Emery, M., & Purser, R. E. (1996). *The search conference: A powerful method for planning organizational change and community action.* San Francisco, CA: Jossey-Bass.

Freire, P. (1972). *Pedagogy of the oppressed.* Harmondsworth, England: Penguin.

Glenn, J. C., Gordon, T. J., & Florescu, E. (2014). *2013–14 state of the future.* Washington, DC: Millennium Project.

Guindon, R. (1990). Designing the design process: Exploiting opportunistic thoughts. *Human-Computer Interaction, 5*(2/3), 305–344. doi:10.1080/07370024.1990.9667157

Gunderson, L. H., & Holling, C. S. (2002). *Panarchy: Understanding transformations in human and natural systems.* Washington, DC: Island Press.

Hill, G. (2014). Cycles of action and reflection. In D. Coghlan & M. Brydon-Miller (Eds.), *The Sage encyclopedia of action research* (pp. 233–237). London, UK: Sage.

Hock, D. (2005). *One from many: VISA and the rise of chaordic organization.* San Francisco, CA: Berrett-Koehler.

Holling, C. S. (1973). Resilience and stability of ecological systems. *Annual Review of Ecology and Systematics*, *4*, 1–23. doi:10.1146/annurev.es.04.110173.000245

Johnston, D. A. (1984). *Psychology in the 1980s: An ongoing search for an education and a career: The experience of recent fourth year psychology graduates of the University of Queensland* (Unpublished honours thesis). St Lucia, North America: Department of Psychology, University of Queensland.

Kahane, A. (2004). *Solving tough problems: An open way of talking, listening, and creating new realities.* San Francisco, CA: Berrett-Koehler.

Kahane, A. (2010). *Power and love: A theory and practice of social change.* San Francisco, CA: Berrett-Koehler.

Kahn, H. (1982). *The coming boom: Economic, political and social.* New York, NY: Simon and Schuster.

Kemmis, S., & McTaggart, R. (2005). Participatory action research. In N. K. Denzin & Y. S. Lincoln (Eds.), *The Sage handbook of qualitative research* (3rd ed., pp. 559–603). Thousand Oaks, CA: Sage.

Kincheloe, J. L. (2001). Describing the bricolage: Conceptualizing a new rigor in qualitative research. *Qualitative Inquiry*, *7*(6), 679–692. doi:10.1177/107780040100700601

Kincheloe, J. L. (2005). On to the next level: Continuing the conceptualization of the bricolage. *Qualitative Inquiry*, *11*(3), 323–350. doi:10.1177/1077800405275056

Kish, L. B. (2002). End of Moore's law: Thermal (noise) death of integration in micro and nano electronics. Physics Letters A, 305, 144–149. *doi:10.1016/S0375-9601*(02)01365-8

Knowles, M. S. (1972). Innovations in teaching styles and approaches based upon adult learning. *Journal of Education for Social Work*, *8*(2), 32–39. doi:10.1080/00220612.1972.10671913

Kolb, D. A. (1984). *Experiential learning: Experience as the source of learning and development.* Englewood Cliffs, NJ: Prentice-Hall.

Korten, D. C. (1995). *When corporations rule the world.* London, UK: Earthscan.

Korten, D. C. (2009). *Agenda for a new economy: From phantom wealth to real wealth.* San Francisco, CA: Berrett-Koehler.

Kurzweil, R. (2005). *The singularity is near.* Harmondsworth, England: Penguin.

Lawlor, A. (1991). The components of action learning. In M. Pedler (Ed.), *Action learning in practice* (2nd ed.) (pp. 247–259). Aldershot, England: Gower.

Lewin, K. (1946). Action research and minority problems. *Journal of Social Issues*, *2*(4), 34–46. doi:10.1111/j.1540-4560.1946.tb02295.x

Lindblom, C. E. (1959). The science of 'muddling through'. *Public Administration Review*, *19*(2), 79–88. Retrieved from http://www.jstor.org/stable/973677

Lindblom, C. E. (1979). Still muddling, not yet through. *Public Administration Review*, *39*(6), 517–526. Retrieved from http://www.jstor.org/stable/976178

List, D. (2006). Action research cycles for multiple futures perspectives. *Futures*, *38*(6), 673–684. doi:10.1016/j.futures.2005.10.001

Moore, G. E. (1965/1998). Cramming more components onto integrated circuits. *Electronics*, April 19, 114–117. doi:10.1109/jproc.1998.658762 [Reprinted in *Proceedings of the IEEE*, *86*(1), 82–85.]

Palmer, A. B. (1981). Learning cycles: Models of behavioural change. In J. E. Jones & J. W. Pfeiffer (Eds.), *The 1981 annual handbook for group facilitators* (pp. 145–154). San Diego, CA: University Associates.

Pedler, M. (2008). *Action learning for managers.* Aldershot, England: Gower.

Piketty, T. (2014). *Capital in the twenty-first century* (E. Goldhammer, Trans.). Cambridge, MA: Belknap Press.

Raelin, J. (2009). Seeking conceptual clarity in the action modalities. *Action Learning: Research and Practice*, *6*(1), 17–24. doi:10.1080/14767330902731269

Reason, P., & Bradbury, H. (2008). Introduction. In P. Reason & H. Bradbury (Eds.), *The Sage handbook of action research: Participative inquiry and practice* (2nd ed., pp. 1–10). Los Angeles, CA: Sage.

Revans, R. W. (1980). *Action learning: New techniques for management.* London, UK: Blond & Briggs.

Revans, R. W. (1982). *The origins and growth of action learning.* Bromley, England: Chartwell-Bratt.

Revans, R. W. (1983). *The ABC of action learning.* Bromley, England: Chartwell Bratt.

Sitrin, M., & Azzellini, D. (2014). *They can't represent us!: Reinventing democracy from Greece to Occupy.* London, UK: Verso.

Stevenson, T. (2009). The future's history: Let's re-frame it. *Futures, 41*(9), 669–671. doi:10.1016/j.futures.2009.04.001

Susman, G., & Evered, R. (1978). An assessment of the scientific merits of action research. *Administrative Science Quarterly, 23*(4), 582–603. doi:10.2307/2392581

Swepson, P. (2003). A history of the Action Learning, Action Research and Process Management Association (ALARPM): From Brisbane (Australia) to the world through inclusion and networks. *Systemic Practice and Action Research, 16*(4), 237–281. doi:10.1023/A:1025085221964

Wadsworth, Y. (2014). World congresses of action research. In D. Coghlan & M. Brydon-Miller (Eds.), *Sage encyclopedia of action research* (pp. 826–829). London, UK: Sage.

Zijderveldt, A. (1972). *The abstract society: A cultural analysis of our time*. Harmondsworth, England: Allen Lane the Penguin Press.

Zuber-Skerritt, O. (1990). Management development and academic staff development through action learning and action research. *Education Training and Technology International, 27*(4), 327–347. doi:10.1080/1355800900270411

Zuber-Skerritt, O. (2001). Action learning and action research: Paradigm, praxis and programs. In S. Sankaran, B. Dick, & R. Passfield (Eds.), *Effective change management through action research and action learning: Concepts, perspectives, processes and applications* (pp. 1–20). Lismore, Australia: Southern Cross University Press.

Zuber-Skerritt, O. (Ed.). (2012). *Action research for sustainable development in a turbulent world*. Bingley, England: Emerald.

Bob Dick
Graduate College of Management
Southern Cross University
Australia

RICHARD BAWDEN

12. RESEARCHING PLAUSIBLE FUTURES

Managing the Process

PROLOGUE

Like other contributors to this Festscrift I am sure, I owe Ortrun Zuber-Skerritt a considerable intellectual debt of gratitude. In my own case this flows from the opportunity that she provided for me to collaborate with her in exploring the vital nexus between learning, researching, process management and change. This collaboration was not simply an academic exercise. In addition to our shared passion for the intellectual foundations of action researching and experience-based learning as critical forms of human inquiry, we were, as we remain, also united in our commitment to putting such processes to practical use. This was most especially within a context of the strategic development of organisations and institutions. In particular, as we submitted in a co-authored piece nearly a quarter of a century ago, our appreciation of process management lay with its focus on change as well as its embrace of relationships rather than tasks, of its basis in human values, and, very significantly as it was to transpire particularly for me, of its orientation to the future.

In this chapter, I explore some of the significance and also challenges of learning both *for* the future and especially *from* it that have become evident to me as I have further pursued their strategic significance. This progression of interest was certainly inspired and informed, at least in part, through my collaboration with Ortrun all those years ago. If we can learn to transform everyday lived experiences into informed action, as both experiential learning and action research insist, then it should be possible to translate what we might learn *from* experiences of futures that 'can be imagined into being' into informed strategic actions that are appropriate *to* the actual future that does unfold.

INTRODUCTION

It is easy, it would seem, to overestimate the capacity of systems of social behaviour to change in response to challenges from the often turbulent environments in which they must operate. The recurrence of systemic failures, generation upon generation, reinforces the often cited claim that so little is learned from past experiences that the same errors are not only repeated into the present but will almost assuredly also

J. Kearney & M. Todhunter (Eds), Lifelong Action Learning and Research: A Tribute to the Life and Pioneering Work of Ortrun Zuber-Skerritt, 147–161.

recur repeatedly into the future. This occurs even under circumstances where the motivation for change comes from the increasingly obvious and urgent necessity to correct systemic failures that we ourselves have generated. In this context, the overall strategic social challenge, as Milbraith (1989) argued a while back now, is for us to have to learn how to 'learn our way out' of the unsustainable social/environmental 'mess' that we have created for ourselves. There are two essential prerequisites for such a learning strategy in the search for a sustainably desirable and ethically responsible future state: (a) the development of learning competencies appropriate to the complexity of the challenge, and (b) the articulation of the characteristics of the desired, sustainable 'destination'. Indeed the creation of a vision of a future for civilisation that is desirable, sustainable, fair, equitable and inclusive of humans and the rest of nature alike has been called the 'greatest task facing humanity today' (Constanza, 2000). This in turn emphasises the argument that 'learning is the basic process to be managed whenever changing circumstances are involved' (Bawden & Zuber-Skerritt, 1991). The context for this statement at the time of writing was the submission that 'a new management style' oriented towards processes rather than products, 'was beginning to pervade Australian businesses and institutions of higher education'. Process management, it was argued, is a learning process that is 'oriented towards change, the future, and the needs of society or a particular group of people' while also encouraging the clarification of goals and the identification of their means of achievement.

In the event, the claim of the pervasiveness of the adoption of a new future-oriented learning focussed 'management style', has proved to be either very premature or a 'false dawn'. Visions of coherent, desirable, inclusive, fair and equitable, and sustainable futures remain rarely encountered within the rhetoric of governments or of commercial or bureaucratic organisations – or most especially (and tragically) of institutions of education, to say nothing of the dearth of actual strategic developments that reflect them. Meanwhile such commitment that has been made to 'learning as the basic process to be managed' has had its progress significantly impeded by the distortions of power in at least two ways. In the first place there is the clear influence that it is those who control resources and provide governance who essentially determine the strategic directions of institutional systems – come what may. Far less evident, but probably even more significant, is the restricting impact that prevailing worldview beliefs and assumptions have on the creation of responsible visions for a desirable future and on the generation of strategies for dealing with the crises that it brings as it continues to unfold; or on any learning for that matter.

Given the significance of worldview perspectives to the ways by which we humans make meaning from the phenomena that we experience in the world about us, and thence to the actions that we take, it is quite amazing that these perspectives have not gained the emphasis that they deserve in management processes. Rarely do they surface as foci in institutional system development and management, and rarely indeed do they appear as central features of cognitive development, in any of the core functions of institutions of higher education: curriculum, operations, research or engagement.

The Nature of Worldviews

It is not as if the matters of worldviews and their impact on learning through the frameworks of what Kitchener (1983) refers to as epistemic cognition, have remained unexplored. In his explication of the history of the concept of worldview (*Weltanschauung*) for instance, Naugle (2002) concluded that it 'has enjoyed a distinguished place in the history of recent thought'. Hiebert (2008) observes further that interest in worldview has, in particular, 'emerged during the past two decades as an important concept in philosophy, philosophy of science, history, anthropology and Christian thought'.

Worldviews are sets of beliefs and assumptions 'that describe reality' where a focus on them allows 'a greater understanding of the human experience' (Kolto-Rivera, 2004). They are the 'usually taken-for-granted and often idiosyncratic values, norms and beliefs that constitute our individual and socialized view of the world' (Plas, 1986). They encompass sets of beliefs and assumptions about the nature of reality (ontologies), the nature of knowledge (epistemologies), and the nature of human nature, with particular respect to values that include ethics and aesthetics (axiologies). Embracing the logic of epistemic cognition proposed by Kitchener (1983) as the highest level of a three level model of learning as cognitive processing, and extending the notion of episteme conceptualised by Foucault (1970) as 'epistemological unconsciousness', it is possible (and pedagogically useful) to present worldviews as epistemic perspectives.

These perspectives are held so deeply that, as one commentator has recently put it, to question them is 'to challenge the very foundations of life' and 'people resist such challenges with deep emotional reactions' (Hiebert, 2008). Others have made similar observations about the tenacity with which worldviews are held, with Checkland (1981) arguing that, as a consequence, major intellectual efforts are needed 'to analysis and dispute them'. Furthermore, subscription to what might be termed the 'official' worldview, the epistemic perspective that comes to prevail within societies and to pervade all institutional systems, invariably results inthe denial of alternative worldviews. Norgaard (1994), for example, has argued that the pervasive societal embrace of the worldview of modernism 'has led us into, prevented us from seeing and kept us from addressing interwoven environmental, organisational and cultural problems'. This epistemic 'myopia' is self-perpetuating within what Yankelovich (1991) refers to as 'an imperative of our Culture of Control', where advanced industrial democracies are characterised by the use of 'expert-driven technology to achieve what is essentially a controlled way of life'.

In this vein, it has recently been argued that the really inconvenient truth about climate change, as a crisis of almost unparalleled dimensions, is that it is not essentially about carbon at all but about capitalism (Klein, 2014): It is a war 'that the prevailing economic model is raging against life on earth'.

The Epistemic Challenge

Given the nature of these intellectual and value-laden cognitive impediments, the strategic challenge for all institutional systems is to elaborate ways to escape the confines of prevailing epistemic perspectives to allow them to 'see' different potential future states of the 'world out there' that otherwise might be beyond their imaginations: To liberate them cognitively such that they then might be able to envisage future circumstances that without epistemic challenge would probably remain 'unseen'. And a primary focus for such liberation for institutional systems is an appreciation of their own functional integrity, of the outcomes of their embeddedness within the 'higher order' supra-systems that comprise their environments, and of their own properties and behaviours that are emergent both through the inter-activeness of their sub-system components and the influence of their supra-systems (Ackoff, 1974). Learning to 'see' situations from such 'three-dimensional perspective' is an example of how changing worldviews can allow 'fresh interpretations of what is happening' as well as providing opportunities to generate 'new ideas as to what can be done about it' (Ackoff, 1974).

Scenario planning is an example of a future-oriented learning process that provides opportunities for the development of what might be termed 'epistemic consciousness' through existential experiences of futures that are imagined into being. Essentially, scenario planning exercises involve the generation and subsequent rigorous consideration of a number of different, but equally plausible future states of the environment of any system under consideration, which planners can use to guide the development of their strategic options for managing their systems in the face of potential changes (Swartz, 1991). In this manner it is possible to learn how to manage *for* the future by learning from imagined experiences *of* it, or as Fahey and Randall (1998) propose as the basic thrust of their notion of scenario learning, to learn *from* it.

It is this idea of scenario learning from the future that provides the basic conceptual foundations of a comprehensive action-researching endeavour to develop a methodology that its founders have called QUEST™ (Bawden & Freeman, 2007). The process is explicitly experiential, exploiting the essence of the cognitive dialectics, as identified by Kolb (1984), between immersion in concrete experience and the abstraction of conceptualisation on the one hand, and between reflective observation and informed actions on the other. Reflecting the conceptual framework of Ackoff (1974), it is also explicitly systemic, especially with regard to its functional integrity, its embedded organisational structure, and its potential for learning. And echoing the cognitive processing model of Kitchener (1983), it explicitly introduces participants in the process to three dimensions of self-reflexivity: cognition, meta-cognition and epistemic cognition.

QUEST™ AS A PROCESS MANAGEMENT APPROACH TO SCENARIO LEARNING

The Nature of Scenario Planning

The QUEST™ methodology shares the essential logic of all approaches to scenario planning. As the future rarely turns out to be a mere extension of the present, it is better to plan within a context of a range of different but plausible futures than it is to rely on a single plan based on the assumptions that a preferred future will unfold (Swartz, 1991). The majority of scenario planning approaches adopt the same basic linear systematic methodology, albeit often with variations on the central theme:

1. a key focal issue is identified within an organisation by a planning team that is regarded as 'future sensitive' and for which strategies therefore need to be developed;
2. key factors within a relatively local environment that might be influential with respect to that issue as the future unfolds are then identified;
3. attention then turns to the identification and rating (by their assumed criticality) of a significant number of 'driving forces' in the macro-environment that have the presumed capacity to influence how the key factors of the micro-environment might behave and these are then typically reduced to a very small number of pairs of critical variables consisting of diametrically opposed positions;
4. scenario logics are then generated from this information to reflect significant variations in the manner by which these environmental driving forces and key factors might plausibly develop as the future unfolds;
5. four or five of these different logics are then typically developed into comprehensive narratives of different potential scenarios of future environments to which the organisation will need to adjust (or, where possible, mitigate), and indicators for their emergence identified;
6. these scenarios are then put to use as different contexts for the development of rigorous strategic plans for dealing with potential future environmental changes.

QUEST™ has a number of significant points of departure from this standard scheme, especially with regard to its experiential nature, its innate systemicity and its emphasis on critical self-reflexivity. Conventional approaches to scenario work are typically systematic (as distinct from systemic) in structure with the scenarios created as outcomes of a linear progression of activities. The QUEST™ process, in contrast, is systemic with the different activities regarded as interacting sub-system components of a functionally integrated whole system of inquiry. The five essential sub-processes (represented by the five letters in the QUEST acronym) are conducted, in a manner inspired particularly by both the soft systems methodology (SSM) (Checkland, 1981) and critical heuristics of social planning (Ulrich, 1983).

Together, they are regarded as a functionally integrated system of interactive human activities that are freely iterative, recursive and critically self-reflexive. From this perspective, the essence of systemicity lies as much with the process of inquiry itself as it does with assumptions about the nature of the world 'out there'.

Q is the search for the *question* that most effectively reflects the 'future sensitive' issue of concern, which then forms the boundary of the system-of-interest that is identified – be it a whole organisation, a profession, a public service, or even a specific concern shared within an amorphous community. U is the generation of the *utopic* vision of the preferred ideal future with respect to the issue in question for the system-of-interest. E is the thorough and rigorous investigation of past, present and future *environments* of the system that are of relevance within the context of the future-sensitivity of the issue in question. S is the set of plausible *scenarios* that emerges from that contextualised environmental supra-system investigation. T are the *transformations* (a) in strategic directions for the system to meet the potential challenges presented by the different scenarios, (b) in the relationships within the groups of participants in the process through their systemic awareness, and (c) in the epistemic perspectives (worldviews) of all who are involved or are likely to be affected in some way or another.

The Essence of Systemicity

The innate systemicity of the approach is emphasised throughout the whole endeavour in two other major ways, the most fundamental of which is that the participants in QUEST™ projects are introduced at the very commencement of the exercise to the notion that they should consider themselves not just as a group of social learners working together on a task, but as a critical learning system. This is a whole system with functional integrity and interactive structure, which has the capacity to transform itself in a variety of ways. Furthermore, in acting in such a mode, participants are made aware that, reflecting Ackoff's (1974) three dimensional systems hierarchy, their system represents a key sub-system that is embedded within the system of their concern. Through its embeddedness in its environmental supra-system, their system in turn is vulnerable to the influences of the turbulent and unpredictable conditions that the latter can present to it.

In QUEST™ projects the participants are regarded not just as remote data collectors, environmental analysts, and creators of abstract scenarios, but also as totally embedded component parts of both the system of their concern and the environments in which that system is embedded. Through the reflexive experiential process, the participants live the process of imagining-into-being (a) themselves as a coherent learning (sub-) system, that (b) is embedded within the system-of-interest that is the focus of their strategic concern, and (c) in turn is potentially embedded in one or another of a panoply of different environments that the future might present to their systems and for which strategic options need to be developed. It is through the explicit experiential focus on the systemic nature of QUEST™ that participants are also existentially exposed to the significance of epistemic perspectives and to the 'felt' discomfort and dissonance that so often accompanies exposure to differences in worldview beliefs and value assumptions. Attention to such feelings and value expressions is encouraged throughout the exercise, as well as to intellect, imagination and intuition. This is achieved through the reflexive character of the process through which participants (the learning sub-systems) come to comprehend and thence express their own wholeness as human beings. They 'live' the different futures with a passion that is rarely encountered in those scenario approaches where the process is essentially an intellectual exercise in which the participants act in a somewhat detached abstract manner.

Systemic Practices

While systems ideas are often encountered within the now extensive literature on scenario planning and learning, they are rarely placed within an epistemic perspective. More typically they are included as aspects of the process, with the focus invariably set within what is referred to as the 'hard systems' tradition. This concerns itself with the nature and dynamics of 'real systems out there in the world' rather than the more abstract notions of self-reflexive inquiry systems with cognitive, meta-cognitive and epistemic dimensions as embraced within the 'soft' and 'critical' schools. These latter constructs reflect what Checkland (1981) describes as 'a shift in systemicity' from the real world to the process by which issues in that world are explored from a systemic perspective. Checkland emphasises that the process of inquiry itself is explicitly systemic, echoing the notion of learning systems presented by Ackoff (1974) and the descriptions of the nature and design of inquiring systems presented by Churchman (1971). In addition to their embrace of a holistic ontology, the 'soft/critical' systems processes assume an epistemology of contextualism in contrast to the objectivism of the logic of 'hard' systems (Bawden, 1998).

Examples of the adoption of 'hard' systemics processes within the scenario literature include systems simulation, system dynamics and causality analysis as included in their text on scenario planning by Lindgren and Bandhold (2003). More basic techniques in this regard are the 'iceberg analysis' for the identification of different layers of causal patterns, as described by van der Heijden (1996) and the 'dynamic scenarios analysis' of Ward and Schriefer (1998) 'where systems thinking meets scenario planning'. Even where planning is presented as 'a system', as in a recent text on scenario planning within organisations (Chermack, 2011), the focus lies with emphasis on the typical elements in 'hard' systems analysis such as inputs and outputs, without clear reference to the other key systemic concepts that include the key characteristic 'three-dimensional' embeddedness. Interestingly, Chermack uses that same 'hard' systems logic and language in presenting 'the scenario development phase' of the planning process as 'a system'.

The QUEST™ methodology is based explicitly on principles and practices of self-reflexive soft/critical learning/researching systems (Bawden, 1998). There is an explicit intention here to create epistemic consciousness through a rigorous process of self-conscious social learning and a tacit hope that such critical appreciation can then lead to actual epistemic transformation as one of the key outcomes of the entire process. In a recent book, Oliver Freeman, one of the founders of the book, and a colleague, describe in imagined detail four scenario narratives of the world in 2040, which they have generated and purposively called Worldview Scenarios 'as they each focus on a different social mindset, or worldview' (Watson & Freeman, 2012).

Critical Reflexivity and Epistemic Dimensions

The focus on systemics, it has been argued above, is one way of introducing the character and significance of epistemic perspectives or worldviews to QUEST™ participants through their reflections on their experiences of the process as they proceed through its various activities. But the epistemic consciousness that emerges from this focus is intentionally amplified by the emphasis on critical reflexivity, which like systemicity, pervades the entire practice. The framework for reflection sessions conducted throughout the process (and which participants are encouraged to pursue through their own personal reflections) is based on Kitchener's model. Again following Ackoff (1974), these three levels are best considered as being systemically embedded each within the other to create a functional whole. In this manner then, participants are expected, both individually and collectively, to reflect critically on, and thus learn (a) from the matter to hand at any given moment throughout the methodology – a cognitive focus; (b) on the process by which they are exploring or researching into that particular matter – a meta-cognitive focus, and (c) on the nature of the assumptions and beliefs that they are bringing to bear as they analyse their activities at the other two 'levels' – an epistemic cognitive focus. It is at this third level of reflection that specific attention is paid to the composition and character of worldviews as epistemic perspectives and to their crucial influence on the entire future-oriented researching endeavour. And once again this consciousness is drawn out from experiences of difference as felt by the participants and as informed by discussions and readings about psychological and philosophical aspects of epistemic perspectives.

This critical reflexive engagement with epistemic dimensions of learning again contrasts with most other practices of reflection within the scenario planning 'movement', although there are a number of clear exceptions to this convention.

In tracing the way of the pathfinders, Swartz, for instance, emphasised the seminal role that Pierre Wack, one of his fellow planners at the Royal Dutch Shell Corporation, played in the development of the scenario planning process.

Of singular significance in this regard was the concern that Wack came to place on 'the mind-set of decision-makers' (Swartz, 1991). The essential purpose of scenarios, Wack would argue in an article that he himself published in the Harvard Business Review, was to help promote changing views of reality; the purpose of scenarios, he submitted, represented the 'gentle art of re-perceiving' (Wack, 1985). This intent has also been captured in a relatively recent article by Wilkinson and Eidinow (2008) who submit that 'the discursive–analytical nature of scenario processes can ensure attention is focussed on different types of knowledge and uncertainty'. This focus, they argue, is especially useful in circumstances akin to what have been referred to as 'wicked problems' (Rittel & Webber, 1973).

In presenting 'aggressive challenges', such problems are characteristically 'messy and circular' with different stakeholders 'seeing' problematic situations, such as those associated with environmental/ecological crises, from different perspectives that lead to contradictory definitions of the actual constitution of the problematique.

This is a theme that has also been recently explored in the context of the development of 'scenario praxis for systemic governance' by Ison and his colleagues (Ison, Grant, & Bawden, 2014) under circumstances where, all too often, there is a systemic failure of governance where 'wicked problems' prevail. As an example they cite the work of Barnett and O'Neill (2010) who identify five maladaptive responses to climate change that result in increased social, environmental and economic adaptation costs because of 'a failure to consider the consequence of actions in relation to wider systemic effects'.

The emphasis on 'systemic failure' here returns us in recursive manner to the signal importance of the explicit systemic nature of QUEST™. As mentioned, the unfamiliarity to most, of the systems construct, of its basic principles and of the practices that reflect them both, provides opportunities for participants to actually experience the 'discomfort of the unfamiliar', which is characteristic of the tensions and cognitive dissonances associated with epistemic challenge. The experience is crucial to Wack's insistence on scenario planning as an exercise in re-perception, although exception can be taken to his submission that it is a 'gentle art'. Evidence to the contrary is provided by work that illustrates that the epistemic challenge essential for the adoption of systemic ways of dealing with world needs is tantamount to a combination of existential shock and both intellectual and ethical demands (Salner, 1986). And this has clear methodological implications both in terms of the provision of appropriate 'shocks and demands' and of support for the vulnerability that the inevitable 'emotional outbursts' display.

Three Final Features

Three further aspects of the QUEST™ methodology approach are worthy of mention in bringing to closure this elaboration of it as a vital expression of the nexus between learning, process management and change.

As mentioned earlier, the U in the acronym represents the generation of the *utopic* vision of the preferred ideal future with respect to the issue in question for the system-of-interest. This is a relatively recent addition to the methodology – so recent in fact that it does not even rate a mention in the version published most recently by Watson and Freeman (2012). There has always been an understandable reluctance, within the entire community of scenario planners, to encourage participants to generate details of their ideal futures lest it detract from the fundamental assertion of the process that it is about avoiding getting the future wrong rather than trying to get it right! Furthermore, the process by which such an ideal state of affairs is generated bears little resemblance to the scenario planning process. It is essentially an unbounded statement of total optimism about the state of the system independent of the environmental supra-systems in which it is embedded, and it is based on a non-reflexive process of envisioning rather than on the analysis/synthesis dialectic of the scenario process.

There are, however, at least four arguments that can be mounted to support the inclusion of a deliberate envisioning activity within the QUEST™ approach. In the first place, and somewhat perversely, it can be included as the very antithesis of the process of scenario planning! In a more positive vein, its inclusion is recognition of the significance of the clarification of goals by any institutional system; it is a cliché, but one really does need to have a destination in mind if one is to design effective ways of getting there. A third rationale in this regard is that collective envisioning provides another milieu for the development of epistemic consciousness through differences between individuals within any group (learning sub-system) that will inevitably emerge with respect to what constitutes the ideal as well as details of the future that is preferred. And these differences can be further amplified if the envisioning process includes a motivation to explore not just what a desired future *would* look like, but, normatively, what it *should* look like. In this context, James Ogilvy is among those who believe that whole scenario planning process itself can be used with a normative thrust as a process that can be used for designing better futures; 'scenario planning as a tool for a better tomorrow' (Ogilvy, 2002).

It is a fourth feature of the envisioning activity that is of most significance to the utopic aspect of QUEST™. Once a vision has been generated for the future of the system-of-interest, an opportunity is provided for the introduction of the crucial task of a 'back-casting' activity that focusses on the imagined circumstances that would have had to have occurred in that system's environments, to have enabled it to achieve its ideal state. This allows the introduction not only of methods of analysis appropriate to the methodology but also of a formal conceptual framework for structuring such an analysis. The framework presents six domains of variables in the environment, which are the sources of the key variables of future change. Given the insistent focus on systemicity throughout this narrative, it might seem a contradiction to introduce the idea of a framework that differentiates the environmental supra-system into different domains as indeed the QUEST™ suggests, with its distinctions between natural, social, political, economic, cultural and technological influences (NSPECT).

During the actual process of exploring the wide range of potential variable factors in the environment of imagined futures, the focus is as much on the possible outcomes of the inter-relationships between variables in the different sectors as it is on plausible dynamics of change within each of them. A rich tapestry of plausible multi-factorial variations that might characterise different future states of the environment emerges, through a combination of the collective imagination, intuition and application of instrumental and systemic logic, by the participants. As it is from this admixture that the logics for different scenarios are generated, it is essential that the 'tapestry of ideas' is as rich as possible in the variations that it identifies. And this in turn dictates that the process is as democratic as possible and, vitally, as unconstrained by the influence of any single dominant epistemic perspective.

In the QUEST™ methodology, attention is drawn to these possibilities by the addition of the letter [I] to the six domains of the environment to create [I]NSPECT. This addition represents I for interpretation, which provides an indication that matters of distortions need to be addressed, be they inter-personal, intellectual, or value-based. The [I] is placed in parenthesis as it is not a domain in the sense of the other six elements, but a focus for interpretation of all of them. Its addition also provides a clever heuristic with its conversion of a set of letters into a true acronym whose meaning is not only relevant to the nature of the process of what might be termed 'environmental imagining', but also conveys an imperative to action.

The [I] also presents a very appropriate segue to the central activity of the creation (some refer to it as the invention) of a small set of plausible scenarios, with each one describing a future state that contrasts markedly with the others in that set. In QUEST™ the practical techniques of scenario generation, refinement, and conversion into compelling narratives, follow the standard practices of most scenario planning processes, with the notable addition that comes with the inherent systemicity of its methodology. In addition to employing the conventional inductive and deductive processes to invent and refine different scenarios, QUEST™ participants are also encouraged to allow these scenarios to 'emerge' somewhat unconsciously or intuitively!

A common criticism of scenario planning endeavours is that with a few notable exceptions, the attention paid to the use of generated scenarios is far less rigorous than that paid to their generation. The T of the QUEST™ acronym represents a response to that inadequacy with its emphasis on transformation as a facet of equal importance to all of the other activities of the methodology. Not to address implementation, of course would be a repudiation of the claim that the approach is explicitly experiential in nature. It would also be a failure to exploit the systemic essence of the entire endeavour. It will be recalled that the identification process of the question-at-issue extended to its inclusion in a system-of-interest. In other words, the character of the question constituted the boundary conditions of a system-of-interest that might be an entire organisation or a coherent public service or a profession or a community group or a specific issue of concern within any of those entities. As the letter T in the acronym suggests, the anticipation is that the scenarios will indicate the need for transformation(s) in the system-of-interest in ways that permit it to develop strategies that allow (a) adaptation to changes in its supra-system, and/or (b) reduction or even eradication of negative impacts that it might be having on that supra-system, and/or (c) mitigation of a range of other potential impacts, and/or (d) the system-of-interest to actually influence the supra-systems in ways that are favourable to it. And of course, as it is the learning sub-system that is responsible for the design of these strategic responses, it too must be open to the prospect of self-transformation, particularly with regard to both its meta- and epistemic dimensions.

A third acronym is TWO CAGES, which is a variation on one developed by Smyth and Checkland (1976) for use with the soft system methodology. It is introduced as appropriate to the matter of implementation where any transformations (T) that are indicated, are subjected to an analysis that embraces the need to address (a) the Worldview (W) or epistemic perspective that supports its rationale, (b) the potential influence – negative as well as positive – of those who constitute the Ownership (O) of the system-of-interest, (c) the Community or Clientele (C) that comprises the intended beneficiaries of any strategic changes, (d) those Agents or Actors (A) who will need to be involved in the actual practical transformative activities, (e) the Guardians (G) who hold the responsibility for the interests of those who might be adversely affected by any strategic changes but whose voices are typically not heard, (f) the nature of the Environment (E) being considered (as represented by the different scenarios), and then finally (g) the System (S) of human activities that will need to be designed to enable any proposed strategic transformations to occur.

CONCLUSIONS/REFLECTIONS

So there it is – an example of how the nexus of learning, process management and change can be practically expressed within a context of learning *from* the future as a guide to learning how to deal with the turbulent changes it characteristically presents as it unfolds in all of its unpredictability, uncertainty, and sheer messiness. While not a direct collaborator with me in my engagement with my endeavours in process management of learning for the future from the future, it was Ortrun Zuber-Skerritt who provided intellectual foundations upon which I have subsequently built. It was she, after all, who in her inimitable style told me the nature of the business that I was really in!

This was, to say the least, a tad unnerving at the time. As a University Dean of Agriculture and Rural Development, I had, to that point in my career, felt fairly clear about the nature of the work that I did. I was also relatively confident about the character of the contributions that I was making as an academic, to those particular societal domains. A Faculty Dean, as I construed the role, had a variety of different functions and responsibilities across all four of the conventional core roles of academia. I had oversight of the experiential curricula of the undergraduate students in our Faculty as well as holding the responsibility for the overall management of the operations of that quite complex organisational unit. My brief also included the leadership of the systemic research and scholarly efforts of our body of academics and graduate students. Finally I was a very active participant in what today would be referred to as critical engagement with a host of stakeholders in the status and fate of rural Australia.

All of that variety notwithstanding, the essential nature of all that I was doing, Ortrun assured me, was managing learning processes. So persuasive was she in that assertion that she convinced me to join her in co-authoring a chapter on learning, process management and change for a monograph that she was editing on action learning and performance improvement (Zuber-Skerritt, 1991)! It was through our collaboration in co-writing that piece in particular that I really did come to re-conceptualise – and indeed re-orient – the 'business that I was in'. Ortrun was correct of course, for while I had never formally articulated my career focus to that point, it really had consistently been on the development of development processes appropriate to 'learning our ways into better futures'.

And then, at the very time that Ortrun and I were working together on our chapter, I had the great fortune of meeting Oliver Freeman who was also involved with exploring avenues into better future. Our grand project, which continues to this day, has been the development of processes of learning how to learn *from* the future *for* the future by researching it. Our collaboration has been especially focussed on the development and application of the QUEST™ scenario methodology as an action researching project.

There is no doubt in my mind that it was through the critical appreciation of process management that Ortrun nurtured in me, that I was in a position to recognise the significance of 'learning critically from the future' when Oliver first suggested that he and I collaborate. As with Ortrun, Oliver and I were not only from different intellectual traditions but we were not even in the same formal business, for he was a publisher at that stage and I, an academic. It was only later that we morphed into consultants.

What the three of us have in common is the shared belief that learning is indeed 'the basic process to be managed whenever changing circumstances are involved' as we had posited all those years ago (Bawden & Zuber-Skerritt, 1991), with QUEST™ an example of the 'new management style' that we asserted was emerging way back then!

REFERENCES

Ackoff, R. L. (1974). *Redesigning the future: A systems approach to societal problems.* New York, NY: John Wiley and Sons.

Barnett, J., & O'Neill, S. (2010). Maladaptation. *Global Environmental Change, 20,* 211–213.

Bawden, R. J. (1998). The community challenge: The learning response. *New Horizons, 99,* 40–59.

Bawden, R. J., & Freeman, O. (2007). Scenario planning as an experiential exercise in social, reflexive and transformational learning. Richmond Occasional Papers. Retrieved December 12, 2014, from http://fuureshouse.com/library.html

Bawden, R. J., & Zuber-Skerritt, O. (1991). Learning, process management and change. In O. Zuber-Skerritt (Ed.), *Action learning for improved performance.* Brisbane, Australia: AEBIS Publishing.

Checkland, P. B. (1981). *Systems thinking systems practice*. Chichester, UK: John Wiley and Sons.

Chermack, T. J. (2011). *Scenario planning in organizations: How to create, use, and assess scenarios*. San Francisco, CA: Berrett-Koehler.

Churchman, C. W. (1971). *The design of inquiring systems*. New York, NY: Basic Books.

Constanza, R. (2000). Visions of alternative (unpredictable) futures and their use in policy analysis. *Conservation Ecology, 4*, 5–22.

Fahey, L., & Randall, R. M. (1998). What is scenario learning? In L. Fahey & R. M. Randall (Eds.), *Learning from the future: Competitive foresight scenarios*. New York, NY: John Wiley and Sons Inc.

Foucault, M. (1970). *The order of things: An archaeology of the human sciences*. New York NY: Pantheon Books.

Hiebert, P. G. (2008). *Transforming worldviews: An anthropological understanding of how people change*. Grand Rapids, MI: Baker Academic.

Ison, R., Grant, A., & Bawden, R. J. (2014). Scenario praxis for systemic governance: A critical framework. *Environment and Planning C: Government and Policy 2014, 32*, 623–640.

Kitchener, K. S. (1983). Cognition, metacognition, and epistemic cognition: A three level model of cognitive processing. *Human Development, 26*, 222–232.

Klein, N. (2014). *This changes everything: Capitalism vs. the climate*. New York, NY: Simon & Schuster.

Kolb, D. A. (1984). *Experiential learning: Experience as the source of learning and development*. Englewood Cliffs, NJ: Prentice Hall.

Kolto-Rivera, M. E. (2004). The psychology of worldviews. *Review of General Psychology, 8*(1), 3–58.

Lindgren, M., & Bandhold, H. (2003). *Scenario planning: The link between future and strategy*. Basingstoke, Hants: Palgrave Macmillan.

Milbraith, L. W. (1989). *Envisioning a sustainable society: Learning our way out*. New York, NY: State University of New York Press.

Naugle, D. K. (2002). *Worldview: The history of a concept*. Grand Rapids, MI: Wm.B.Eerdmans Publishing Co.

Norgaard, R. B. (1994). *Development betrayed: The end of progress and a co-evolutionary revisioning of the future*. London, UK: Routledge.

Ogilvy, J. A. (2002). *Creating better futures: Scenario planning as a tool for a better tomorrow*. Oxford, UK: Oxford University Press.

Plas, J. M. (1986). *Systems psychology in the schools*. New York, NY: Pergamon Press.

Rittel, H., & Webber, M. (1973). Dilemmas in a general theory of planning. *Policy Sciences, 4*, 155–169.

Salner, M. (1986). Adult cognitive and epistemological development in systems education. *Systems Research, 3*, 225–232.

Smyth, D. S., & Checkland, P. B. (1976). Using a systems approach: The structure of root definitions. *Journal of Applied Systems Analysis, 5*, 75–83.

Swartz, P. (1991). *The art of the long view: Planning for the future in an uncertain world*. New York, NY: Currency Doubleday.

Ulrich, W. (1983). *Critical heuristics of social planning: A new approach to practical philosophy*. Chichester, UK: John Wiley & Sons.

van der Heijden, K. (1996). *Scenarios: The art of strategic conversations*. Chichester, UK: John Wiley and Sons Inc.

Wack, P. (1985). The gentle art of re-perceiving. *Harvard Business School Working Paper*. Cambridge, NY: Cambridge University Press.

Ward, E., & Schriefer, A. E. (1998). Dynamic scenarios: Systems thinking meets scenario planning. In L. Fahey & R. M. Randall (Eds.), *Learning from the future: Competitive foresight scenarios*. New York, NY: John Wiley and Sons Inc.

Watson, R., & Freeman, O. (2012). *Futurevision: Scenarios for the world in 2040*. Brunswick, Victoria, Australia: Scribe Publications.

Wilkinson, A., & Eidinow, E. (2008). Evolving practices in environmental scenarios: A new scenario typology. *Environmental Research Letters, 3*, 1–11.

Yankelovich, D. (1991). *Coming to public judgment: Making democracy work in a complex world.* Syracuse, NY: Syracuse University Press.

Zuber-Skerritt, O. (Ed.). (1991). *Action learning for improved performance.* Brisbane, Australia: AEBIS Publishing.

Richard Bawden
Emeritus Professor
University of Western Sydney
Australia

RICHARD TEARE

13. APPLYING THE CONCEPT OF LIFELONG ACTION LEARNING

Learning and Development for a Better World

INTRODUCTION

Ortrun Zuber-Skerritt's contemporary ideas about Lifelong Action Learning (LAL) are grounded in the work of the Global University for Lifelong Learning (GULL). This chapter profiles Ortrun's contribution to the LAL concept and to GULL's work since its launch in 2007. The chapter also outlines how Ortrun's personal and scholarly insights have helped to shape an inclusive approach to learning and development that encourages and strengthens low income and subsistence communities. As a vehicle for LAL, GULL aims to harness the potential of people to bring about positive change and in particular, greater self-reliance and financial independence. It is a self-directed process of learning and growth that can be shared with others. The importance of LAL is also reflected in sustainable transformation – a form of practical 'self-help' that yields on-going personal and community benefits.

Ortrun's substantial contribution to the literature on aspects of Action Learning and Action Research (ALAR) is internationally recognised and widely acknowledged by people all over the world who draw on her work. To shed light on *why* her contribution is so significant, I aim to highlight some of the ways in which Ortrun's generosity of spirit, visionary thinking and commitment to action underpin her many books. The chapter opens with a personal tribute to Ortrun (modelling action leadership) and continues by tracing her contribution to GULL's work with reference to five books she has authored, co-authored and edited since 2009. This chapter 'Applying the Concept of Lifelong Action Learning' is divided into two parts, 'Learning Communities' (2009–2012) with reference to *Action Learning and Action Research: Songlines through Interviews* (2009); *Action Leadership: Towards a Participatory Paradigm* (2011) and *Action Research for Sustainable Development in a Turbulent World* (2012), and 'Self-directed community development' (2013–2015) with particular reference to *Lifelong Action Learning for Community Development: Learning and Development for a Better World* (2013) and also *Professional Learning in Higher Education and Communities: Towards a New Vision of Action Research* (2015). Given that the majority of the world's population lack options for personal and professional development, the final section, 'Learning and Development for

J. Kearney & M. Todhunter (Eds), Lifelong Action Learning and Research: A Tribute to the Life and Pioneering Work of Ortrun Zuber-Skerritt, 163–177.

a Better World', highlights the significance of Ortrun's contribution in relation to GULL's inclusive approach to learning and development.

MODELLING ACTION LEADERSHIP

It is both a pleasure and a privilege to contribute to a book about Ortrun Zuber-Skerritt's lifelong learning but it is also a rather daunting assignment as there is so much to say about Ortrun – an exceptional character who has generated a rich body of work throughout her career. To obviate the risk of duplication (others have known Ortrun and her scholarly contribution for much longer than I), this chapter centres on Ortrun's practical and theoretical contributions to a network movement initiated in 2007 by the Global University for Lifelong Learning (GULL). The chapter spans a relatively short time frame, beginning in 2008 when Ortrun and I began to discuss GULL's work. Since then, Ortrun has given freely of her time and energy and devoted space in five of her books to lead GULL's thinking about the concept of Lifelong Action Learning (LAL) and specifically how this can be applied in low income and subsistence communities settings. I am deeply grateful to Ortrun for her friendship, kindness and commitment to action leadership. Prior to sharing some personal reflections, I should like to outline the purpose of GULL and its vision for inclusive learning.

Enabling YOU to Make a Difference in OUR World

The official launch of the Global University for Lifelong Learning (hereafter referred to as GULL) took place on Friday 5 October, 2007 in the State Function Room, National Parliament House, Port Moresby, Papua New Guinea (PNG). The event was attended by both of GULL's founding Co Chancellors, Sir Paulias Matane, eighth Governor-General (Head of State) and Sir Michael Somare, PNG's Prime Minister. Among other acts of generosity by these two visionary national leaders, a limited edition stamp was issued in PNG to commemorate the launch event.

Why is this event relevant to the development of a new framework for lifelong action learning? The story began long ago in PNG and is mirrored by the early life of Paulias Matane. He was born in 1931 in a remote subsistence community in East New Britain Province, PNG. As both his parents died when he was a young boy, he was raised by his elderly grandparents. His grandfather told him that if he wanted to succeed in life, he had to be focussed, have a vision, set an objective, plan for it, and with total honesty, commitment and perseverance, he would reach his goal. Paulias followed his grandfather's advice and at the age of 16, he was able to attend school for the first time. He later became a Teacher, Headmaster, Schools Inspector and then National Superintendent of Teacher Education. After that, he served his country as a Permanent Secretary, an Ambassador, a High Commissioner, and as a Vice President of the United Nations General Assembly. On 26 May 2004 he was elected as the eighth Governor-General of PNG.

So what is the connection? During the late 1990s, I began to see for myself the myriad difficulties faced by a high proportion of the world's population and in particular, the limited educational provision available to them. It has always been and remains grossly unfair that the place where a person is born determines whether (or not) they have access to affordable education and other options for on-going personal development. Given this, a helpful response would be to establish an inclusive network in support of people like Paulias – *but how?* A credible alternative to the expensive and relatively narrow 'validated' or 'accredited' academic approach would be needed. A credible alternative finally began to take shape during a visit to the UK made by Sir Paulias in 2004. As a newly appointed Commonwealth Governor-General, he had travelled for an audience with Her Majesty the Queen. We met prior to this, and quickly discovered that we shared a similar vision. So we began to correspond by email about the basis for what became GULL's mandate to award professional qualifications. This took the form of a 'Statement of Recognition', which was signed by Sir Paulias and Sir Michael Somare on 10 April 2007. This Statement, which was offered in perpetuity, can be viewed in the 'Recognition' section at the GULL website, www.gullonline.org.

As GULL's work began, we sought to establish a decentralised network as a deliberate strategy for ensuring national and local ownership at the lowest possible cost. We wanted to base the network on traditional know-how and knowledge so that anyone could participate. GULL's approach is based on action learning 'pathways' to reflect the fact that lifelong learning is a continuing journey centred on the unique needs and aspirations of its participants. Above all, we wanted to offer a process that would enable participants to help themselves and then to help others, which is why we adopted the motto 'Enabling YOU to make a difference in OUR world'.

Among the government ministers and organisational leaders from other countries who have since endorsed GULL, the late Sir Howard Cooke, a former Governor-General of Jamaica used a memorable phrase to describe the essence of GULL's work. I met Sir Howard at his home in Jamaica in February 2008 and after explaining the concept of GULL, he responded by saying that he believed that a 'Genius of God' resides in each and every person and that GULL's approach to lifelong action learning would enable participants to discover and use their own unique 'genius' to help themselves and others. This is a concise and powerful summary of GULL's mission.

A Personal Tribute to Ortrun

While I was busy developing the GULL network, Ortrun observed with keen interest and offered to help shape and develop GULL's conceptual framework for LAL. She did this as she always does through stimulating discussion at her home during my annual visits to Australia and PNG and between visits by email. But Ortrun didn't stop there, she convened meetings with policy makers, academics, community leaders and others to sharpen our debates and she began to draw on the emerging body of GULL's experiences in the field to help shape, refine and better explain GULL's approach. It is hard to imagine how so much progress could have been made in just a few years without Ortrun's inputs.

Although we have known each other for a long time, we only began to collaborate in 2008 and these visits, once or twice a year, have been enormously fruitful. Ortrun has always offered to host my visits and has looked after me better than any upscale hotel ever could! She is an outstanding host with an eye for detail, a discerning palate and wonderful company with an ever-present zest for life. Among other wise suggestions, Ortrun felt that there should be a serious book about GULL's vision, mission and approach. Initially I resisted, countering that GULL's website (with almost 800 pages of information) was a 'living book' and that I didn't have time left over to write a book too. As anyone who knows Ortrun will testify, her intellect, determination and enthusiasm are among her outstanding qualities and gradually I began to accept that Ortrun – as ever – was right about this. GULL did merit a book and our collaborative effort (Zuber-Skerritt & Teare, 2013) is a highlight in my own writing career that had already spanned authorship and editorship of 20 books. I learned so much from co-authoring with Ortrun – her tenacity, focus, attention to detail and determination to ensure that we produced the best possible account of our work together is a reflection of her inquiring mind, resolve and professionalism.

My aim here is to draw on some of the scholarly contributions that Ortrun has initiated to support me, GULL and the many millions of people who we hope will benefit from GULL and/or from GULL's approach in years to come. Thanks to Ortrun, GULL has a robust conceptual framework, supported by her rigorous scholarship, and it is with heartfelt gratitude that I now reflect on some of Ortrun's notable contributions over the past few years.

APPLYING THE CONCEPT OF LIFELONG ACTION LEARNING

Learning Communities

As noted earlier, Ortrun and I re-connected in 2008 and at that time, work on her book *Action Learning and Action Research: Songlines through Interviews* (Zuber-Skerritt, 2009) was at a fairly advanced stage. Yet she found space and time to include a summary of our many long discussions in Chapter 9. The book focusses on how people can help themselves, improve their situation and their personal and professional lives through mutual support, collaborative problem solving, and action learning methodology. As Ortrun felt that GULL exemplifies this, we discussed how GULL's action learning pathways provide an enabling framework for self-directed development.

Initially we sought to follow the book's standard interview format which would have involved me posing questions to Ortrun about lifelong learning and GULL. After several attempts, Ortrun felt that it would be more informative and interesting if we reversed roles and in the end, Ortrun presented me with a skilfully crafted set of questions that drew out my experiences as an initiator, co-founder and designer of the GULL framework and lifelong learning system. This demonstrates Ortrun's pragmatism and determination to craft the book and this particular chapter in a way that would provide as much information as possible to the reader. It is the only chapter in the book in which Ortrun is the interviewer rather than interviewee.

In her postscript, Ortrun says that she is convinced that action learning at work is the best way of operationalising lifelong learning for personal, professional, community and organisational development. She adds that it was not until we met again that she realised that she hadn't yet succeeded in her wider objective of providing direct help to the poorest and disadvantaged. She had, though, provided indirect assistance over many years as a facilitator of 'train the trainer' and leadership development workshops. Ortrun felt that GULL provided a new channel that would enable her to re-think her work so that her future writing might focus on accessibility and inclusion at both conceptual and practical levels and she concludes by affirming her support for GULL in the following statement (Zuber-Skerritt, 2009, p. 182):

I have used and promoted action learning for more than 30 years in higher education and in professional and management development around the world and in the context of organisation development and leadership programmes in developing countries. It is in developing countries that action learning is particularly well suited to the challenges faced by the disadvantaged and the poorest. In view of my own experience and observations, I was delighted to hear about the launch and development of the GULL system and I am honoured to support GULL as one of its honorary officers. I wholeheartedly support GULL's philosophy, mission, method and philanthropy.

Ortrun's 2011 book *Action Leadership: Towards a Participatory Paradigm* ably demonstrates her willingness to reflect, to re-conceptualise and to take action in order to generate new thinking about learning and development. In re-reading the book, I noticed two key indicators in the preliminary pages. First, Ortrun had dedicated the book to the disadvantaged and oppressed and to those who help them: '...those with little hope and spirit, whether poor or rich, and to those who help these people attain empowerment, confidence and self-worth'. Then I read in the Foreword written by Morwenna Griffiths the following insight about Ortrun's own action leadership: '... Ortrun is able to be *of* academia but also to reach *beyond* it. She also makes her work relevant to a range of government and business organisations, all the while remaining interested in, and attuned to, recent academic theorising'. This is a very accurate comment on Ortrun's approach to scholarship and to cross-checking and adjusting conceptual frameworks until they accurately reflect practical realities.

The book goes on to exemplify Ortrun's resolve to build on earlier discussions about inclusive approaches to learning and her ability to be *of* academia but also to reach *beyond* it. As an illustration of this, Ortrun planned what turned out to be a memorable 'think tank' session, which took place on 22 April 2010. As is typical of her own action leadership style, she invited to her home a wide range of her friends, colleagues and others who she felt would have insights and expertise to share. The aim of the session was to discuss possible opportunities for disadvantaged communities in Australia and participants included representatives from the Samoan community, community educators working with migrants, progressive university academics and consultants in government and industry. Nineteen people participated in the think tank discussions and later enjoyed Ortrun's characteristically generous hospitality in the form of a sumptuous meal prepared with the assistance of several of her close friends.

The think tank participants came up with a long list of community groups that would benefit from GULL's approach, including refugees in camps; indigenous communities; illiterate and homeless people; certain migrant groups without government support for education; youth and school leavers who cannot find employment or apprenticeships; and the elderly or those in forced early retirement. The list of community groups also promoted an even longer list of ideas on how to approach and forge links and partnerships with existing networks, associations, foundations, organisations, and indigenous and other support groups.

At the end of the think tank session, participants were asked to devise a final statement and an interesting observation made by Ron Passfield drew on Seth Godin's (2008) book, *Tribes: We Need You to Lead Us*. Ron felt that GULL's model for self-directed learning mirrored Godin's rather visionary concept, namely that an action leadership network: Transforms shared interest into a goal and a desire for change; Provides tools to allow participants to communicate; and Leverages its 'tribe' to allow it to grow and gain new members (Godin, 2008, p. 25).

Ortrun's *Action Leadership* book opens by making the case for fresh thinking about ways to improve how people and organisations learn. As a vehicle for this discussion, Ortrun advocates for Participatory Action Learning and Action Research (PALAR), which she defines here as a way of thinking, feeling, living and being that is influenced by personally held values, worldviews and paradigms of learning. These in turn influence our behaviour, strategies, methods and ultimately our capacity for improvement and self-directed development. Ortrun links her own professional development journey with an evolving role for PALAR in relation to community development, action leadership development and the development of lifelong learning, and observes that GULL's approach integrates all three! In this context, it is helpful to summarise the key points made about each of these components:

- *Community development* can be viewed as a process of action learning and lifelong learning for individuals, groups and entire communities. The process can be led by an external facilitator, but ideally should become a self-sustained, self-directed and ongoing process in the communities where people have learnt to analyse and solve their own problems and improve their life and work situations themselves. Ortrun highlights the potential for assets-based community development as a means of identifying assets (skills, resources), strengths and issues in communities, social groups or informal networks. After this, community members can begin to build on strengths and encourage members to find their own solutions. In this way, assets-based community development is capacity and empowerment building and it helps to free communities from over-dependence on outside help.

• *Action leadership development* (for community development) is characterised by strategic vision, collaboration and networking, and by coordination, cooperation, commendation and communication. Action or collaborative leadership requires the leader to be concurrent, collective, mutual and compassionate with other leaders on an equal basis. In low income communities with limited opportunity for external networking, community leaders may need to prioritise the development of other leaders from within. In this context, the tools for envisioning, equipping and team-building and for action planning are likely to be important components of leadership development programs for community members as they must assume action leadership roles.

• *Development of lifelong learning* (for action leadership) is especially important in communities that have historically depended on outside help and assistance. Preparation for lifelong learning rarely features in traditional systems of formal education that are more often characterised by a teacher-led, content-centred, curriculum-oriented approach. If it is to succeed, lifelong learning must be learner-centred, self-directed, question/issue focussed, problem-oriented, participatory and collaborative, and an effective approach to developing lifelong learning is through participatory action learning and action research.

Ortrun concludes that an effective and affordable system is needed to foster and encourage action leadership and lifelong learning for community development and that GULL's approach meets this requirement.

Published in 2012, *Action Research for Sustainable Development in a Turbulent World* (Zuber-Skerritt, Ed.) explores the concept of sustainable development in both community and workplace settings. Ortrun's rationale for this broad-based review is driven by a desire to further explore contemporary approaches to individual and organisational learning in the context of rapid societal change. As ever, Ortrun builds on her prior work with a convincing case for an action leadership approach that is characterised by flexibility and responsiveness to change, and that encourages innovation in problem-solving. These features tend to ensure that action leaders are themselves experienced, open-minded people with an other-centred rather than self-centred approach and commitment to lifelong learning.

As a starting point, the book draws on prior descriptions of the learning organisation as a work environment that encourages members to draw from knowledge within the work organisation to strengthen their ability to think critically and creatively. The concept assumes that learning is an ongoing, creative and lifelong process, one that adapts and transforms in response to the needs and aspirations of people inside and outside the organisation. Building on this, Ortrun and her colleagues argue that these principles can and should be applied in other settings too, and that the collective of community – where people share interests, goals and resources – can become a vibrant learning community. Ortrun portrays a learning community as a place where its members live, act and interact as equals, express their ideas and challenge themselves and each other to achieve shared goals. If constraints relating to factors such as ethnic and cultural traditions and practices can be overcome, a learning community could in turn foster on-going or self-sustaining community development. The challenge, though, is to secure cooperation between individuals and groups, open and honest communication, and a culture of trust and respect. To reach this level of collaboration a community has to undergo several stages of dynamic change so that the learning community adopts and absorbs the features often attributed to the learning organisation.

As an enabler of change and of securing sustainable learning community status, Ortrun again concludes that PALAR coupled with GULL's approach to self-directed lifelong learning offers the toolkit needed for this purpose. To test this, the book features a case study that traces a Samoan learning community development project. The case study is set in Logan City, on the outskirts of Brisbane in Australia, and it outlines some of the benefits for the Samoan community relating to positive change that participants identified within their wider community. Participants' feedback and evaluative comments suggest both intangible and tangible outcomes. Intangible outcomes involve enhanced relationships amongst teachers, parents and children; better understandings of cultural issues by teachers; increased engagement of parents in their children's learning; improved behaviour and better learning by Samoan students at school; and more confident leadership within their community. By drawing on the participants' written and video-recorded comments on their experiences, it was possible to derive a learning community framework that is characterised by transformational lifelong learning, and as a result, by new ways of doing, knowing and being.

These three pillars of positive, sustainable change in the learning community are outlined in Table 13.1.

Table 13.1. Characteristics of a sustainable learning community

New ways of doing:	Action planning; communicating; collaborating; seeking opportunities; finding and implementing solutions
New ways of knowing about:	Self; others
	New concepts (Lifelong learning; action learning; action leadership)
New ways of being:	Optimistic; motivated; resilient; confident; persistent; reflective

Participant feedback relating to the development process was positive and constructive, and all participants felt that they had been able to develop personal skills relating to their own lifelong learning needs and aspirations, and that by sharing or cascading these skills to other community members, they had succeeded in building a stronger, broader capacity for sustainable community development.

Self-directed Community Development

The book, *Lifelong Action Learning for Community Development: Learning and Development for a Better World* (2013), aims to explain and demonstrate how indigenous communities can be extended and strengthened by the integrated methodology of Lifelong Action Learning (LAL) and by new approaches to learning and development as exemplified by the GULL system. As noted earlier, GULL aims to harness the potential of people to bring about positive change together, characterised by self-reliance, financial independence, and cascading learning and benefits to others. It is a self-directed and self-sustaining process of learning and growth. The case studies in the book provide evidence that over time, low income communities can achieve transformations that bring with them many benefits personally, professionally and for the community.

In Chapter 1, Ortrun provides a theoretical framework for integration of the main concepts of action learning and lifelong learning, and an explanation of a new paradigm of learning and development as an alternative to (but not in competition with) the formal educational system. As she observes, there are many publications that deal discretely with community development *or* action learning *or* action research *or* lifelong learning. The significance of this book is that it seeks to integrate these concepts.

As a starting point, Ortrun clarifies that action learning is learning *from* and *for* action. Learning *from action* means we learn by doing and reflecting on what went well and what did not, how and why. Learning *for action* means we learn for future action by drawing from and adapting our learning from past experience to create best possible outcomes. So action learning is an iterative, cyclical process of action–reflection–learning, and continuing to the next cycle of action–reflection–learning is always new but always informed by learning from previous cycles. It is especially effective if pursued collaboratively, while working with others in groups on work-based problems. Group working is important as it provides an informal vehicle for members to allocate time and space for reflective learning through dialogue and discussion.

Next, Ortrun contrasts Lifelong Learning (LL), which is mostly individual, with Action Learning (AL), which is mainly collaborative and developed intentionally. However, LL and AL share the philosophical understanding that knowledge can be created by 'reflective practitioners', that is, by anybody who learns how to create knowledge through experiential learning and solving real-life problems. In view of this, Ortrun argues that it is feasible to integrate the two concepts as Lifelong Action Learning (LAL). The integrated concept includes on the one hand the time and space of LL from birth to death and in participants' contemporary cultural contexts, and on the other the system and processes of action learning. Ortrun builds on this characterisation using the six interrogatives: who, what, when, where, how and why:

Who plays the main role? Who assumes the main responsibility for learning outcomes? Who is in the centre of attention? – It is the learner, not the teacher, who identifies and decides what needs to be learned. There is no fixed curriculum and participants formulate their own personal learning statement and work on this with support from a personal coach or mentor and share their learning with action learning group colleagues.

What is the content of learning? – It addresses a significant problem, issue or concern in the learner's life or workplace, which needs to be understood and solved collaboratively with others.

When does the learning take place? – Learners apply the principles of lifelong action learning as needed in daily life so learning is lifelong, active, continuous and recursive, irrespective of age, experience, and level of formal/ institutionalised education the learner has completed.

Where can LAL be practised? – Wherever it is needed to enable people to address and overcome difficulties and improve their lives in a sustainable way. It does not require established physical infrastructure such as learning centres, lecture halls or qualified teachers; participants continue to collaborate, reflect and learn wherever they are in physical space and time.

How does the learner learn? – Through developing an ability to understand and acquire or create knowledge continuously through experience, reflection on that experience, critical thinking, conceptualisation and innovative action, in other words through lifelong action learning – not by being told what to do and how to do it.

Why is this kind of learning important in the twenty-first century? – Because regardless of time and place it is effective in addressing the needs of the people involved and the communities in which they live. It leads to continuing improvement of life circumstances; sustainable community development; personal growth, empowerment and confidence; and importantly, then, to the learners' quality of life: physically, mentally, psychologically and spiritually.

The notion of 'emergent learning' is also a feature of LAL. Learning emerges in relation to a specific context so what we come to know is embedded, and its meaning and value are linked to a particular time and place. Emergent learning arises from our direct experience of the practical world; it is triggered by an unpredicted event. The process that follows has the possibility to create not only knowledge but also the wisdom we need to engage productively and effectively in a world of uncertainty. Emergent learning also means more than acquiring knowledge over a lifetime; it means that we create new knowledge continuously as we encounter new conditions and challenges. In this sense LAL is emergent, creating new knowledge continuously, and embedded in a particular context. In addition, LAL is developed collaboratively with others in groups, communities or organisations, in an intentional and systematic way, and is then cascaded to others.

As noted earlier in this chapter, GULL aims to provide an enabling framework for sustainable community development and, at the outset, facilitation of LAL provides a starting point so that individuals, groups and whole communities can begin to analyse and improve their real-life situations. Beyond this, GULL aims to enable learners to take charge of their own lives and work, discussing and reflecting with others on what has or has not worked, why and why not and how, and what needs to be done next, how and to what end. As a result of this approach to problem-solving through trial and error, discussion, reflection and learning, learners are able to apply their learning from one task to other tasks. This is essentially 'double-loop learning' that is reflected in changes made to goals, assumptions, values and/or standards for performance through mindful appreciation of the change process. As a precursor to this, single-loop learning occurs when the learner has changed action strategies, but as yet, the learner has not yet identified or digested the principles of the process for application elsewhere. It is a mechanical, technical or surface approach to learning, whereas double-loop learning takes a deeper and transformational approach that enables positive change. That said, in the context of twenty-first century living, GULL seeks to facilitate learning that extends far beyond the technical and superficial; it ideally needs to be transformational by registering at a deeper level and this is termed 'triple-loop learning'.

Applying these three levels or loops to community development, Ortrun observes that single-loop learning equates with the imposition of existing knowledge and strategies on the communities that are seeking help. Here, community members would do what they are told, how they are told, without learning how to learn reflectively and critically, to create knowledge for addressing future challenges. At the next level, double-loop learning encourages inquiry to find out what the community needs, using cross-cultural communication, dialogue and feedback, and in so doing, external facilitators would know what we didn't know before. Finally, by raising the proverbial bar, triple-loop learning encourages community members to question what they historically took for granted and as this level of learning is not imposed or predetermined, it is emergent, transformational and sustainable.

Transformational, sustainable community learning and development contrasts sharply with historical approaches that have tended to adopt a methodology that views 'development' as a process designed and directed from outside and then implemented in the community. LAL methodology is more radical than this – it is community improvement and development that is designed, directed and implemented from inside the community, by and for the community itself. In this

173

way, knowledge emerges to best suit what the community identifies as its needs and draws deeply on its ability to satisfy these needs in a sustainable way.

In a more recent book (Zuber-Skerritt, Fletcher, & Kearney, 2015), effective self-directed change is linked to the time spent thinking about the actions needed for transformational learning to occur. This is because critical reflection is a core component of holistic change and for GULL, it is the essence of 'professional learning' – a collaborative and holistic process that helps the learner to make deeper level behavioural changes too. The concept of 'professionalism' is generally considered to encompass mastery of a body of knowledge and skills and the appropriate mental framework to apply it effectively in different situations. In exploring this concept, Zuber-Skerritt, Fletcher and Kearney observe that professional learning applies across the spectrum of human activity, from technically qualified professionals like medics to unqualified subsistence farmers with technical mastery based on traditional knowledge. Furthermore, professional learning is a challenging, active process because to adapt, change, learn and re-learn, a practitioner must think and act differently. It also requires an open mind and a willingness to learn from work – whether it is paid or voluntary – and from others.

LEARNING AND DEVELOPMENT FOR A BETTER WORLD

The 2013 book with its sub-title *Learning and Development for a Better World* is the first in a series of three books with this sub-title about GULL's work and LAL. The book sought to address the question: How might we encourage those in low income and subsistence communities to discover and fully utilise their talents along with other like-minded people? To summarise and conceptualise the book's main outcomes, Ortrun proposes a descriptive model and in conclusion, I should like to draw on this.

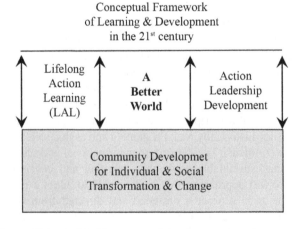

Figure 13.1. Model of learning and development for a better world
(See also Zuber-Skerritt & Teare, 2013, p. 228)

The elements in this model are (1) the overarching 'Conceptual framework of learning and development in the twenty-first century' supported by two main pillars, (2) 'Lifelong action learning', and (3) 'Action leadership development'. These are grounded in (4) 'Community development for individual and social transformation and change'. All four elements contribute to the central focus on (5) 'A Better World'. These five elements are briefly explained below.

1. *A conceptual framework of learning and development in the twenty-first century*: The overarching framework of learning and development in the twenty-first century is called Lifelong Action Learning (LAL) as a concept, methodology, practice, strategy and a way of life. The concept of LAL is based on the philosophical assumption that every person is capable of learning and creating knowledge on the basis of concrete experience, reflecting on this experience and formulating general, abstract concepts. The person can then test these new concepts in new situations and thus have a new concrete experience. Therefore LAL is not linear, but is circular, ongoing and lifelong. It is not taught from outside or above, but motivated from inside and self-directed. It is the product not of instruction, but of action, interaction and reflection. It is developed continuously through experience, practice and dialogue with peers, mentors and coaches, all learning from and with one another. In this context, Ortrun argues that the best way to help people learn is to adopt a self-directed approach to sustainable community development whereby learning is elicited and new knowledge created by asking questions. It is process-oriented and here, the practice of LAL is inclusive. As the methodology is collaborative and relational and both flexible and systematic, the GULL system with its simple yet powerful tools to facilitate change can be deployed and customised in any setting and environment.

2. *Lifelong action learning (LAL)*: Although LAL is rooted in collaborative learning from and with others in action learning groups or project teams, each individual member is normally motivated to find the answer/solution to a shared question/problem/issue/concern. In the context of this shared vision, each individual defines and states their personal learning goal and, step by step reaches this goal on a learning journey of professional development, with the help of a mentor and/or coach, who in turn has undergone professional development as an action leader.

3. *Action leadership development (ALD)*: Within the LAL paradigm, leadership is not conceived as a position of control reserved for those in leadership roles, but rather it can be achieved by all participants. As Ortrun points out, action leaders delight in helping others succeed. They are experienced, wise, and other-centred rather than self-centred. Action leadership can be developed through LAL in partnership with others, through collaboration, participation, reflection on one's own practices, and conceptualising on the possibilities and barriers for sustainable development.

4. *Community development for individual and social transformation and change*: The most important task in any model of learning and development for

transformational change is to ignite a flame or spark that generates in all participants a strong motivation, commitment and passion for real, transformational change in their organisation or community. Therefore, time and effort are well spent on structured and unstructured discussions, and on defining and analysing individual and mutual interests, needs and goals before embarking on the journey of designing a strategic plan, implementing the plan and evaluating the results and learning outcomes. Another important task is to facilitate the process of LAL for individuals and project teams and Action Leadership Development (ALD) for facilitators, mentors and coaches who help and support the individual participants and project teams in achieving their goals. GULL's methodology is now widely used in this context to maximise the outcomes from LAL and ALD for individual and social transformation and change, beginning in one community and later cascaded by members of that community to others. After they gain confidence and have been recognised and certified by GULL, they are equipped and motivated to help others by facilitating the full process for small groups in other communities, thereby consolidating and sharing their own learning.

5. *Community development for a better world*: Both action leadership and individual LAL are embedded in the new conceptual framework introduced in this book. As the arrows in Figure 13.1 suggest, they contribute to and are required for, effective and sustainable community development if it is to lead to substantial personal and social change. Transformational, sustainable community development begins when people at the grassroots level become engaged, and by understanding their cultures and traditions it is possible to empower them to find their own solutions to problems of poverty, health and learning to learn by developing their confidence and skills in LAL and action leadership.

To conclude, I should like to quote from Ortrun's closing remarks at the end of the book as her insights here help to explain why Ortrun has achieved so much and is held in such high regard by her peers, colleagues and friends (Zuber-Skerritt & Teare, 2013, p. 235):

... being located and living in a LAL paradigm can often be likened to being a 'stranger in a foreign land' and sometimes being the odd ones out or swimming against a very strong cultural current. It takes courage and confidence to march to a different drumbeat instead of conforming to the status quo. In my experience, it is more productive to relate to like-minded people who support one another in working together towards positive common goals, rather than wasting time and energy fighting against and responding to constant, destructive criticism. We in LAL learn from constructive criticism from 'critical friends' who, because they are loving and caring, are carefully constructive and cooperative with others ...We hope that this book will encourage readers, communities, development agencies and creative system designers to adopt or adapt the GULL system or to create their own innovation system that enables all people, especially the hitherto excluded, poor and disadvantaged, to unlock their human potential for positive social change and transformation.

Thank you Ortrun for modelling action leadership to me and to many others around the world, and for lifelong action learning outcomes that really do promote learning and development for a better world.

REFERENCES

Global University for Lifelong Learning (GULL). Retrieved from www.gullonline.org

Godin, S. (2008). *Tribes: We need you to lead us.* New York, NY: Portfolio.

Zuber-Skerritt, O. (2009). *Action learning and action research: Songlines through interviews.* Rotterdam, The Netherlands: Sense Publishers.

Zuber-Skerritt, O. (2011). *Action leadership: Towards a participatory paradigm.* Dordrecht, The Netherlands: Springer International.

Zuber-Skerritt, O. (Ed.). (2012) *Action research for sustainable development in a turbulent world.* Bingley, UK: Emerald Group Publishing Limited.

Zuber-Skerritt, O., & Teare, R. (2013). *Lifelong action learning for community development: Learning and development for a better world.* Rotterdam, The Netherlands: Sense Publishers.

Zuber-Skerritt, O., Fletcher, M., & Kearney, J. (2015). *Professional learning in higher education and communities: Towards a new vision for action research.* London, UK and New York, NY: Palgrave Macmillan.

Richard Teare
President
Global University for Lifelong Learning (GULL)

PART V

CONCLUDING REFLECTION

MAUREEN TODHUNTER

14. A FITTING CELEBRATION

INTRODUCTION

Critical reflection is intrinsic to action learning and action research, as it is to the life and work of Ortrun Zuber-Skerritt. It is fitting, then, to conclude this tribute to her life and work with critical reflection. I use 'reflection' in two of its meanings: thinking through carefully, and mirroring back. Ironically, my most penetrating learning at university – to think, question and analyse *critically* – was with academics who were then collaborating with Ortrun to improve the quality of their teaching. So here is testament to that collaborative work some 25 years back. I reflect critically as co-editor of this Festschrift, while admittedly sliding across other avenues of knowing Ortrun as her colleague, collaborator, copy editor and friend. I reflect critically on this Festschrift for what we may learn through it, identifying at least some of its contributions to knowledge, and affirming its celebration of the life of this practical visionary (hat tip to Ron Passfield!).

Preparing this Festschrift is a story of things fitting well at many turns, some happily serendipitous. People from Ortrun's world, their ideas, stories, creative abilities and actions have come together, into place, piece by piece. Why so? It is not that those who helped bring this Festschrift to life distorted their truth; the authors present their narratives and Ortrun's place in these narratives with sincerity and care. The artists likewise. Those who read the text for formatting (Robyn White) and proofing (Jo Anne Pomfrett), who are both familiar with Ortrun's work through formatting and proofing her book manuscripts, nodded with familiar smiles page after page. Through critical reflection I recognise some key reasons. The 'fitting together' that shapes this book and is evident literally from cover to cover, flows from the synthesis between Ortrun's ideals and visions and her life as she actually lives, with ALAR and action as primary anchors. As Ortrun herself says, she practises what she preaches.

In this concluding chapter I consider how Ortrun's worldviews, epistemology and personal qualities are enmeshed in her life within and beyond higher education, giving full life to her passion for action, action learning and action research for a better world, and so to the paradigm of ALAR and its various epistemological relatives. This exploration may open windows or wonderings about our own life journeys as they parallel or stray from Ortrun's along the Action learning/research paths.

J. Kearney & M. Todhunter (Eds), Lifelong Action Learning and Research: A Tribute to the Life and Pioneering Work of Ortrun Zuber-Skerritt, 181–188.

WORLDVIEW

I believe that central to understanding Ortrun's pioneering life and work is her world view. By its very nature, a worldview helps to condition one's values and thinking and one's actions as a human being living in the world with others. As I observe Ortrun, three elements in particular stand out when we consider the fit between her worldview and her life/work.

One is her deep appreciation of knowledge and its utility. This helps us to understand Ortrun's lifelong concern for learning, research, knowledge creation and knowledge transmission. The vignettes of her professional life revealed in the Festschrift stories from her colleagues illustrate this quest, usually not simply for her own interest but for common interest as well. Knowledge is Ortrun's passion, as manifest still in her keen involvement in knowledge creation and transmission, relentlessly, some 70 years after beginning her own classroom education at school in Germany.

The second element is her understanding that humans have great capacity to help themselves, and have responsibility to help others so that others can help themselves. This means pursuing solutions to shared problems collectively. It may entail liberating the minds of others from the oppression of their perceived helplessness. Little wonder that in recent years Ortrun explains her motivation through the proverb, 'Give a man a fish and you feed him for a day; teach him how to fish and you feed him for a lifetime'.[1]

The third element is effectively the nexus between the first two and is captured in the latter half of this giving/teaching adage. It refers to the need to take action – to create, use and share knowledge with others to address real life problems and improve human lives. Ortrun sees that problems require us to engage actively, to identify what is entailed and pursue resolution as creatively as needed and as ably as we can. The rationale is to collectively achieve sustainable solutions and to learn in the process, creating practical and conceptual knowledge that others can use. This understanding mobilises Ortrun into action to guide and nurture others in their quest to solve real life problems, to help educate, enable and empower them. In the spirit of action research, these actions usually move to a celebration of shared achievements – and when Ortrun's on the scene, soon enough to a publication, to share the lessons publicly! This understanding fuses 'work' with the rest of Ortrun's life. Jonathan Jansen (2009) speaks of knowledge in the blood.[2] Ortrun has action in her blood.

EPISTEMOLOGY

This discussion alerts us to characteristics of Ortrun's conception of knowledge that have profoundly shaped her life and work, and have influenced development of the comprehensive worldview, the *Weltanschauung*, of the ALAR paradigm. She has a broad and inclusive view not just of the utility of knowledge but quintessentially of what knowledge is. This gives her a distinctive take on who has or can have knowledge, who can create it, and how they can create it. Ortrun understands that knowledge includes the lessons we learn from life through reflecting mindfully on experience such as through problem solving, to create practical and conceptual knowledge useful for other circumstances. Usually this is a process carried out with others sharing the problem-solving experience. True to ALAR understanding, it means that any person thinking and acting in this way can have knowledge and can create it.

Such an outlook universalises human capacity to know and to create knowledge, and so serves to break down intellectual hierarchies of knowledge. Nurturing the capacity for knowledge creation in people neither living nor educated in the dominant European thinking encourages these people to have confidence in their own abilities. It helps to offer alternative visions and understandings of reality that are rooted in the lived experiences of communities where people live their lives, at local, subnational and national levels. We see this in Ortrun's work with people in Africa, Latin America and Asia, as the chapters by Doris Santos, Chris Kapp, Lesley Wood and Richard Teare illustrate. We also see this in Ortrun's work geographically much closer to home, as evident in her efforts working through ALAR initiatives in her own local context in Southeast Queensland.

The acknowledgement by Ortrun and others that local people create local knowledge does not presuppose a single universal culture or set of understandings, or worldwide conformity. Rather, it speaks to the diversity of people and their circumstances, their ability to identify and address local concerns collectively and to learn and create knowledge in the process, alongside the human qualities shared by people worldwide. The scale and pace of socio-political, economic and technological transformations under way globally at the present historical moment highlight the invalidity of knowledge hierarchies still remnant from an earlier era. Now the so-called west is losing reason to maintain both the empowering confidence of its assumed knowledge superiority and the sense of the universalism of its knowledge, which for centuries the west has assumed. As Hamid Dabashi (2013) explains, 'People from every clime and continent are up and about claiming their own cosmopolitan worldliness and with it their innate ability to think beyond the confinements of that Eurocentrism'.

Understandings of the who, what, how and why of knowledge creation are long contested epistemological issues. The views of Ortrun and others acting within and advocating action learning and action research challenge the powerful, entrenched philosophical assumptions about knowledge still dominant in higher education institutions in most parts of the world. That is true in Australia where Ortrun worked as an academic in three universities for roughly 30 years. Dominant understandings and epistemologies and the power that attaches to them have continued to shift since the 1980s when neoliberal policy logic began to drive change across all sectors of education and every other field of life in Australia (Connell, 2012). This transformative shift has shaped not just the politics of gaining acceptance for action learning and action research, but also the ways in which the task can be approached most effectively.

Ortrun and all who use/live/advocate for action learning and action research within the higher education system in Australia and similar contexts know all too well the systemic resistance to what opponents disparage as 'alternative' understandings of knowledge and its creation. They have needed to work flexibly, creatively and collaboratively, supporting each other where possible to try to build the legitimacy of ALAR and extend its reach. This is something of a Kuhnian struggle (Kuhn, 1962) to mainstream the ALAR paradigm across the education sectors in pursuit of what ALAR advocates recognise as common interest. It is a struggle that Ortrun has embraced with spirited determination, with people who she has helped to mobilise and/or have helped her to pursue the passions they share for ALAR. As we may expect here, action is vital in this picture. So too is celebration!

PERSONAL QUALITIES

It is not just her worldview and epistemological understandings that orient Ortrun towards ALAR. Ortrun's personal qualities also synchronise with ALAR and its various Action relatives, which is why Ortrun has been a vital energy in shaping the evolution of the 'Action' family now including PALAR (Participatory ALAR) and LAL (Lifelong Action Learning). Ortrun is surely capacious. She is generous, thoughtful and caring, while also determined and tenacious, with a drive to maximise opportunities as creatively and daringly as needed. Her spiritual beliefs are not just consistent with ALAR but are also validation and motivation. And rather than resisting what some fear as difference and change, Ortrun relishes diversity and possibility for improvement or growth. The tribute notes at the start of this Festschrift encapsulate these qualities; the narratives across its chapters illustrate them.

Ortrun is a people person – with great capacity for connecting, for fitting together, as if a dispenser of multipurpose social glue. Inclusive seems a pale term to describe this ability. Rather, she is a master at interweaving people, ideas, needs and action. She happily draws together a nucleus of people with ability, connections and shared concerns, and galvanises them into action to serve shared interests. She inspires, motivates and cultivates capacities. She builds confidence, offers guidance. She extends people beyond what they thought was their capacity. She is supportive and nurturing of her wide circle of colleagues, friends, their colleagues and friends and anyone else who may fit into the picture. The circle continues to expand in size and geographic reach. Perhaps most importantly of all, she loves warmly – not just as a feel-good sentiment, but in a way that gives life to the fuller transformative possibilities of love. These personal qualities equip Ortrun as a mover and shaker in academic life and at the forefront of ALAR scholarship.

But there is also a grittier side that compels and enables humane, social Ortrun. Here her strength of will and courage come to the fore. These have been vital qualities when working to resolve tensions on the academic landscape, whether for her own or for others' careers or more generally to overcome hurdles to the success of ALAR scholarship, research, conferences, publication and so forth. They are still so. Ortrun also has high expectations, which can make working with her a test of one's resolve but ultimately a rewarding learning experience – and testament to the value of collaborative relationships. Her fixed commitment to time line can also test, but also ensures timely completion of tasks – including publication.

A final quality, one that has fired Ortrun's life at all turns, is her adventurous spirit. Her son Carsten speaks in his Foreword of the courage and quest for adventure that drove his mother some 45 years ago to a new life in Australia, thousands of miles from her family and home in Germany. Ortrun found Australian soils adventure fertile and where not so, or not enough so, fertilised these with her magnetism for people and action and fun. That grand antipodean adventure is still evolving – with people and action and fun, and links still to family and home in Germany. Thirst for adventure certainly added flavour to the way she navigated the sometimes stormy seas of academic life while performing her best professionally in her career. So too in her intrepid approach to scholarship and research at the frontline of ALAR, to affirm its legitimacy within the higher education system and beyond. We may be sure that without the grittier side of Ortrun's character, neither she nor ALAR and the Action family would be where they are today.

FITTING CONTENT FOR A FESTSCHRIFT

The synthesis between Ortrun's worldview, epistemology and personal qualities places ALAR and the Action paradigm family in a prominent place in her life. The synthesis also places a supportive, cooperative stream of like-minded people in a prominent place in her life. It means that in preparing this Festschrift, people from this stream – colleagues from across the world – have happily come to the fore with their tributes. And so the fit between chapters from far flung ALAR-minded folk discussing intersections between their own work and Ortrun's. A typical sentiment here comes from long-standing colleague and friend Eileen Piggot-Irvine, who explained her chapter as 'a tribute to her [Ortrun's] generosity of wisdom, facilitation, sharing friendship, warmth, fun, and love of action research: of her mentoring of my own and others' learning at an authentically transformational level'.

In Part I on *Higher Education*, Mary Brydon-Miller and David Coghlan have sought to build on Ortrun's work as they explored how ALAR can be used to challenge the nature of the contemporary university. Chris Kapp has discussed an action learning approach to workshops in South Africa on writing academic journal articles, an approach inspired by Ortrun's leadership, coaching, example and enthusiasm. Colombian academic Doris Santos has considered how Ortrun's work inspired her as an early-career researcher and how Ortrun personally supported her in two endeavours aimed at weaving the fragile web of relationships that underlie the politics of Participatory Action Research (PAR) in Colombia.

In Part II on *Organisations*, Shankar Sankaran has explored ways to achieve synergy through combining action learning with action research, drawing from Ortrun's examples and guidance. Ron Passfield has discussed the numerous ALAR initiatives he has worked on with Ortrun, identifying her as a practical visionary across their long-standing professional relationship. Eileen Piggot-Irvine has outlined Ortrun's contribution to her work on evaluating the process and impact of action research projects aiming for a better world.

In Part III on *Communities of Practice*, Lesley Wood has examined the postgraduate voice in PALAR programs for community engagement in South Africa, considering Ortrun's collaboration and influences. Pip Bruce Ferguson has explored her own work, and Ortrun's collaborative efforts and other influences, in building national and international communities of practice for and through action research. Yoland Wadsworth has discussed the creation of World Congresses of ALAR to network an international community, explaining how the congresses owe their existence to the driving determination and personal networking of Ortrun.

In the final part, Part IV on *Futures*, Bob Dick has discussed the interest he shares with Ortrun in ALAR's possible role in the potentially more turbulent world now emerging. Richard Bawden considers managing the process of research into plausible futures while noting Ortrun's contributions to this research. And finally Richard Teare highlights how Ortrun's theoretical contributions through the Lifelong Action Learning (LAL) concept have helped to shape an inclusive approach to learning and development through GULL, the Global University for Lifelong Learning that strengthens low-income and subsistence communities and continues to contribute to learning and development for a better world in the future.

This collection of stories from colleagues has provided useful glimpses of Ortun's contributions to the ALAR paradigm conceptually and in practice. The stories cast some light on the value, extent and diversity of initiatives and actions Ortun has pursued, the people she has worked with and encouraged into the ALAR fold, and the expansive reach of her guidance and personal support. Although this is a bare dozen stories, they indicate the action in mind and heart that continues to drive Ortrun in lifelong action learning and research.

A FITTING TIME FOR THIS FESTSCHRIFT

Discussion above of Ortrun's worldview, epistemology and personal qualities helps us to understand the tapestry of her professional life. The chapters here reveal some of its distinctive threads, and how her passions, abilities, motivation and determination weave in texture and colour. We see that the Ortrun tapestry portrays her enormous contributions to learning and research through higher education. Through the academic discourse. An Everest of publications. Seminars, workshops, conferences, congresses. Conceptual and practical models. Promoting ALAR inside and outside its various organisational forms. Mentoring and personal support for students and colleagues. And always through the care that flows straight from her heart. We can therefore better imagine how the Ortrun tapestry itself weaves texture and colour into the extraordinary tapestry of Knowledge Creation across time and place. So it's fitting that this Festschrift tells these stories of Ortrun's contributions, as a well-deserved tribute to her life's work for a better world.

Time has significance here for two reasons linked inextricably with Ortrun's concern for knowledge and its creation. Today a new imperative compels us to better understand knowledge for life in the twenty-first century. The pace, scale and nature of change force new requirements upon knowledge creation and so upon our shared need to understand what knowledge is, and how, for whom and why people create it. Knowledge creation in this century requires forms of cooperation that are responsive to rapidly – through global warming, dramatically – evolving circumstances. This cooperation depends on trust and reciprocity among all who are involved. Bob Dick observes in Chapter 11 how what seems to be an ever more turbulent world requires an increasingly responsive and flexible approach to research and change, the very type of approach that ALAR entails. Richard Bawden and Richard Teare in their chapters in the *Futures* part of this book also make clear the utility of an ALAR approach to knowledge for creating a better world for all for the long term. These circumstances suggest the time for ALAR, or for greater use of ALAR, is now.

These circumstances also shine the light on why timing of this Festschrift is fitting, since future is informed by past. History of ALAR and of the Action family, which can provide a constructive guide for future conceptual development and practice, is not recorded in a coherent form. As a tribute to Ortrun's contributions to conceptual and practical knowledge in pursuit of a better world, this Festschrift serves as a contribution to recording ALAR history through the life of one of its key movers and shakers. Timing also fits here with the launching of this Festschrift at the ALAR World Congress in Pretoria in November 2015, 25 years after the inaugural ALARPM (ALAR with Process Management) World Congress in Brisbane in 1990, where Ortrun was more than an instrumental organiser.

TO CONCLUDE

Early in this volume Mary Brydon-Miller and David Coghlan recall that in the story of Snow White the magic mirror tells the truth. The stories in all these chapters tell their authors' truths – anecdotal, illustrative, instructive – without magic mirrors. So with critical reflection upon these stories, how can I but conclude that through her lifelong action learning and research Ortrun Zuber-Skerritt has made truly valuable contributions to knowledge and practice in higher education, organisations, communities of practice and understandings of our shared future. These are contributions to theoretical and practical knowledge in pursuit of a better world – a world whose people are more inclusive, egalitarian and caring, more thoughtful, mindful and capable, because they act constructively and collectively in pursuit of shared interests.

Co-editor Judith Kearney noted in her opening chapter that a Festschrift celebrates the life of an academic luminary. And that Ortrun loves to celebrate, purposefully and collectively. This Festschrift is surely a fitting celebration of the pioneering life and work of Ortun Zuber-Skerritt. Judith and I and all who have contributed to this volume respect you, love you and thank you sincerely, Ortrun. This is our tribute.

NOTES

[1] This proverb appears to have fallen foul of the rule 'if you don't know the origin of an enigmatic proverb, say it is ancient Chinese'. It appears to derive from the story written by Anne Isabella Ritchie in the 1880s, *Mrs. Dymond*, which includes a line explicitly with this meaning. http://www.phrases.org.uk/meanings/give-a-man-a-fish.htm. Such genesis also explains the proverb's unconsciously gendered language.

[2] Jonathan Jansen's study explores how white South African university students imagine and enact an Apartheid past through the stories they have inherited, the knowledge 'in their blood'.

REFERENCES

Connell, R. (2012). My university: Neoliberalism and knowledge. *Advocate: Journal of the National Tertiary Education Union, 19*(3), 26–27.

Dabashi, H. (2013). Can non-Europeans think? *Al Jazeera*, 15 January, 2013. Retrieved from http://www.aljazeera.com/indepth/opinion/2013/01/2013114142638797542.html

Jansen, J. (2009). *Knowledge in the blood: Confronting race and the apartheid past.* Stanford, CA: Stanford University Press.

Kuhn, T. (1962). *The structure of scientific revolutions.* Chicago, IL: The University of Chicago Press.

Maureen Todhunter
Griffith University
Brisbane
Australia

Lightning Source UK Ltd.
Milton Keynes UK
UKOW06f1105210915

258995UK00001B/76/P